D1794979

CISCO.

Implementing Cisco Secure Access Solution
Technology Workbook
Exam 300-208

CISCO.

Document Control

Proposal Name	:	SISAS Workbook
Document Version	:	1.0
Document Release Date	:	07 Dec 2017
Reference	:	CCNP_SECURITY_WorkBook

Feedback:
If you have any comments regarding the quality of this book, or otherwise alter it to better suit your needs, you can contact us through email at info@ipspecialist.net
Please make sure to include the book title and ISBN in your message

About IPSpecialist

IPSPECIALIST LTD. IS COMMITTED TO EXCELLENCE AND DEDICATED TO YOUR SUCCESS.

Our philosophy is to treat our customers like family. We want you to succeed, and we are willing to do anything possible to help you make it happen. We have the proof to back up our claims. We strive to accelerate billions of careers with great courses, accessibility, and affordability. We believe that continuous learning and knowledge evolution are most important things to keep re-skilling and up-skilling the world.

Planning and creating a specific goal is where IPSpecialist helps. We can create a career track that suits your visions as well as develop the competencies you need to become a professional Network Engineer. We can also assist you with the execution and evaluation of proficiency level based on the career track you choose, as they are customized to fit your specific goals.

We help you STAND OUT from the crowd through our detailed IP training content packages.

Course Features:

- Self-Paced learning
    - O Learn at your own pace and in your own time
- Covers Complete Exam Blueprint
    - O Prep-up for the exam with confidence
- Case Study Based Learning
    - O Relate the content with real life scenarios
- Subscriptions that suits you
    - O Get more pay less with IPS Subscriptions
- Career Advisory Services
    - O Let industry experts plan your career journey
- Virtual Labs to test your skills
    - O With IPS vRacks, you can testify your exam preperations
- Practice Questions
    - O Practice Questions to measure your preparation standards
- On Request Digital Certification
    - O On request digital certification from IPSpecialist LTD.

About the Authors:
This book has been compiled with the help of multiple professional engineers. These engineers specializes in different fields e.g. Networking, Security, Cloud, Big Data, IoT etc. Each engineer develops content in its specialized field that is compiled to form a comprehensive certification guide.

About the Technical Reviewers:

Nouman Ahmed Khan

AWS-Architect, CCDE, CCIEX5 (R&S, SP, Security, DC, Wireless), CISSP, CISA, CISM is a Solution Architect working with a major telecommunication provider in Qatar. He works with enterprises, mega-projects, and service providers to help them select the best-fit technology solutions. He also works closely as a consultant to understand customer business processes and helps select an appropriate technology strategy to support business goals. He has more than 14 years of experience working in Pakistan/Middle-East & UK. He holds a Bachelor of Engineering Degree from NED University, Pakistan, and M.Sc. in Computer Networks from the UK.

Abubakar Saeed

Abubakar Saeed has more than twenty-five years of experience, Managing, Consulting, Designing, and implementing large-scale technology projects, extensive experience heading ISP operations, solutions integration, heading Product Development, Presales, and Solution Design. Emphasizing on adhering to Project timelines and delivering as per customer expectations, he always leads the project in the right direction with his innovative ideas and excellent management.

Muhammad Yusuf

Muhammad Yousuf is a professional technical content writer. He is Cisco Certified Network Associate in Routing and Switching, holding bachelor's degree in Telecommunication Engineering from Sir Syed University of Engineering and Technology. He has both technical knowledge and industry sounding information, which he uses perfectly in his career.

Table of Contents

About this Workbook

This workbook covers all the information you need to pass the Implementing Cisco Secure Access Solution 300-208 exam. The workbook is designed to take a practical approach of learning with real life examples and case studies.

> ➢ Covers complete Route blueprint
> ➢ Summarized content
> ➢ Case Study based approach
> ➢ Ready to practice labs on VM
> ➢ Pass guarantee
> ➢ Mind maps

Cisco Certifications

Cisco Systems, Inc. is a global technology leader, specializing in networking and communications products and services. The company is probably best known for its business routing and switching products, which direct data, voice and video traffic across networks around the world.

Cisco offers one of the most comprehensive vendor-specific certification programs in the world. The Cisco Career Certification program begins at the Entry level, then advances to Associate, Professional and Expert levels, and (for some certifications) caps things off at the Architect level.

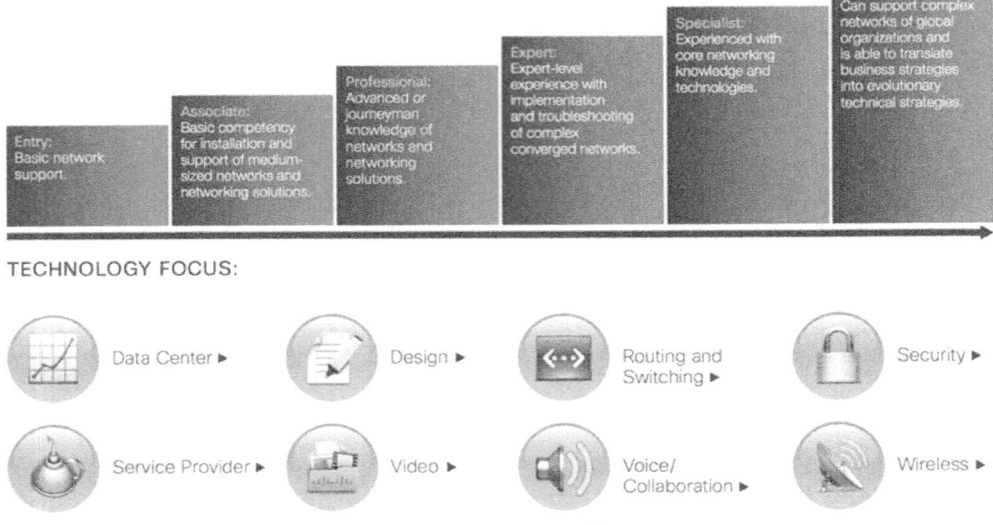

TECHNOLOGY FOCUS:

Data Center ▶

Design ▶

Routing and Switching ▶

Security ▶

Service Provider ▶

Video ▶

Voice/ Collaboration ▶

Wireless ▶

Figure 1 Cisco Certifications Skill Matrix

How does Cisco certifications help?

Cisco certifications are a de facto standard in networking industry help you boost your career in the following ways,

1. Gets your foot in the door
2. Screen job applicants
3. Validate the technical skills of the candidate
4. Ensure quality, competency, and relevancy
5. Improves organization credibility and customers loyalty
6. Required to maintain organization partnership level with OEMs
7. Helps in Job retention and promotion
8. Boosts your confidence level

Cisco Certification Tracks

Certification Tracks	Entry	Associate	Professional	Expert	Architect
Collaboration				CCIE Collaboration	
Data Center		CCNA Data Center	CCNP Data Center	CCIE Data Center	
Design	CCENT	CCDA	CCDP	CCDE	CCAr
Routing & Switching	CCENT	CCNA Routing and Switching	CCNP	CCIE Routing & Switching	
Security	CCENT	CCNA Security	CCNP Security	CCIE Security	
Service Provider		CCNA Service Provider	CCNP Service Provider	CCIE Service Provider	
Service Provider Operations	CCENT	CCNA Service Provider Operations	CCNP Service Provider Operations	CCIE Service Provider Operations	
Video		CCNA Video			
Voice	CCENT	CCNA Voice	CCNP Voice	CCIE Voice	
Wireless	CCENT	CCNA Wireless	CCNP Wireless	CCIE Wireless	

Figure 2 Cisco Certifications Track

About the Route Exam

- ➢ **Exam Number:** 300-208
- ➢ **Associated Certifications:** CCNP Security
- ➢ **Duration:** 90 minutes (55-65 questions)
- ➢ **Exam Registration:** Pearson VUE

The Implementing Cisco Secure Access Solutions (SISAS) (300-208) exam tests whether a network security engineer knows the components and architecture of secure access, by utilizing 802.1X and Cisco TrustSec. This 90-minute exam consists of 55–65 questions and assesses knowledge of Cisco Identity Services Engine (ISE) architecture, solution, and components as an overall network threat mitigation and endpoint control solutions. It also includes the fundamental concepts of bring your own device (BYOD) using posture and profiling services of ISE. Candidates can prepare for this exam by taking the Implementing Cisco Secure Access Solutions (SISAS) course

The following topics are general guidelines for the content likely to be included on the exam

- ➢ Identity Management / Secure Access   33%
- ➢ Threat Defence   10%
- ➢ Troubleshooting, Monitoring and Reporting Tools   7%
- ➢ Threat Defence Architectures   17%
- ➢ Identity Management Architectures   33%

The complete list of topics covered in the SISAS 300-208 exam can be download from here:
https://learningcontent.cisco.com/cln_storage/text/cln/marketing/exam-topics/300-208-sisas.pdf

Prerequisites

Valid Cisco CCNA Security certification or any Cisco CCIE certification can act as a prerequisite.

How much does an exam cost?

Computer-based certification exam (written exam) prices depend on scope and exam length. Please refer to the "Exam Pricing" webpage for details.

Step 4: Getting the Results

After you complete an exam at an authorized testing centre, you'll get immediate, online notification of your pass or fail status, a printed examination score report that indicates your pass or fail status, and your exam results by section.

Congratulations! You are now CCNP-Security-SISAS certified.

Chapter 1: Identity Management/Secure Access

Technology Brief

AAA Concepts

In the previous section, different techniques are explained to stop an attacker from getting unauthorized access to network infrastructure. Those users who are required to access networking devices for maintenance or for configuration also needs to have authorization as well as a proper audit trail so that the culprit will be identified at the hour of need. AAA is all about implementing the above-mentioned goals with some centralization command can control. For example, an organization has 100 devices located at different locations geographically. One method is to access these devices one by one and to add a local database containing usernames and passwords of all authorized persons. The second solution is to have a centralized server containing the database with each device pointing to server for taking decision.

AAA Components

AAA is a modular framework and it tries to cater all kinds of traffic over the network either as a network administrator trying to access a networking device or as an end user trying to send data traffic out of local LAN.

The three main components of AAA are:

Authentication: Authentication is the process of proving identity to the system. It is used in every system not just in computer networking. In a banking system, we need to prove the identity by entering the password before making a transaction. Similarly, if a network administrator needs to access a router or a switch and make some changes, some kind of authentication must be defined on the device. The first but least usable practical solution would be to define the usernames and passwords database inside the device. The second option would be the use of some centralized server like Cisco ACS or ISE. In Cisco devices, we can use the combination of both options by defining a *method list* that states the list of preferred methods for authentication. If one option is not available, then the second option will be used and so on. Examples of these methods are explained in Lab Section of AAA.

Authorization: After authentication of user succeeds, the next problem to deal with is the level of clearance that a user needs to perform his legal actions. Another example in a banking system would perfectly illustrate this. After entering the correct password, we get authorization to withdraw the maximum cash possible depending on the balance available in our bank account. Similarly, there are similar scenarios in computer networking where we need to restrict the access to the user. For example, an end user may need network resources for eight hours a day. Similarly, a network administrator may need commands associated with privilege level 4. Custom lists as well as default method lists are used to define the authorization in Cisco devices.

Accounting: The third element of AAA is accounting or auditing. Whenever a user gets authenticated and authorized to a specific set of commands in Cisco devices, the set of commands he used must be recorded while accessing the specific device during a specific time. Like authentication and authorization, we also use either *default* or *custom method list* to define what should be accounted for and where to send this information.

Mind Map

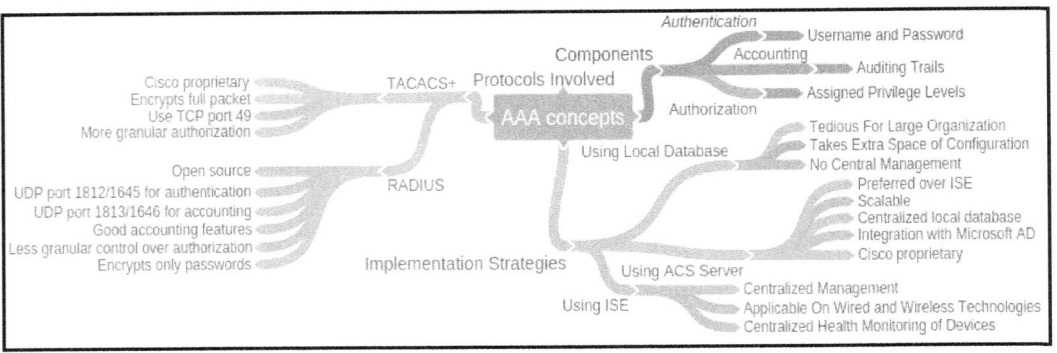

Device Administration

Device administration is a process of AAA for controlling the access to a network device via telnet session, SSH session, console. Imagine a scenario in which your company has an Active Directory for Secure Network Access, and you have privilege 15 (Full Access). In this case, you can do anything you want with the network device. If you have limited access, you are restricted for some particular commands

Network Access

Secure network access is necessary in order to identify the user or endpoint before permitting it to communicate or access the network. Secure Network Access is the main topic covered in this course. AAA has an important role in Network Access authentication and authorization. Nowadays, organizations require remote user, Sites, BYOD and many more. To filter legitimate user AAA Network access authentication is required. AAA authenticates these devices and control what these users are authorized for.

Options for implementing AAA

Cisco provides a number of ways to implement AAA. Over the years, many names have been used for appliance which implements centralized list of usernames and passwords for access. Two examples are ACS server and Radius Server. Today, two kinds of such proprietary servers exist, namely ACS server and ISE. Few open source implementations like *Free Radius* implemented in Linux is also very popular in ISP environment.

The following are different options of centralized servers:

Cisco Secure ACS solution Engine: In the past, Cisco sold this solution as hardware appliance with Cisco Access Solution (ACS) server preinstalled. However, it can also be installed on virtualized environment like VMWare in production environment. Any network device that wishes to implement AAA becomes the client of this server, which

contains usernames passwords, and associated level of authorization with each username. Two protocols are commonly used in communication between client and ACS server namely *TACACS+* and *RADIUS*. Generally, TACACS+ is used for communication between client device and server for giving access to network administrator. Similarly, RADIUS is normally preferred as protocol between device and ACS server for allowing access to end-users of network. However, it is not a hard and fast rule; we can use any of both of them at the same time.

It may be time-consuming to enter every single username, password, and associated level of authorization in ACS, as majority of organizations that can afford ACS have a very large number of employees. ACS has a nice feature of integration with already running databases containing every single username and passwords. An example of this would be integrating AAA with Microsoft Active Directory.

ACS comes in different forms. It can be installed in older versions of ACS already running Windows- based server. Another option is to purchase hardware appliance from Cisco with preinstalled ACS. The third and most convenient option is to install ACS in VMWare on ESXi server. The basic functionality and purpose of ACS remains the same regardless of which method of deployment is used.

ACS in a nutshell:

In order to explain the full process of ACS giving access to a user over the network, consider the scenario on the next page.

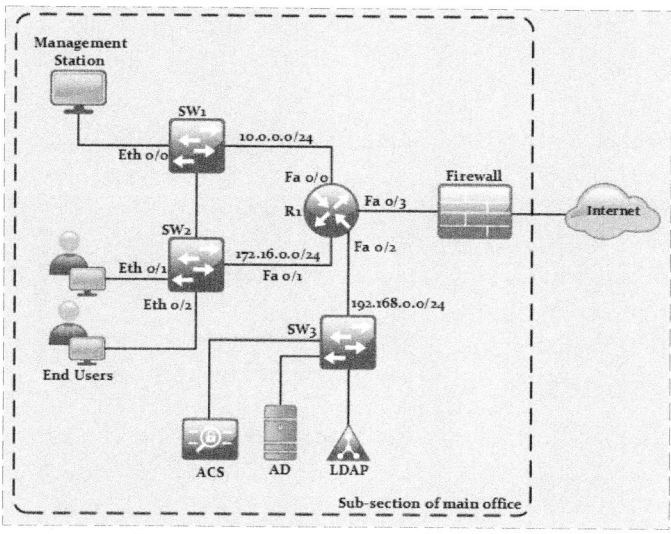

Figure 1-1. ACS in working environment.

Consider an end user coming to an office and tries to login in the workstation. Or a network administrator who tries to login to a switch or a router or even a firewall. Assume the router is configured with using ACS as primary tool for AAA and it is also

integrated with Microsoft Active Directory (AD) and LDAP servers. So, the request will first come to a router, which in turn prompts a username and password request in front of user. Upon submission, the router will send the requested query to the ACS server, which in turn contact the LDAP or AD for authenticity of provided username and password. Upon green signal from LDAP or AD, ACS can verify the authorization level of that user and gives the green signal to originating network device to allow the specific user for authorized access.

Identity Service Unit (ISE): ISE is used for secure access management like ACS. It is a single policy control point for an entire enterprise including wired and wireless technologies. Before giving access to endpoints or even networking devices itself, ISE checks their identity, location, time, type of device and even health of endpoints to make sure that they comply with company's policy like antivirus, latest service pack and OS updates etc. Most of the time people prefer ACS to ISE, although ISE can implement AAA but it is not a complete replacement of ACS.

Protocol Selection between ACS and Client: In general, TACACS+ is preferred over RADIUS when you need to give access to the network administrator, say, CLI access of some router as well as do some authorization of a specific group of commands, and ensure audit trail. This is due to its granular control in authorizing which commands should be allowed.

When configuring for end-clients to enable them to send their traffic over the network, RADIUS is always preferred over TACACS+. It is not compulsory to follow this convention. TACACS+ and RADIUS can also be used simultaneously between ACS server and its client devices.

This table summarizes and compares the unique features of RADIUS and TACACS+.

TACACS+	RADIUS
TCP port 49.	UDP ports. 1812/1645 for authentication 1813/1646 for accounting.
Encrypts full payload	Encrypts only passwords.
Cisco proprietary	Open Standard.
Use for Device Administration	Use for Network Access

Separate Authentication and Authorization	Combine Authentication and Authorization

Table 1. Comparison between RADIUS and TACACS+

TACACS+

TACACS is a set of protocol created and intended for controlling access to Unix terminals. Cisco created a new protocol called TACACS+, which was released as an open standard in the early 1990s. TACACS+ may be derived from TACACS, but it is a completely separate and non–backward-compatible protocol designed for AAA. Although TACACS+ is mainly used for device administration AAA, you can use it for some types of network access AAA.

TACACS+ Authentication Messages

Action of Determination of a user is called Authentication. It may be by using Username and Password combination or like modern authentication requirement such as a one-time password or a challenge. When using TACACS+ for authentication, only three types of packets are exchanged between the client (the network device) and the server:

- Authentication START—This packet is used to begin the authentication request between the AAA client and the AAA server.
- Authentication REPLY—Messages sent from the AAA server to the AAA client.
- Authentication CONTINUE—Messages from the AAA client used to respond to the AAA server requests for username and password.
- Authorization REQUEST—Fixed set of fields describing the authenticity of the user, and a variable set of arguments that describes the services and options for which authorization is requested.).
- Authorization RESPONSE—It contains a variable set of response arguments.
- Accounting REQUEST—It conveys information used to provide accounting for a service provided to a user.).
- Accounting REPLY—It is used to indicate that the accounting function on the server has completed and securely.

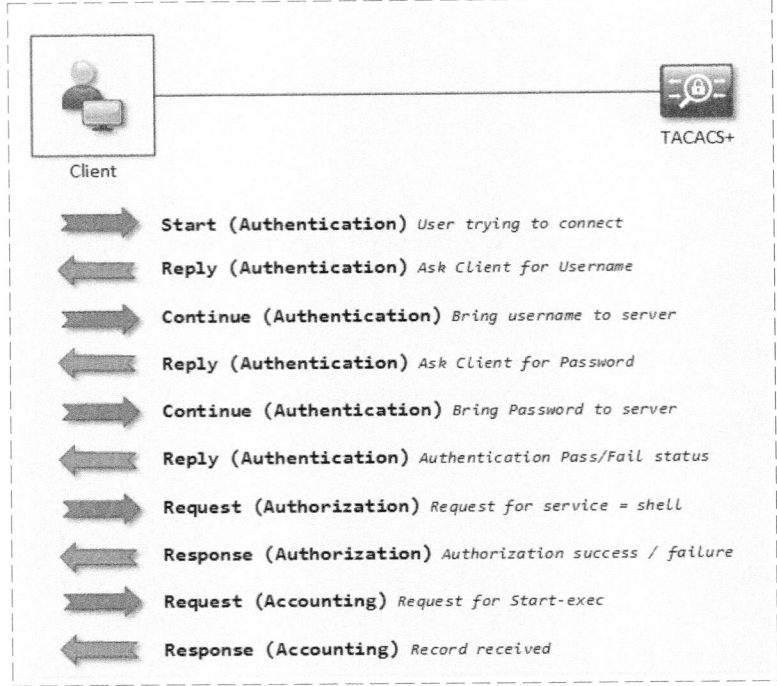

Figure 1-2. TACACS+ Packets

RADIUS

RADIUS is an IETF standard for AAA. As with TACACS+, RADIUS follows a client/server model in which the client initiates the requests to the server. RADIUS is the protocol of choice for network access AAA, and it's time to get very familiar with RADIUS. If you connect to a secure wireless network regularly, RADIUS is most likely being used between the wireless device and the AAA server. Why? Because RADIUS is the transport protocol for EAP, along with many other authentication protocols.

Originally, RADIUS was used to extend the authentications from the Layer-2 Point-to-Point Protocol (PPP) used between the end user and the Network Access ...

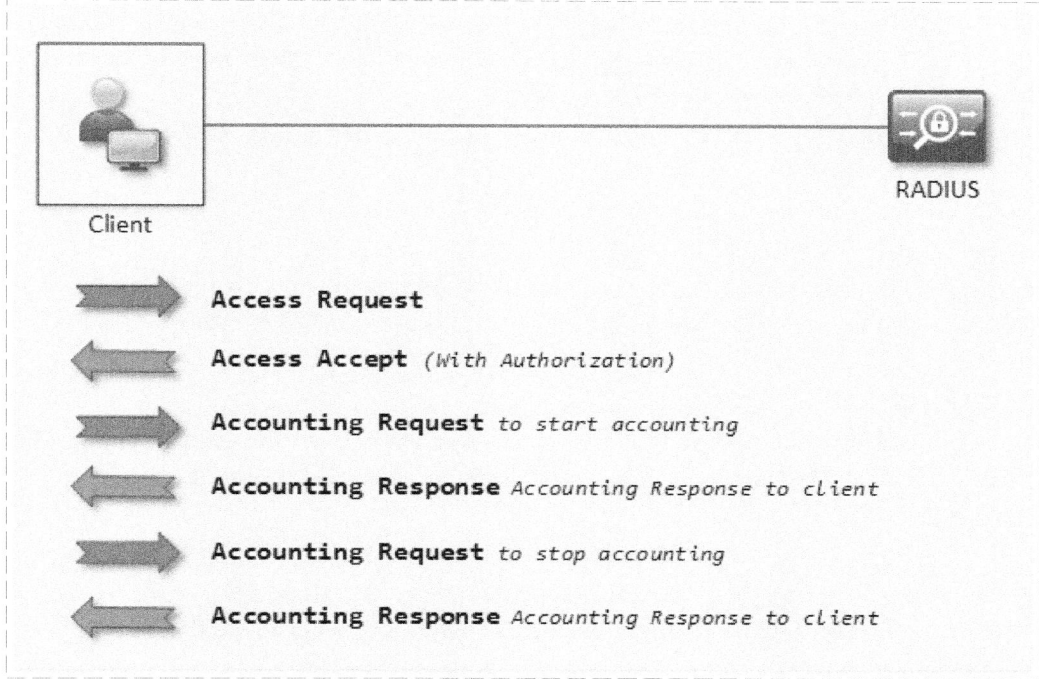

Figure 1-3. RADIUS Packets

TACACS+ vs RADIUS: Two protocols used in ACS as a language of communication between a networking device and ACS server are RADIUS and TACACS+. TACACS+ stands for *Terminal Access Control Access Control Server* and it is Cisco proprietary. Anytime TACACS+ is used for communication between device and server, it will encrypt the full payload of packet before sending it over the network.

Another possible protocol to be used is RADIUS which is an acronym for *Remote Authentication Dial-in User Service*. RADIUS is an open standard meaning that all vendors can use it in their AAA implementation. One main difference between RADIUS and TACACS+ is that RADIUS only encrypts password and sends other RADIUS packets as clear text over the network.

UDP and TCP

RADIUS uses UDP as a transport protocol while TACACS+ uses TCP. There are several advantages of TCP over UDP. As the characteristic of TCP and UDP, TCP offers a connection-oriented transport, while UDP offers best-effort delivery. RADIUS requires additional variables such as re-transmit attempts and time-outs to compensate for best-effort transport. But it lacks the level of built-in support that a TCP transport offers:

- TCP provides separate acknowledgment within (approximately) a network round-trip time (RTT), regardless of how loaded and slow the backend authentication mechanism (a TCP acknowledgment) might be.
- TCP provides immediate indication of a crashed, or not running, server by a reset (RST).
- Using TCP keepalives, server crashes can be detected out-of-band with actual requests.
- Connections to multiple servers can be maintained simultaneously,
- TCP is more scalable and adapts to growing, as well as congested, networks.

Packet Encryption

RADIUS Protocol encrypts the password of the access-request packet only from Client to server. The remaining packet is unencrypted. Hence, other information can be captured by a third party.

TACACS+ encrypts the entire body of the packet but leaves a standard TACACS+ header. Within the header is a field that indicates whether the body is encrypted or not. For debugging purposes, it is useful to have the body of the packets unencrypted. However, during normal operation, the body of the packet is fully encrypted for more secure communications.

Authentication and Authorization

RADIUS combines authentication and authorization processes. The access-accept packets sent by the RADIUS server to the client contain authorization information. This makes it difficult to decouple authentication and authorization.

TACACS+ uses the AAA architecture, which separates AAA. This allows separate authentication solutions that can still use TACACS+ for authorization and accounting. For example, with TACACS+, it is possible to use Kerberos authentication and TACACS+ authorization and accounting. After a NAS authenticates on a Kerberos server, it requests authorization information from a TACACS+ server without having to re-authenticate. The NAS informs the TACACS+ server that it has successfully authenticated on a Kerberos server, and the server then provides authorization information.

During a session, if additional authorization checking is needed, the access server checks with a TACACS+ server to determine if the user is granted permission to use a particular command. This provides greater control over the commands that can be executed on the access server while decoupling from the authentication mechanism.

Multiprotocol Support
RADIUS does not support these protocols:
- AppleTalk Remote Access (ARA) protocol
- NetBIOS Frame Protocol Control protocol
- Novell Asynchronous Services Interface (NASI)
- X.25 PAD connection

TACACS+ offers multiprotocol support.

Router Management
RADIUS does not allow users to control which commands can be executed on a router and which cannot. Therefore, RADIUS is not as useful for router management or as flexible for terminal services.

TACACS+ provides two methods to control the authorization of router commands on a per-user or per-group basis. The first method is to assign privilege levels to commands and have the router verify with the TACACS+ server whether or not the user is authorized at the specified privilege level. The second method is to explicitly specify in the TACACS+ server, on a per-user or per-group basis, the commands that are allowed.

Interoperability
Due to various interpretations of the RADIUS Request for Comments (RFCs), compliance with the RADIUS RFCs does not guarantee interoperability. Even though several vendors implement RADIUS clients, this does not mean they are interoperable. Cisco implements most RADIUS attributes and consistently adds more. If customers use only the standard RADIUS attributes in their servers, they can interoperate between several vendors as long as these vendors implement the same attributes. However, many vendors implement extensions that are proprietary attributes. If a customer uses one of these vendor-specific extended attributes, interoperability is not possible.

Active Directory (AD)
In a network, keeping track of everything is a very difficult, and time consuming task. If the network is wide enough, it becomes impossible to manage and find resources on a network. Microsoft Windows 2000 server launches Active Directory (AD) to replace Domain functionality. Active Directory is like a phonebook. As a phonebook stores information like Name, Contact No, Business, similarly, Active Directory stores the information about organization, sites, system, user, share and much more. It is much more flexible as well. Active Directory is the more efficient way to perform these tasks. Another advantage of Active Directory is it can be replicated between multiple domain controllers.

Components of Active Directory:

- **Name space or Console tree:**

Active Directory as define stores information about multiple users and allow the clients to find objects within namespace or console tree. Namespace or Console tree is like DNS, resolving hostname to IP address, similarly, namespace resolve Network object to object themselves.

- **Object:**

Object may be a User, Resource, or System that can be tracked within Active Directory. These Objects can share common attributes.

- **Attributes:**

In an Active Directory, Attributes describe objects like username, full name, description, hostname, IP address and location etc. It may depend upon the type of object.

- **Schema:**

The Schema is the set of attributes for any particular object type. It differentiates object classes from each other.

- **Name:**

Each object has a name. These are LDAP distinguished names. LDAP distinguished names allow any object within a directory to be identified uniquely regardless of its type.

- **Site:**

Sites correspond to logical IP subnets, and as such, they can be used by applications to locate the closest server on a network. Using site information from Active Directory can profoundly reduce the traffic on wide area networks.

Lightweight Directory Access Protocol (LDAP)

The Lightweight Directory Access Protocol LDAP is an open standard, application protocol. LDAP is for accessing and maintaining distributed directory information services. A directory service plays an important role by allowing the sharing of information like user, system, network, service etc. throughout the network. LDAP provide a central place to store usernames and passwords. Applications and Services connect to the LDAP server to validate users.

Identity Stores:

An Identity Store is a store or database that is used to authenticate users or endpoints. This Identity Store may reside in AAA Server (Internal Identity store) or additional external database (External Identity Store) can also connect. These Identity Stores can also be used for attributes required for authorizing policies.

- **Internal Identity Store**

Internal identity store or local database that can be used for internal username and password accounts like Cisco ISE has an internal user database. User accounts stored in the internal user database are referred to as internal users in this Internal Identity store. The internal user database can be used as an internal identity store for local authentication and authorization policies.

- **External Identity Store**

External Identity stores are the external databases which are used for authentication for internal and external users. Some external identity stores are LDAP, Active Directory, RSA SecureID Token Server and RADIUS Identity Server. Attributes, Configuration parameters can be defined over External Identity store user records.

Other Identity stores Options:

One-Time passwords:

OTP stands for One-Time Password. OTP are valid for single use for login or sign up or transaction etc. from a device. Due to its one-time validity, it is more secure than ordinary password- based authentication such as they are not vulnerable to replay attacks as well as OTP also ensure sessions are not intercepted or impersonated. These one-time passwords are made difficult to memorize or decode to make them stronger. One-Time password depends upon the algorithm of pseudo randomness and hash functions. They are very hard to reverse hence difficult for attackers to get data used for hashing. Generation of One-Time password may use any of these approaches:

- Time-Synchronization (Valid for short interval)
- Algorithm to generate new password based on previous password (Predefined Order)
- Algorithm to generate new password based on a challenge. (Random number)

To send user a new OTP, several channels can be used such as Security tokens, Software's, Out-of-band channels etc.

Public Key Infrastructure (PKI)

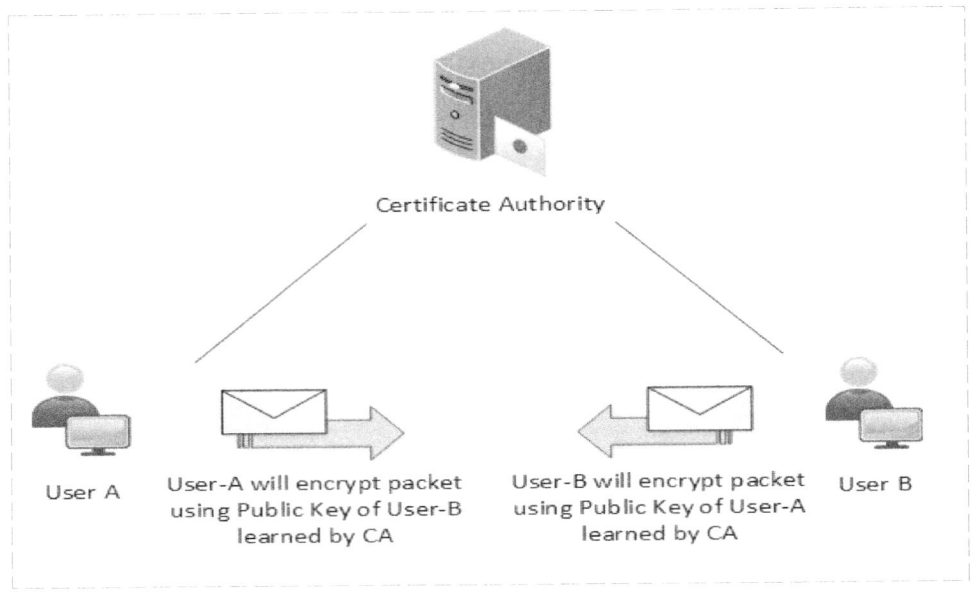

Figure 1-4. PKI

Public-key cryptography is also called asymmetric-key cryptography. In Public Key Cryptography, a key pair is used to encrypt and decrypt content. Two key pairs are used in Public Key Cryptography technique named as Public Key and Private key. These Public and Private keys are related to each other so that the data encrypted with one key can only be decrypted with the other key. Public key can be distributed and private key must be kept secure and secret. Any one try to communicate with another will encrypt the content with Public key of the receiver and receiver will decrypt the content by its private key. Public Key infrastructure (PKI) depends upon software and hardware. A trusted third party called as Certificate Authority (CA) is also used integrity and the ownership of public keys. This Certificate Authority issues encrypted, signed binary certificates.

Element	Description
Certification Authority	Acts as the root of trust in a public key infrastructure and provides services that authenticate the identity of individuals, computers, and other entities in a network.
Registration Authority	Is certified by a root CA to issue certificates for specific uses permitted by the root. In a Microsoft PKI, a registration authority

	(RA) is usually called a subordinate CA.
Certificate Database	Saves certificate requests and issued and revoked certificates and certificate requests on the CA or RA.
Certificate Store	Saves issued certificates and pending or rejected certificate requests on the local computer.
Key Archival Server	Saves encrypted private keys in the certificate database for recovery after loss.

Table 2. Elements of PKI

Implement Accounting:

In an AAA model, accounting features is also very much important in security. Accounting command enables tracking the commands, services and resources used by user while accessing the network. Accounting is the measure of resources consumed by a user during access. In accounting, it includes amount of time, amount of data user has send or received during a session. This accounting is carried in the form of logs of session statistics and usage information. This accounting data is used for authorization control, analysis of resources utilization, billing and planning as well. This accounting is also very much helpful to troubleshoot if network devices are not functioning properly. An example is when someone tries to access the network device and issued a wrong command which stops the device forwarding the packets. Accounting logs will verify the user who is responsible to issue that command. AAA Accounting is disabled by default.

AAA Accounting Types

- **Network**

To enable Accounting for all network-related service requests (including SLIP, PPP, PPP NCPs, and ARAP protocols), use the network keyword.

- **Exec**

To create a method list that provides accounting records about user EXEC terminal sessions on the network access server, including username, date, start and stop times, use the exec keyword.

- **Commands**

To create a method list that provides accounting information about specific, individual EXEC commands associated with a specific privilege level, use the commands keyword.

- **Connection**

To create a method list that provides accounting information about all outbound connections made from the network access server, use the connection keyword.

- **Resource**

To create a method, provide accounting records for calls that have passed user authentication or calls that failed to be authenticated.

Accounting Commands

Generating records when Client is authenticated and after client disconnection.

```
Router(config)# aaa accounting network default start-stop group radius local
```

Generates records when client disconnected

```
Router(config)# aaa accounting network default stop group radius local
```

Generates records for authentication and negotiation failure

```
Router(config)# aaa accounting send stop-record authentication failure
```

It enables full resources accounting

```
Router(config)# aaa accounting resource start-stop
```

Wired/Wireless 802.1x

802.1x Port-Based Authenticaiton

IEEE 802.1x is a Port-Based Authentication. This Port-Based Authentication prevents unauthorized user or client devices to access the network. Client may be Wired or Wireless. In 802.1x authentication, authentication is a Client and Server based authentication protocol, which prevents or restricts unauthorized supplicants or Clients from accessing the network via connecting to LAN through publicly accessible ports. Authentication server (RADIUS) validates each client connected to publically accessible port of Authenticator switch, also called as Network Access Switch (NAS) before permitting the access. 802.1x authentication required authentication server configured for Remote Authentication Dial-In User Service (RADIUS). It is necessary that switch can communicate Authentication server for 802.1x authentication. When Client is successfully authenticated, normal traffic can pass through the port.

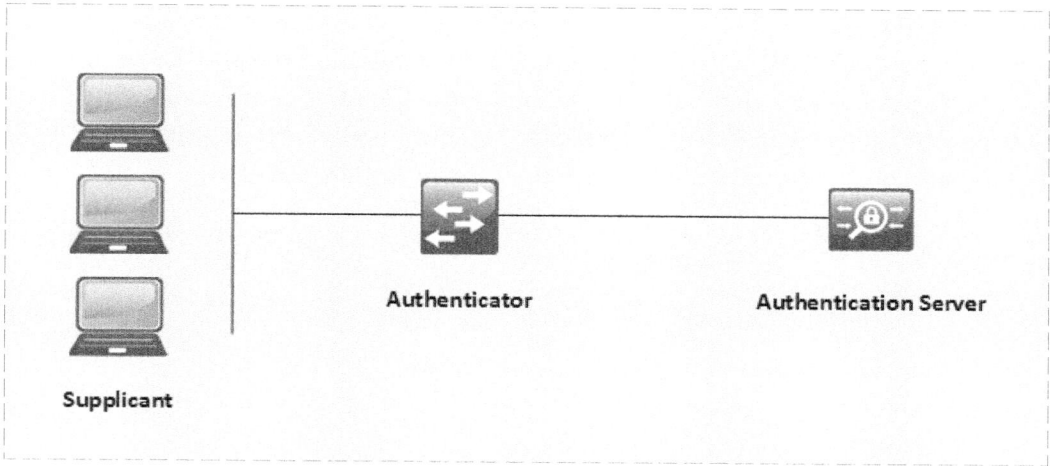

Figure 1-5. 802.1x Devices role

Client:

Client, also known as Supplicant is 802.1x Port-Based Authentication. Client is the Workstation that is connected through Network Access Switch (NAS) to the LAN and request for accessing the network resources. This Workstation or Client must be using 802.1x Client software.

Authenticator:

Authenticator is basically a device that authenticates Client to restrict or permit to use network resources. Normally Network Access Switch (NAS) plays the role of Authenticator. Authenticator controls the access of Client depending upon the status of Authentication. Switches get requests from Clients, it forwards this identity information to authentication server, which validate and verify the information. This Switch encapsulate and de-capsulate the frames using Extensible Authentication Protocol (EAP) to communicate RADIUS authentication server.

Enabling Router for Dot1x Authentication
Router# configure terminal Router(config)# aaa new-model Router(config)# aaa authentication dot1x default group radius Router(config)# dot1x system-auth-control Router(config)# interface [Interface-name] Router(config-if)# dot1x port-control auto Router(config-if)# end

Authentication Server:

Authentication server (RADIUS) performs the real authentication of the Supplicant or Client. Authentication server check for the identity of the Client, if verifies, allow the user by acknowledging the switch that this client is authorized to access the LAN. (The only supported Authentication server is RADIUS with EAP Extensions)

Configuring RADIUS server on Router

Router# configure terminal
Router(config)# ip radius source-interface [Source-Interface]
Router(config)# radius-server host [Server-IP Address]
Router(config)# radius-server key [Server-Key]
Router(config)# end

Attribute-Value (AV) Pairs

The authenticator sent the information of 802.1x authentication to the Authentication server is represented as Attribute-Value Pairs (AV-Pairs). These Attribute Value Pairs provide information to different applications for use. Authenticator Switch configured for Accounting sends these AV pairs. Three types of RADIUS accounting packets are

START   -   Sent when new user session start
INTERIM   -   Sent During a session for Updates
STOP   -   When Session terminates

Attribute Number	AV Pair Name	START	INTERIM	STOP
Attribute [1]	User-Name	Always	Always	Always
Attribute [4]	NAS-IP-Address	Always	Always	Always
Attribute [5]	NAS-Port	Always	Always	Always
Attribute [6]	Service-Type	Always	Always	Always
Attribute [8]	Framed-IP-Address	Never	Sometimes	Sometimes
Attribute [25]	Class	Always	Always	Always
Attribute [30]	Called-Station-ID	Always	Always	Always
Attribute [31]	Calling-Station-ID	Always	Always	Always
Attribute [40]	Acct-Status-Type	Always	Always	Always
Attribute [41]	Acct-Delay-Time	Always	Always	Always

Attribute Number	AV Pair Name	START	INTERIM	STOP
Attribute [42]	Acct-Input-Octets	Never	Always	Always
Attribute [43]	Acct-Output-Octets	Never	Always	Always
Attribute [44]	Acct-Session-ID	Always	Always	Always
Attribute [45]	Acct-Authentic	Always	Always	Always
Attribute [46]	Acct-Session-Time	Never	Never	Always
Attribute [47]	Acct-Input-Packets	Never	Always	Always
Attribute [48]	Acct-Output-Packets	Never	Always	Always
Attribute [49]	Acct-Terminate-Cause	Never	Never	Always
Attribute [61]	NAS-Port-Type	Always	Always	Always

Table 3. Accounting AV pairs

Periodic Reauthentication

Router(config)# interface [Interface-name]
Router(config-if)# dot1x reauthentication
Router(config-if)# dot1x timeout reauth-period [Period]
Router(config-if)# end
Router# show dot1x all

Router-Client Transmission Time

Router(config)# interface [Interface-name]
Router(config-if)# dot1x timeout tx-period [Period]
Router(config-if)# end

Troubleshooting Dot1x from NAD

Router# show dot1x all

```
NAD                                              —   □   ×
Router#show dot1x all
Sysauthcontrol              Enabled
Dot1x Protocol Version         2

Dot1x Info for FastEthernet0/1
-------------------------------------
PAE                    = AUTHENTICATOR
PortControl            = AUTO
ControlDirection       = Both
HostMode               = SINGLE_HOST
ReAuthentication       = Enabled
QuietPeriod            = 60
ServerTimeout          = 30
SuppTimeout            = 30
ReAuthPeriod           = 4000 (Locally configured)
ReAuthMax              = 2
MaxReq                 = 2
TxPeriod               = 60
RateLimitPeriod        = 0
Mac-Auth-Bypass        = Enabled

Router#
```

Extensible authentication protocol (EAP)

EAP-MD-5 (Message Digest) Challenge is an EAP authentication. EAP-MD5 provides base-level EAP support, it is not recommended for Wi-Fi LAN implementations. It provides only one-way authentication. There is no mutual authentication of Wi-Fi client and the network. It does not provide a means to derive dynamic, per session wired equivalent privacy (WEP) keys.

EAP-TLS (Transport Layer Security) provides certificate-based and mutual authentication process between client and the network. EAP-TLS relies on certificates of client-side and server-side for authentication. It can dynamically generate user-based and session-based WEP keys to secure subsequent communications.

EAP-TTLS (Tunnelled Transport Layer Security) is an extension of EAP-TLS. This security method provides for certificate-based, mutual authentication of the client and network through an encrypted channel (or tunnel), as well as a means to derive dynamic, per-user, per-session WEP keys. Unlike EAP-TLS, EAP-TTLS requires only server-side certificates.

EAP-FAST (Flexible Authentication via Secure Tunnelling) mutual authentication is achieved by means of a PAC (Protected Access Credential) instead of using a certificate, which can be managed dynamically by the authentication server. The PAC can be provisioned (distributed one time) to the client either manually or automatically.

Extensible Authentication Protocol Method for GSM Subscriber Identity (EAP-SIM) is a mechanism for authentication and session key distribution. EAP-SIM uses the Global System for Mobile Communications (GSM) Subscriber Identity Module (SIM). EAP-SIM uses a dynamic session-based WEP key, which is derived from the client adapter and RADIUS server, to encrypt data. EAP-SIM requires you to enter a user verification code, or PIN, for communication with the Subscriber Identity Module (SIM) card. A SIM card is a special smart card that is used by Global System for Mobile Communications (GSM) based digital cellular networks.

EAP-AKA (Extensible Authentication Protocol Method for UMTS Authentication and Key Agreement) is an EAP mechanism for authentication and session key distribution, using the Universal Mobile Telecommunications System (UMTS) Subscriber Identity Module (USIM). The USIM card is a special smart card used with cellular networks to validate a given user with the network.

LEAP (Lightweight Extensible Authentication Protocol), is an EAP authentication type used primarily in Cisco Aironet* WLANs. It encrypts data transmissions using dynamically generated WEP keys, and supports mutual authentication. Heretofore proprietary, Cisco has licensed LEAP to a variety of other manufacturers through their Cisco Compatible Extensions program.

PEAP (Protected Extensible Authentication Protocol) provides a method to transport securely authentication data, including legacy password-based protocols, via 802.11 Wi-Fi networks. PEAP accomplishes this by using tunnelling between PEAP clients and an authentication server. Like the competing standard Tunnelled Transport Layer Security (TTLS), PEAP authenticates Wi-Fi LAN clients using only server-side certificates, thus simplifying the implementation and administration of a secure Wi-Fi LAN. Microsoft, Cisco and RSA Security developed PEAP.

Mind Map

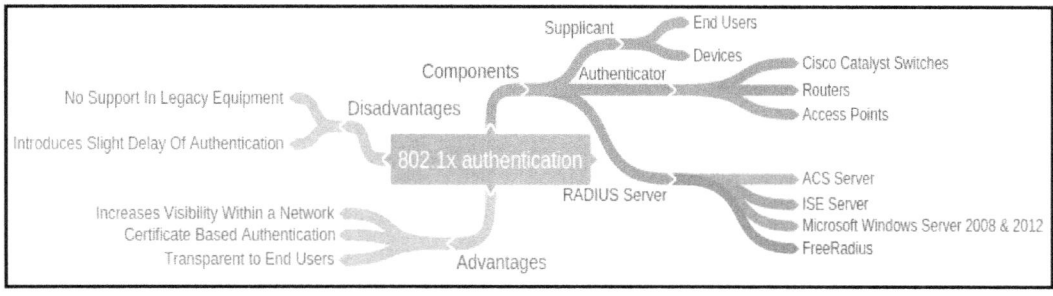

Lab 1.1: Configuring Dot1x Port-based Authentication Using Cisco ISE

Case Study:

In a small network of an organization, Administrator is deploying 802.1x Port-based Authentication. Router is used as Network Access Device (NAD) and Dot1x Client is using Window 7 PC. Requirement of the Lab is to configure 802.1x Port-based Authentication with Microsoft Challenge Handshake Authentication Protocol (MS-CHAP v2) for Window7 Client. Cisco ISE Internal Datastore can be used for User registry.

Topology Diagram:

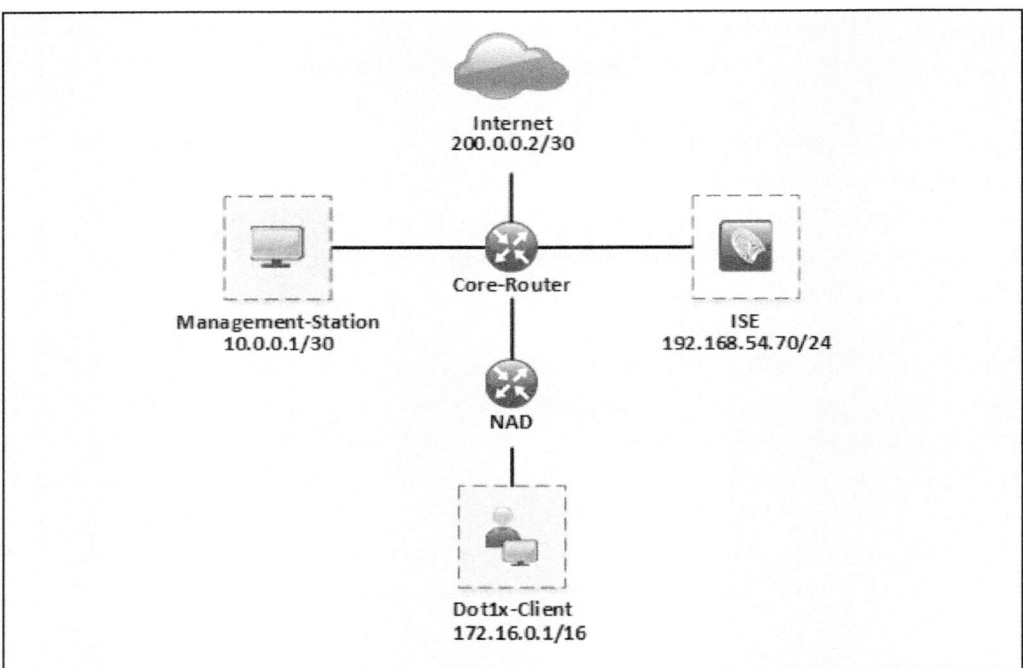

Configuring Core Router

Router(config)#hostname Core-Router

Core-Router(config)#int fastethernet 1/0
Core-Router(config-if)#ip address 192.168.0.1 255.255.255.252
Core-Router(config-if)#no sh
Core-Router(config-if)#ex
*Mar 1 00:03:10.271: %LINK-3-UPDOWN: Interface FastEthernet1/0, changed state to up
*Mar 1 00:03:11.271: %LINEPROTO-5-UPDOWN: Line protocol on Interface FastEthernet1/0, changed state to up

Core-Router(config)#int fastethernet 0/0
Core-Router(config-if)#ip add 10.0.0.2 255.255.255.252
Core-Router(config-if)#no sh
Core-Router(config-if)#ex
*Mar 1 00:03:56.663: %LINK-3-UPDOWN: Interface FastEthernet0/0, changed state to up
*Mar 1 00:03:57.663: %LINEPROTO-5-UPDOWN: Line protocol on Interface FastEthernet0/0, changed
state to up

Core-Router(config)#int fastethernet 0/1
Core-Router(config-if)#ip address 192.168.54.1 255.255.255.0
Core-Router(config-if)#no sh
Core-Router(config-if)#ex
*Mar 1 00:04:12.211: %LINK-3-UPDOWN: Interface FastEthernet0/1, changed state to up
*Mar 1 00:04:12.211: %LINEPROTO-5-UPDOWN: Line protocol on Interface FastEthernet0/1, changed
state to up

Core-Router(config)#int fa 2/0
Core-Router(config-if)#ip address 200.0.0.2 255.255.255.252
Core-Router(config-if)#no sh
Core-Router(config-if)#ex
*Mar 1 00:04:32.201: %LINK-3-UPDOWN: Interface FastEthernet2/0, changed state to up
*Mar 1 00:04:32.211: %LINEPROTO-5-UPDOWN: Line protocol on Interface FastEthernet2/0, changed
state to up

Core-Router(config)#router eigrp 10
Core-Router(config-router)# network 10.0.0.0 0.0.0.3
Core-Router(config-router)# network 192.168.0.0 0.0.0.3
Core-Router(config-router)# network 192.168.54.0
Core-Router(config-router)# network 200.0.0.0 0.0.0.3
Core-Router(config-router)# no auto-summary
Core-Router(config-router)#ex
Core-Router(config)#end

Configuring NAD Router

Router(config)#hostname NAD

NAD(config)#interface fastethernet 0/0
NAD(config-if)#ip add 192.168.0.2 255.255.255.252
NAD(config-if)#no shutdown
NAD(config-if)#ex
*Mar 1 00:10:27.383: %LINK-3-UPDOWN: Interface FastEthernet0/0, changed state to up

```
*Mar  1 00:10:28.383: %LINEPROTO-5-UPDOWN: Line protocol on Interface FastEtherneto/0, changed
state to up

NAD(config)#interface fastethernet 0/1
NAD(config-if)#ip address 172.16.0.254 255.255.0.0
NAD(config-if)#no sh
NAD(config-if)#ex
*Mar  1 00:10:57.895: %LINK-3-UPDOWN: Interface FastEtherneto/1, changed state to up
*Mar  1 00:10:58.895: %LINEPROTO-5-UPDOWN: Line protocol on Interface FastEtherneto/1, changed
state to up


NAD(config)#router eigrp 10
NAD(config-router)#network 1.1.1.1 0.0.0.0
NAD(config-router)#network 172.16.0.0 0.0.255.255
NAD(config-router)#network 192.168.0.0 0.0.0.3
NAD(config-router)#no auto-summary
NAD(config-router)#ex

NAD(config)#interface loopback 0
*Mar  1 00:11:28.639: %LINEPROTO-5-UPDOWN: Line protocol on Interface Loopbacko, changed state
to up
NAD(config-if)#ip address 1.1.1.1 255.255.255.255
NAD(config-if)#ex


NAD(config)#aaa new-model
NAD(config)#aaa authentication dot1x default group radius
NAD(config)#dot1x system-auth-control
NAD(config)#ip radius source-interface loopback 0
NAD(config)#radius-server host 192.168.54.70
NAD(config)#radius-server key cisco123
NAD(config)#interface FastEtherneto/1
NAD(config-if)#dot1x ?

  credentials      Credentials profile configuration
  default          Configure Dot1x with default values for this port
  host-mode        Set the Host mode for 802.1x on this interface
  max-reauth-req   Max No.of Reauthentication Attempts
  max-req          Max No.of Retries
  max-start        Max No. of EAPOL-Start requests
  pae              Set 802.1x interface pae type
  port-control     set the port-control value
  reauthentication Enable or Disable Reauthentication for this port
  timeout          Various Timeouts
```

```
NAD(config-if)#dot1x timeout reauth-period ?
  <1-65535>  Enter a value between 1 and 65535
  server    Obtain re-authentication timeout value from the server

NAD(config-if)#dot1x timeout reauth-period 4000

NAD(config-if)#dot1x port-control auto
NAD(config-if)#dot1x host-mode single-host
NAD(config-if)# dot1x reauthentication
NAD(config-if)# dot1x timeout tx-period 60
NAD(config-if)#dot1x pae authenticator
NAD(config-if)#ex
```

Configuring Cisco ISE

Go to the Management-Station and check if IP Address is properly configured. If not, Set the IP address to 10.0.0.1 /30 and gateway 10.0.0.2 as shown in the figure below

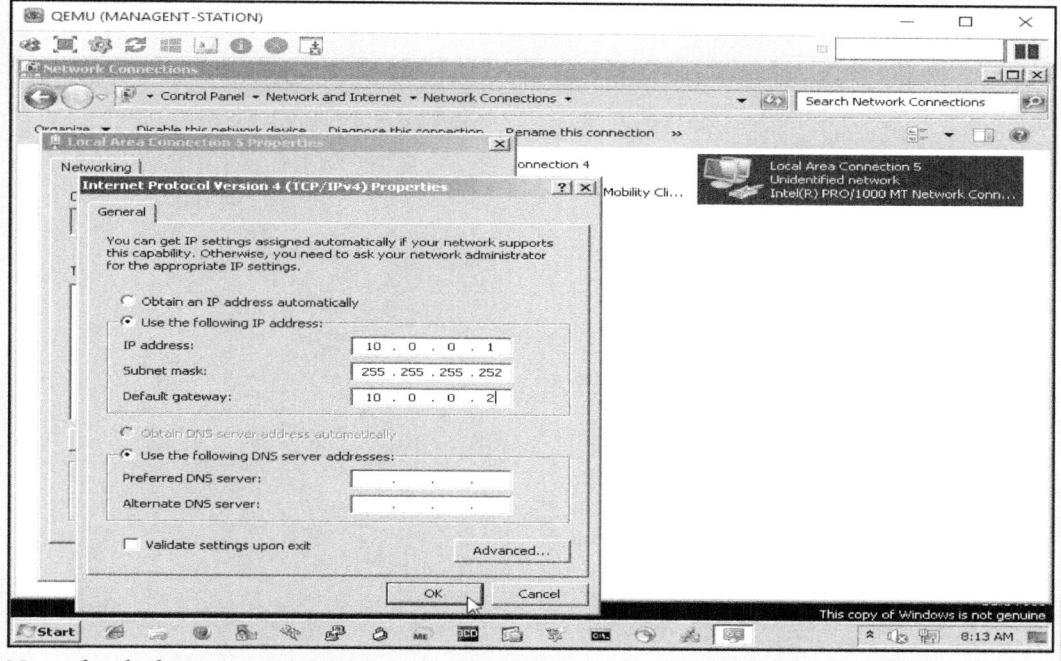

Now check the connectivity between Management-Station and ISE server by Pinging.

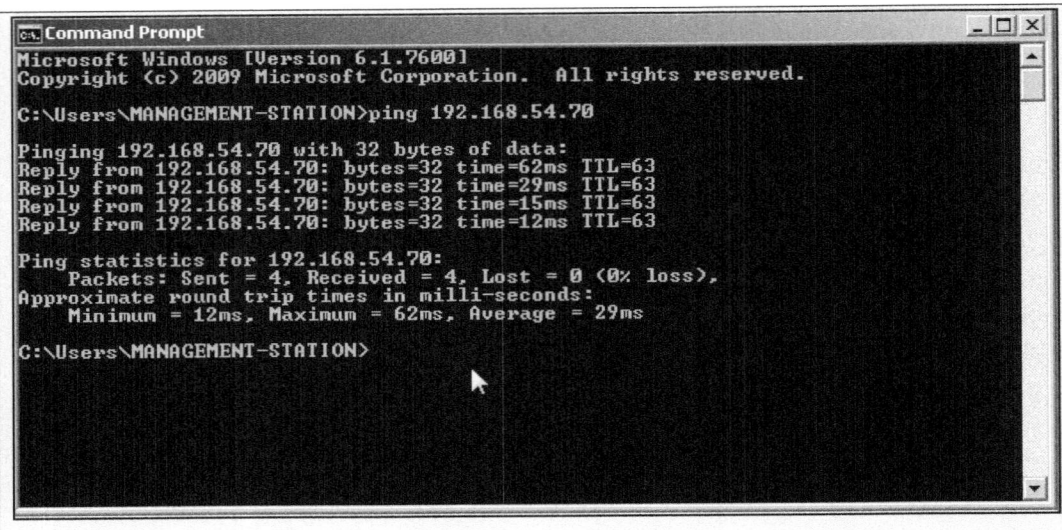

Now go to Internet Explorer and go to URL https://192.168.54.70

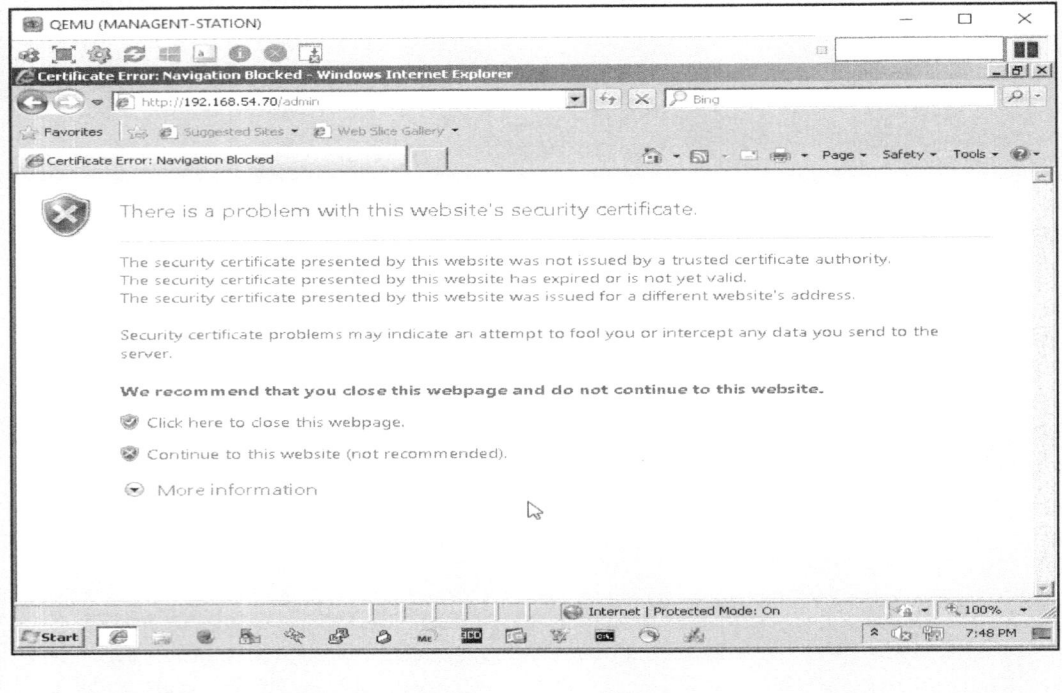

Click on **Continue to this Website**

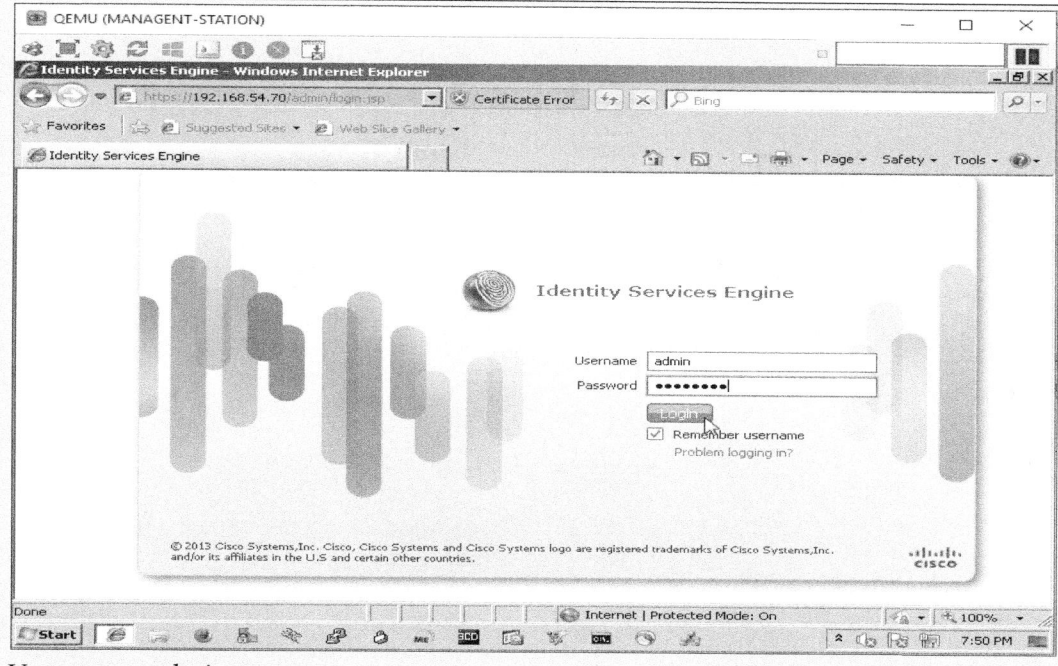

Username : admin

Password : Cisco123

After Successful Login, Go to **Administration > Network Resources > Network Devices** to add the Device (NAD-Router), which will request to authenticate Dot1x Client as shown below.

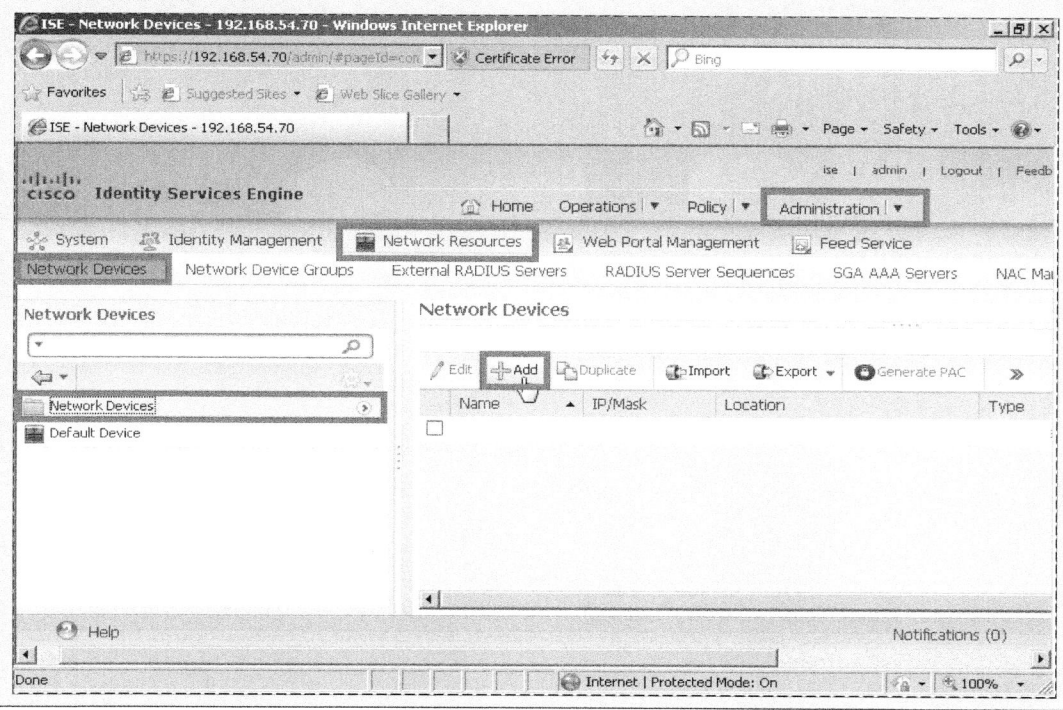

Click on Add button to add Device

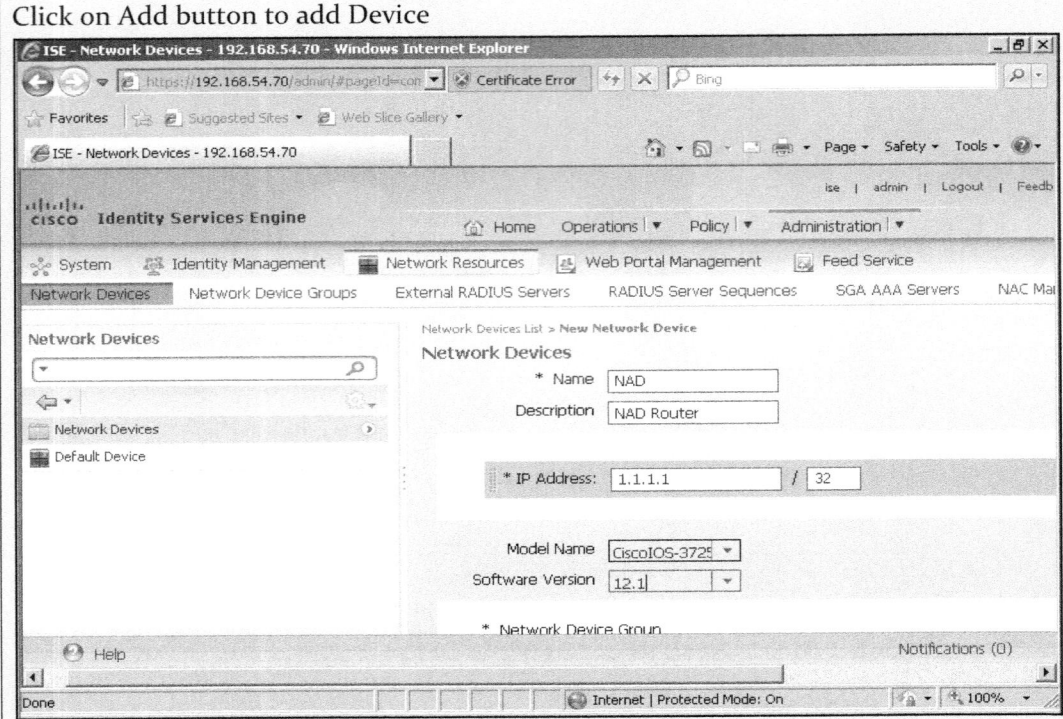

Configure NAME of the device, IP address configured as Source-Interface on NAD.

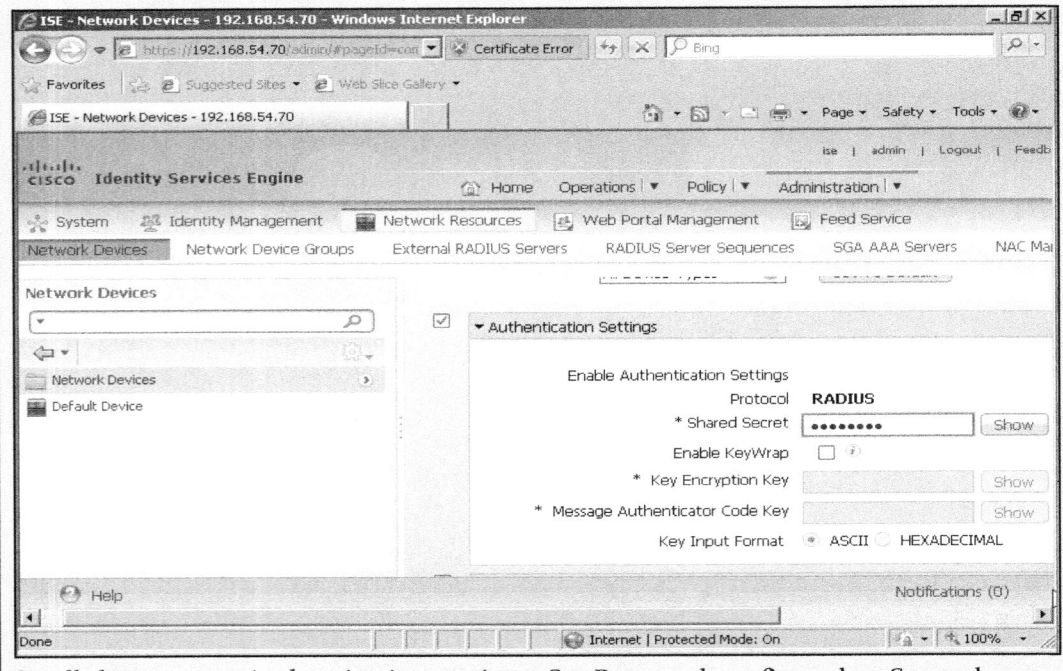

Scroll down to set Authentication settings. Set Password configured as Server key on NAD device " **cisco123**" and save settings.

Now go to **Administrations > Identity Management > Groups > User identity Groups > Add**

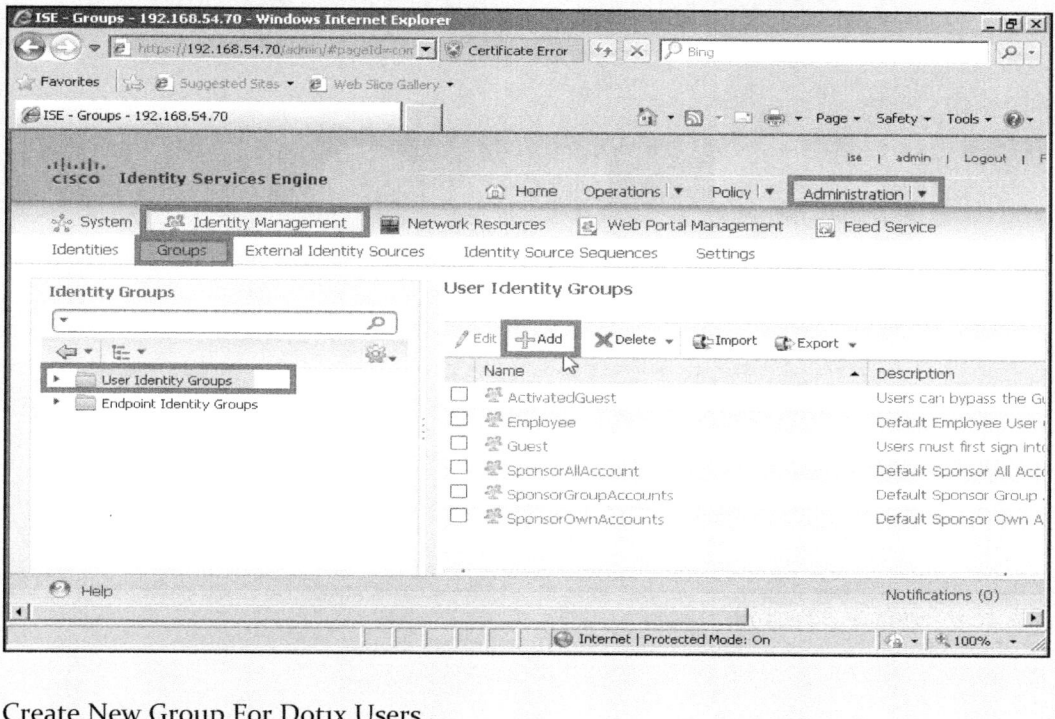

Create New Group For Dotix Users.

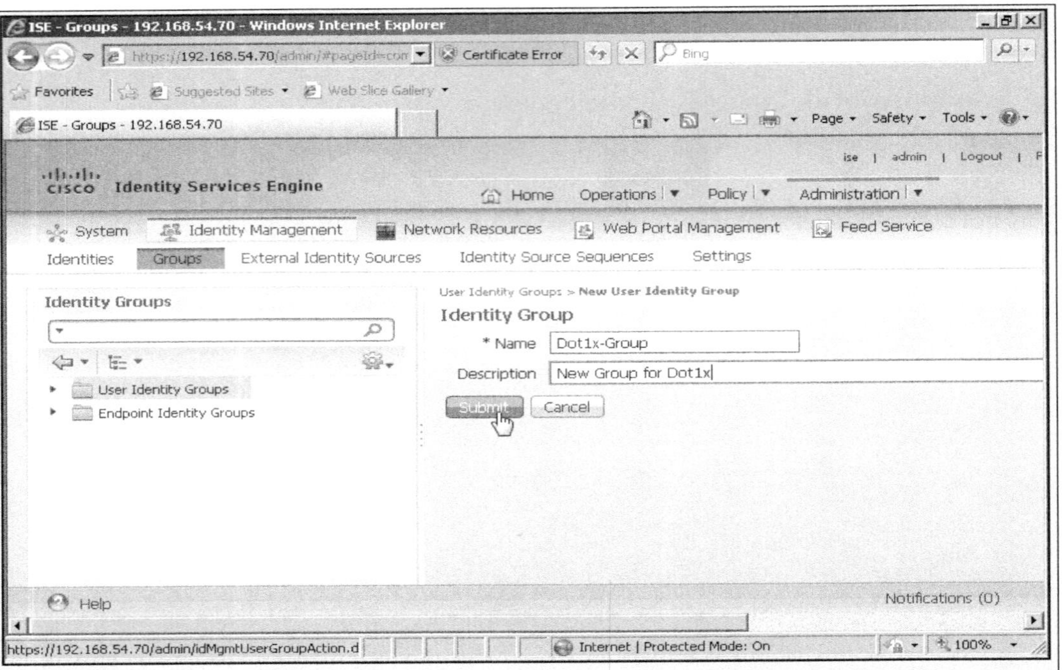

Check if the group is successfully added

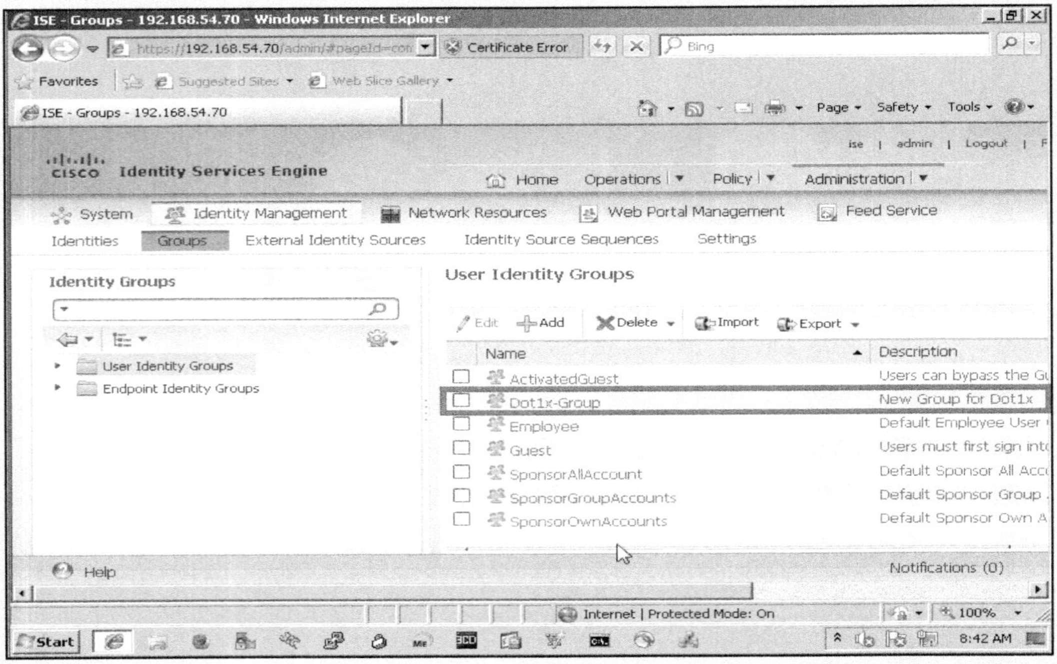

Now go to **Administrations** > **Identity Management** > **Identities** > **add**

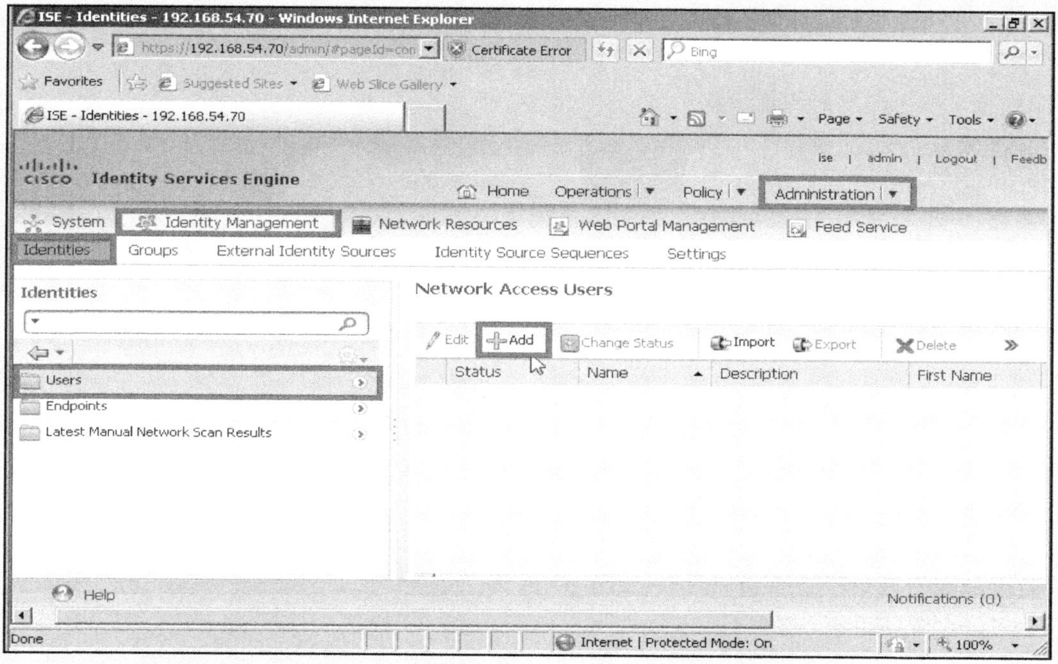

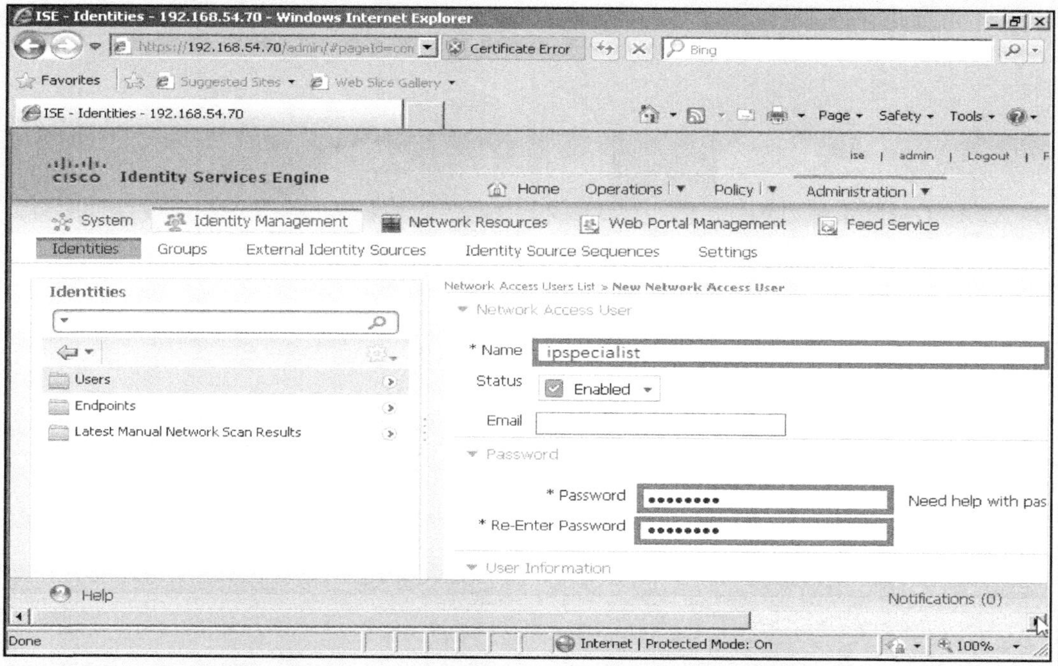

Set Username and Password for Dot1x Port-based Authentication.

Username : **ipspecialist**

Password: **P@$$word:10**

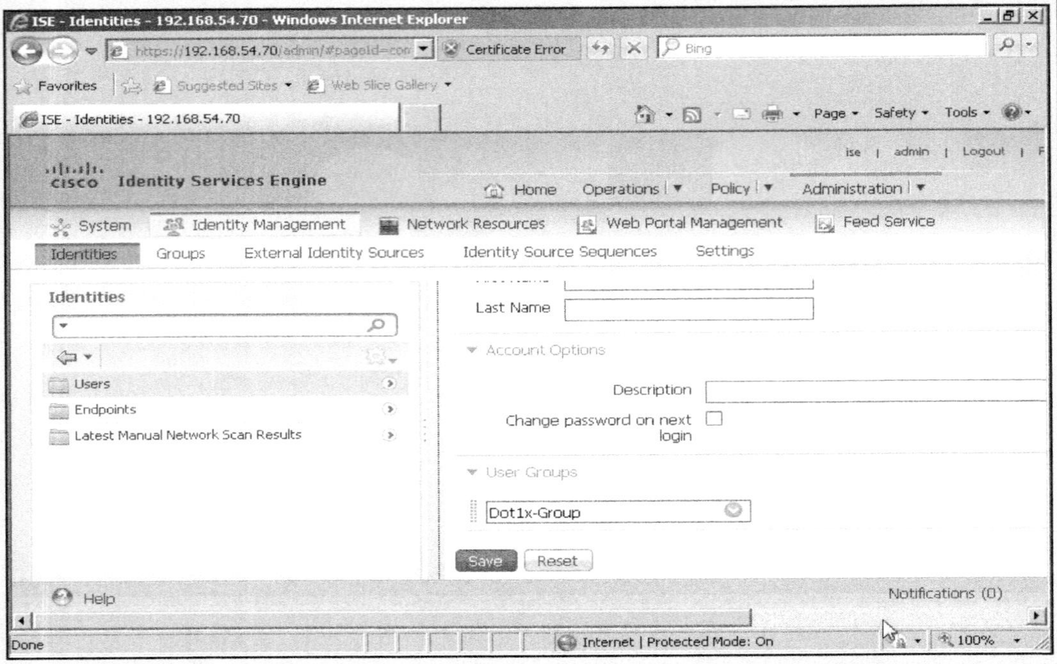

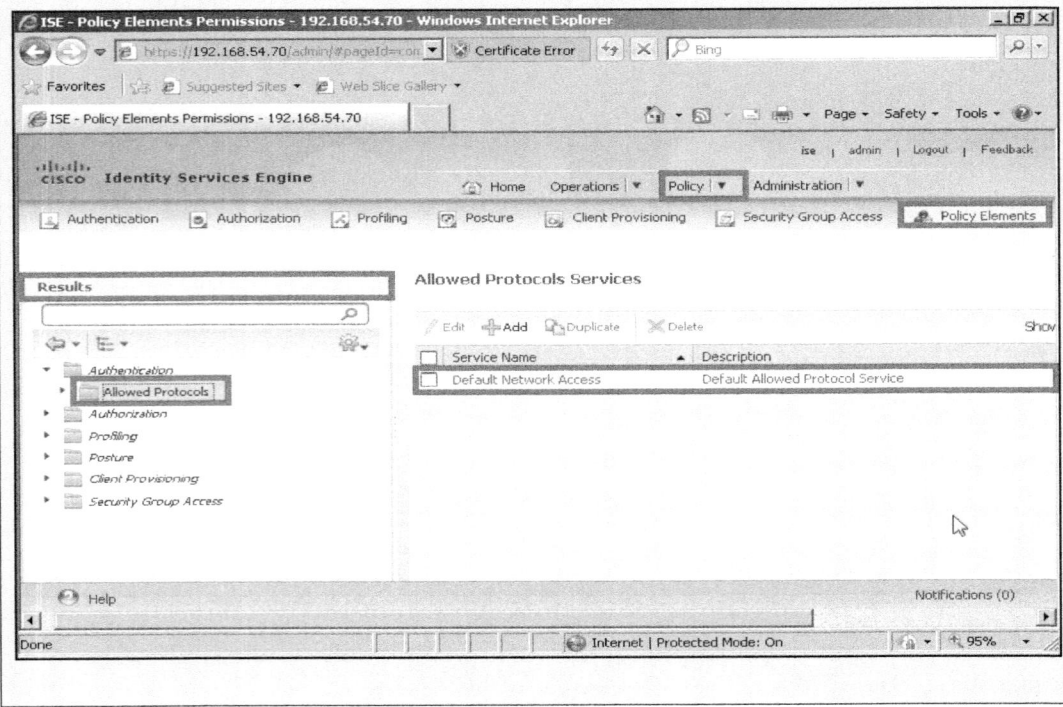

Scroll down and Select the user group to Dot1x-Group and Save Settings.

Now go to **Policy > Policy Elements > Results > Authentication > Allowed Protocols > Default Network Access** and Edit, Check MS-CHAP v2 and Uncheck EAP-TLS from all Locations.

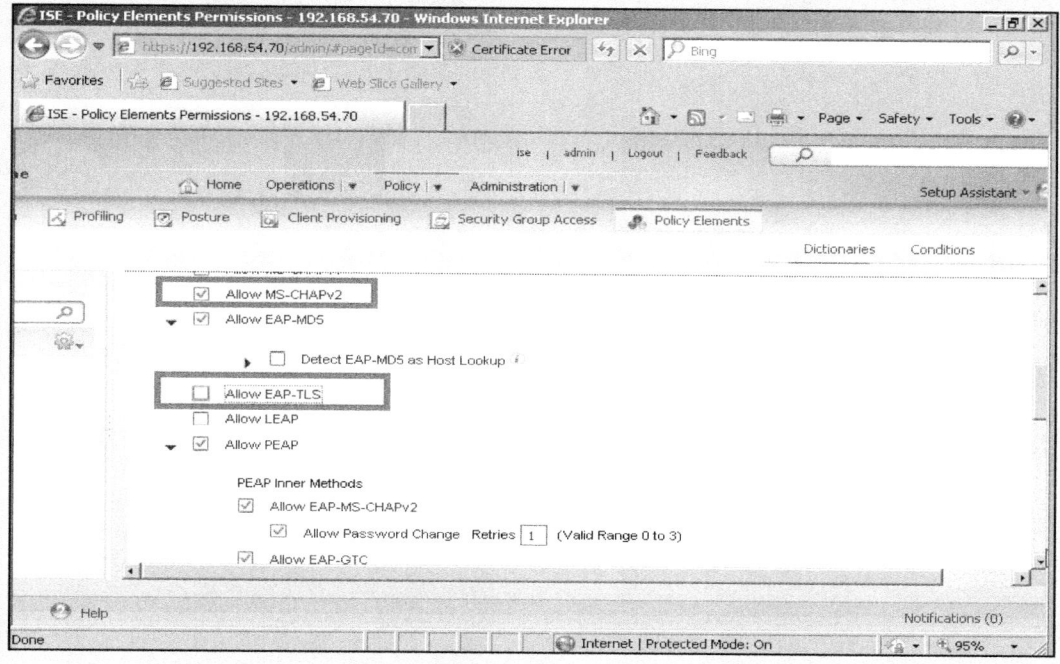

Check MS-CHAPv2 and UnCheck EAP-TLS. There will be three Locations of EAP-TLS that are to be unchecked. Now save the settings

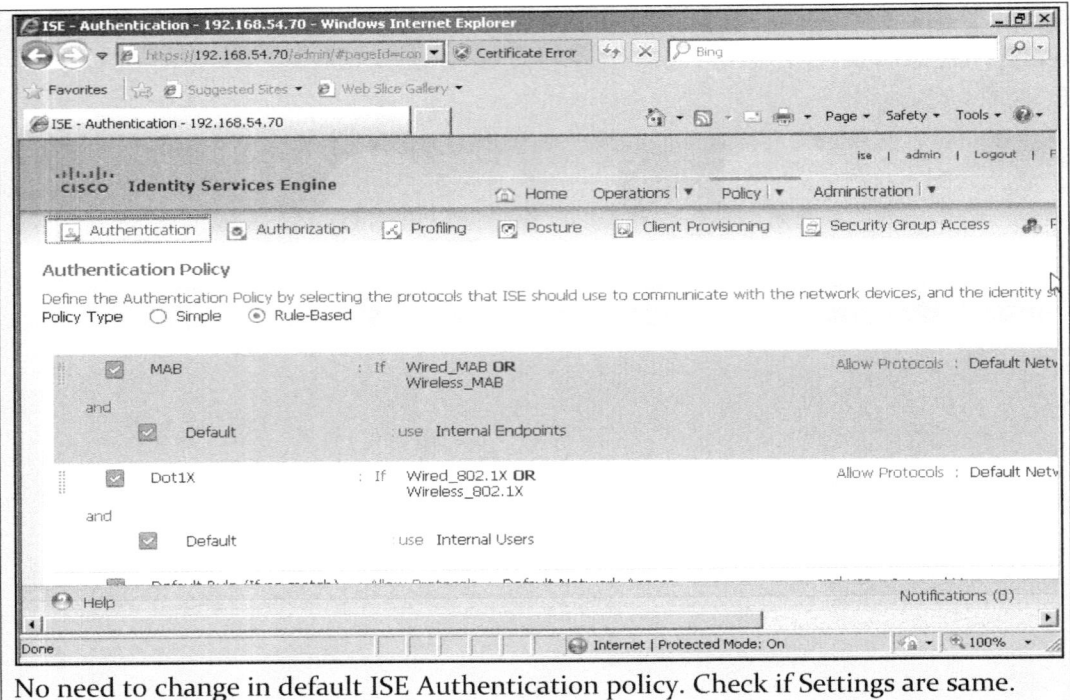

No need to change in default ISE Authentication policy. Check if Settings are same.

Dot1x Client Configuration:

Now, Go to Dot1x-Client PC and from start menu, Search for Service.msc

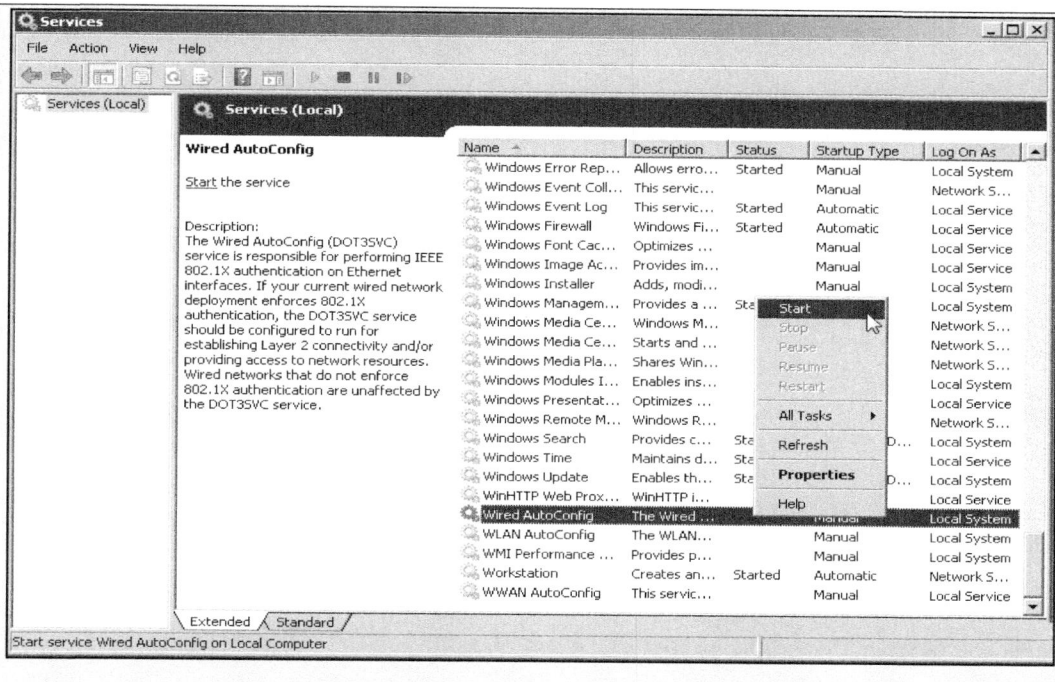

Go to **Wired Auto Config** and Start the service.

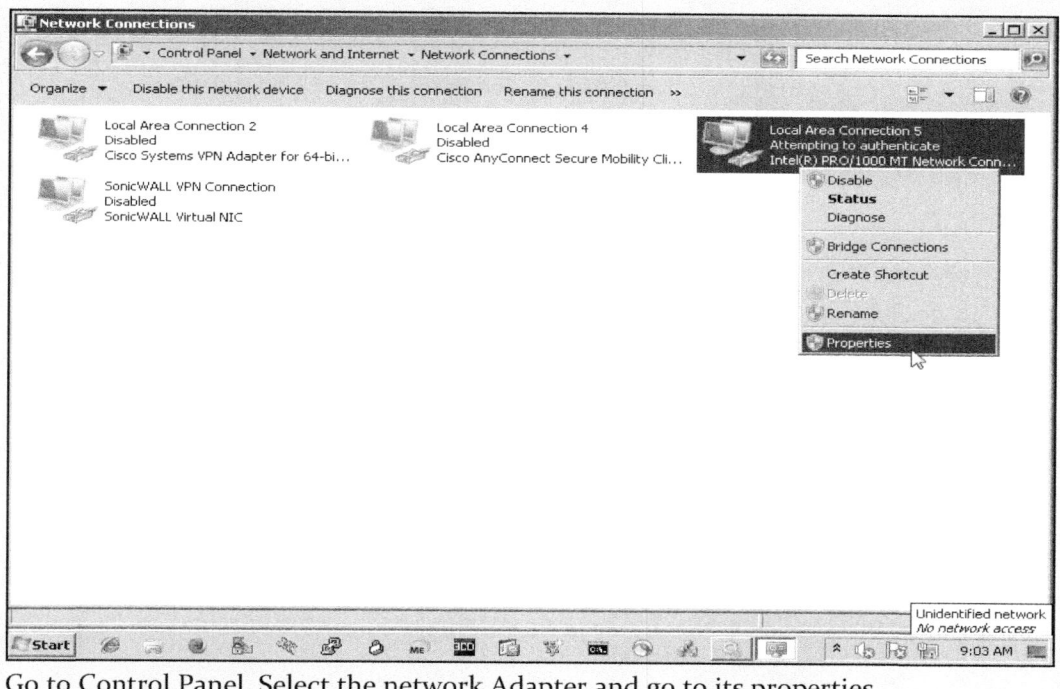

Go to Control Panel, Select the network Adapter and go to its properties.

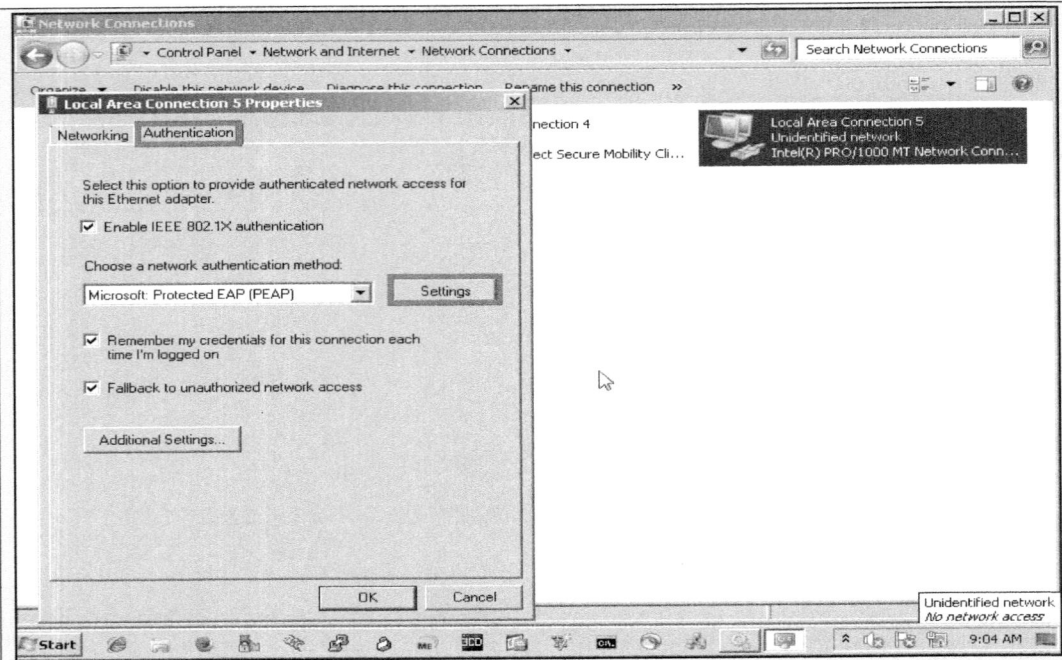

Authentication tab should appear after running **Wired Auto Config** service. Go to Authentication tab and Make sure IEEE 802.1x Authentication is enabled with **EAP(PEAP).** Now Go to Settings for more settings

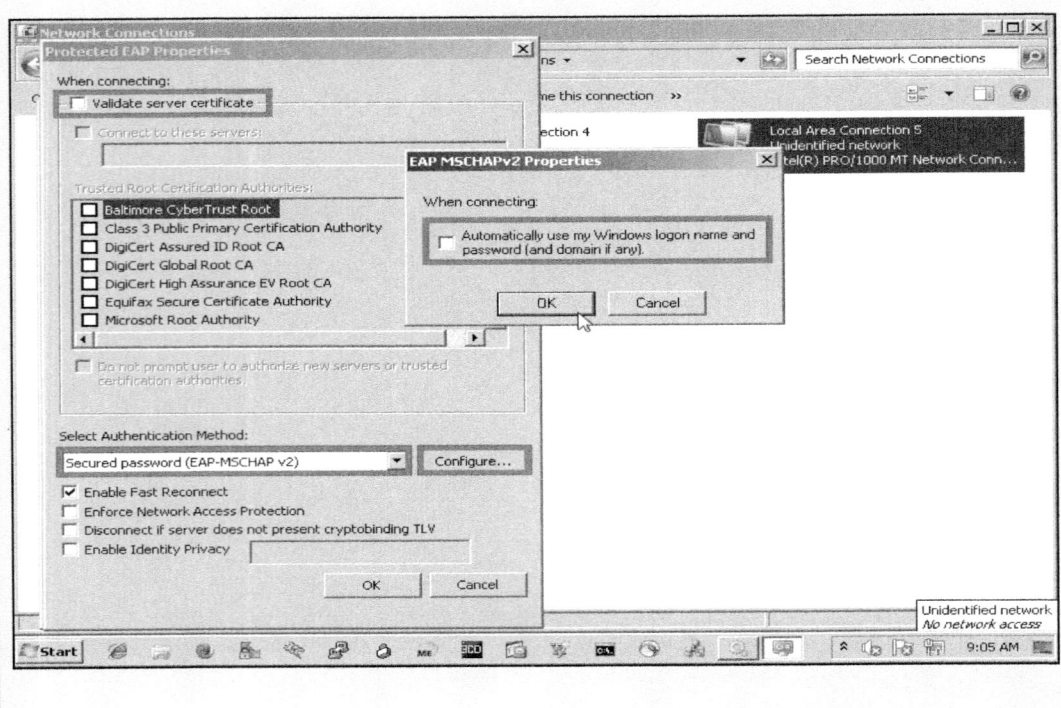

Uncheck Server certificate validation, Set Authentication method **EAP-MSCHAP-v2.**
Click **Configure** button and Uncheck to Auto usage of Windows Session credentials.

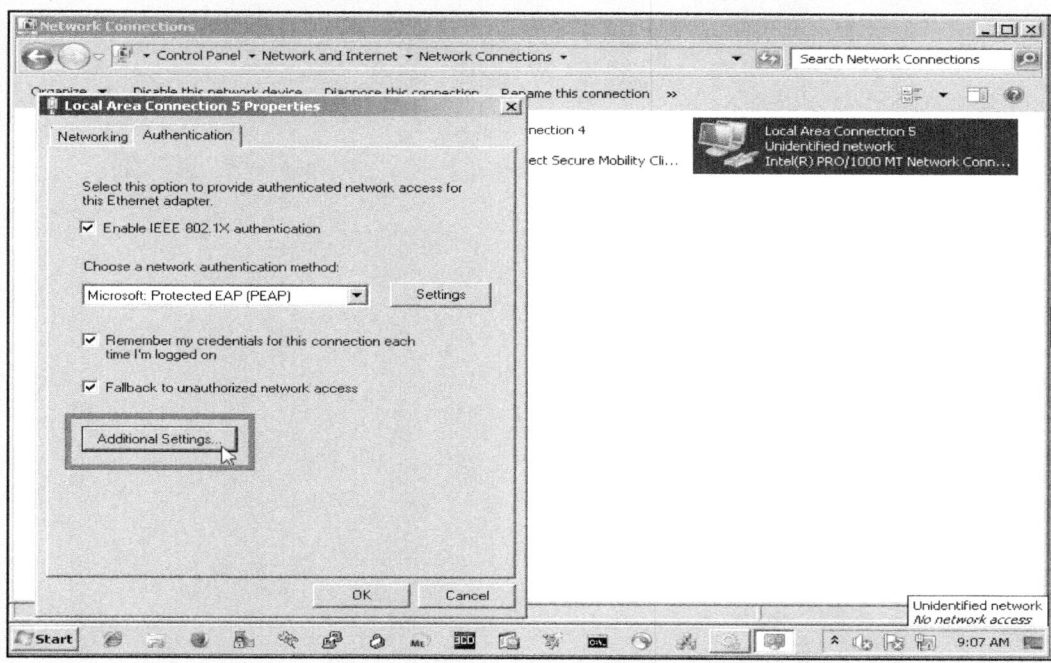

Click on **Additional Settings** button to set Credentials

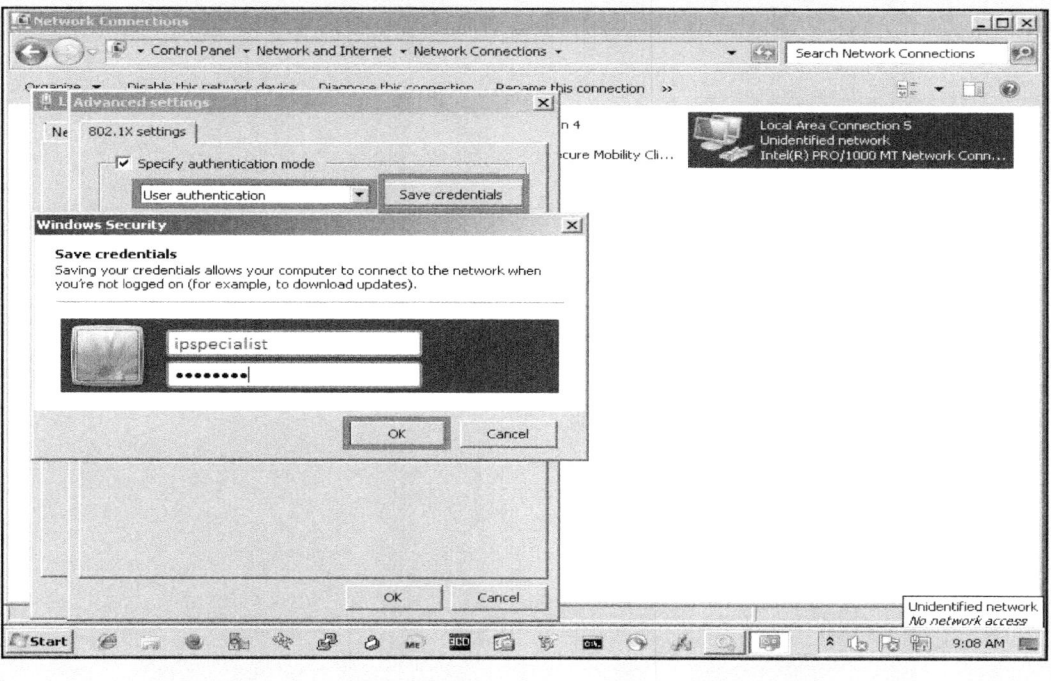

Set Authentication mode to **User Authentication** and Click on **Save Credentials** to Save Credentials. Username is configured as "**ipspecialist**" and password is "**P@$$word:10**"

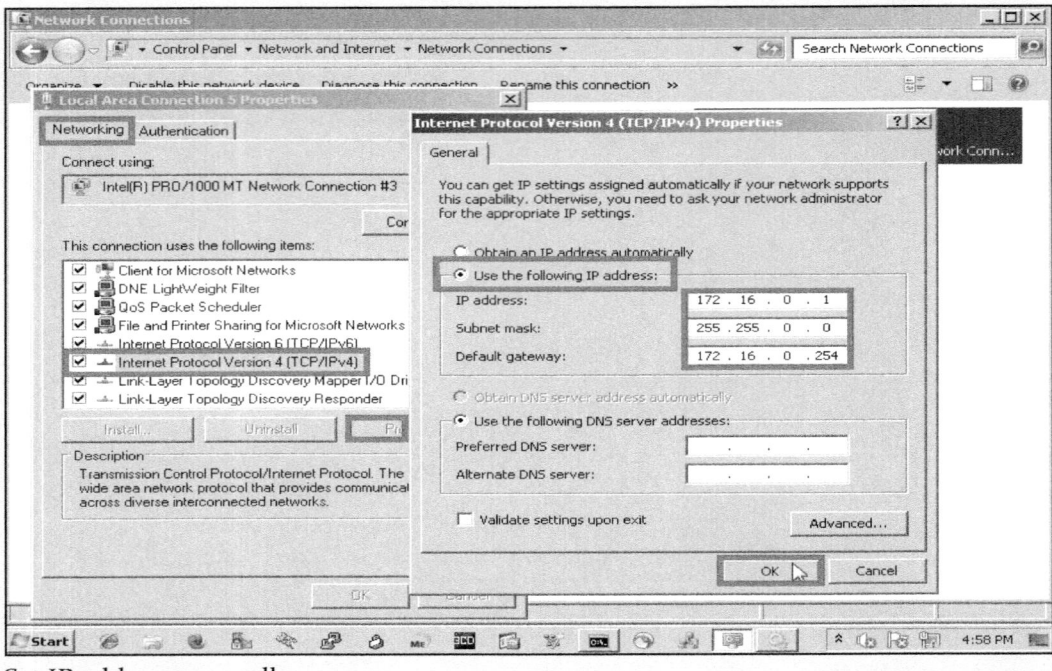

Set IP address manually.

Verification:

Go to **Control Panel > Network And Sharing > Change Adapter Settings**

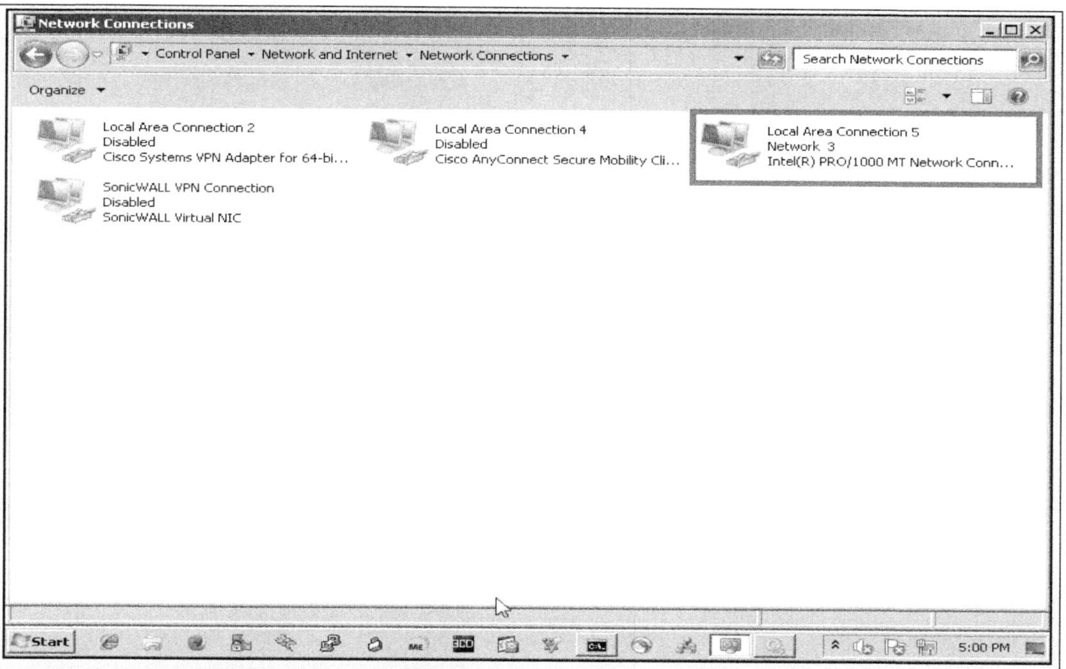

Network is identified and set as **Network 3.**

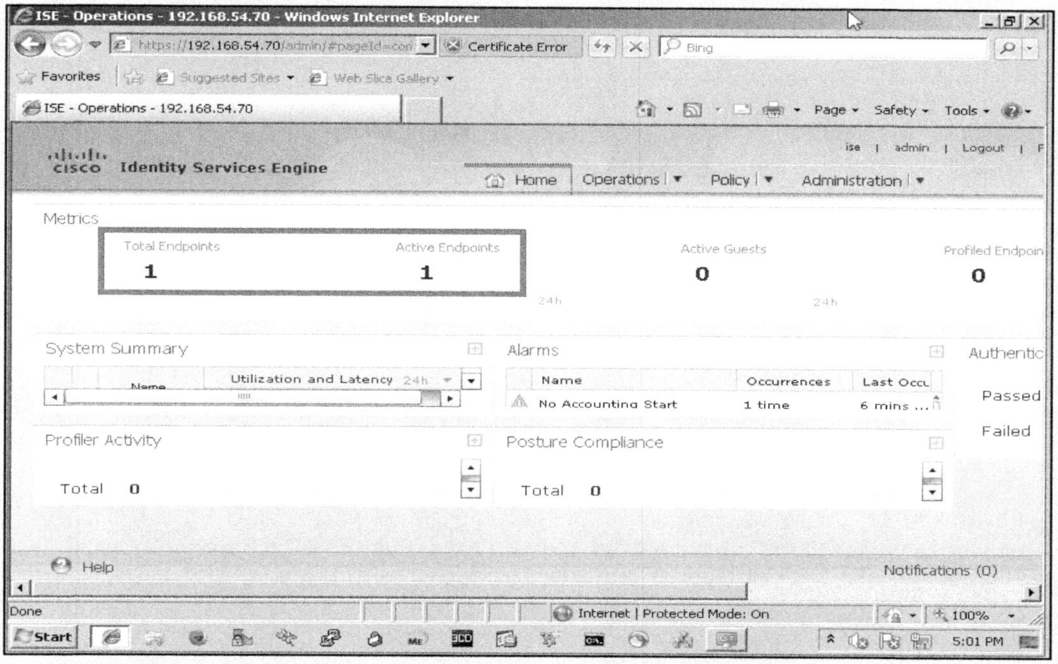

ISE Dashboard showing Successful Authentication count

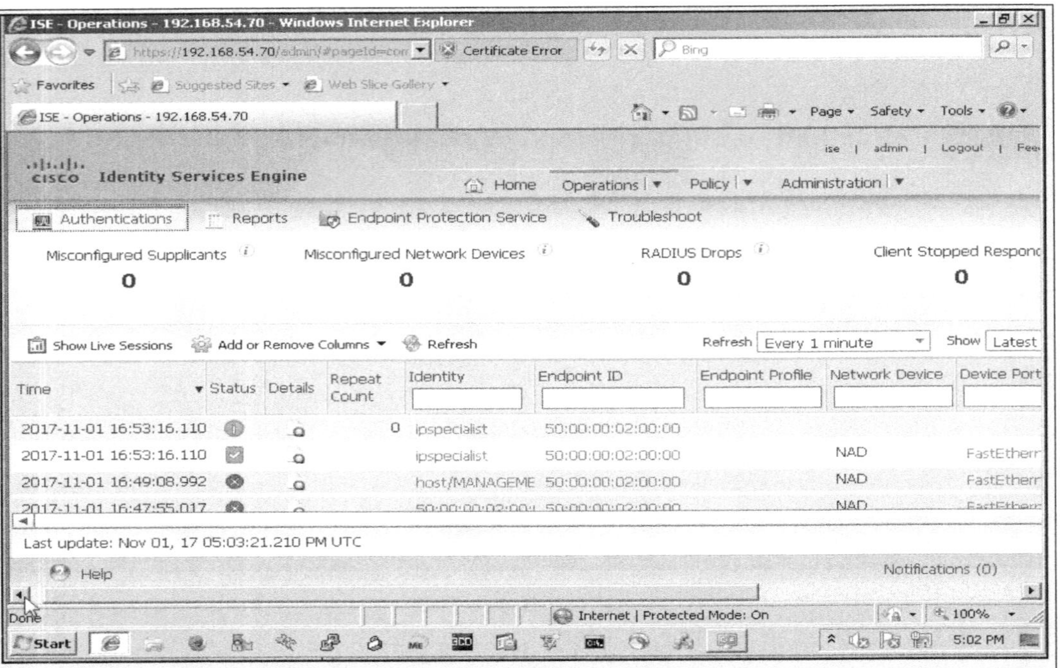

Operation > Authentication showing Authentication session

NAD# **show dot1x all**

```
NAD#show dot1x all
Sysauthcontrol                Enabled
Dot1x Protocol Version          2

Dot1x Info for FastEthernet0/1
----------------------------------
PAE                = AUTHENTICATOR
PortControl        = AUTO
ControlDirection   = Both
HostMode           = SINGLE_HOST
ReAuthentication   = Enabled
QuietPeriod        = 60
ServerTimeout      = 30
SuppTimeout        = 30
ReAuthPeriod       = 4000 (Locally configured)
ReAuthMax          = 2
MaxReq             = 2
TxPeriod           = 60
RateLimitPeriod    = 0
Mac-Auth-Bypass    = Enabled

NAD#
NAD#
```

Dot1x parameters configured on interface fast Ethernet 0/1

NAD# **Show radius statistics**

```
NAD                                                            —    □    ×

NAD#show radius st
NAD#show radius statistics
                                    Auth.        Acct.        Both
           Maximum inQ length:       NA           NA           1
         Maximum waitQ length:       NA           NA           1
         Maximum doneQ length:       NA           NA           1
          Total responses seen:      12           0           12
        Packets with responses:      12           0           12
      Packets without responses:     0            0           0
      Access Rejects         :       2
    Average response delay(ms):      555           0           555
    Maximum response delay(ms):     5292           0          5292
      Number of Radius timeouts:     1            0           1
           Duplicate ID detects:     0            0           0
     Buffer Allocation Failures:     0            0           0
    Maximum Buffer Size (bytes):    417           0           417
    Source Port Range: (2 ports only)
    1645 - 1646
    Last used Source Port/Identifier:
    1645/12
    1646/0

    Elapsed time since counters last cleared: 35m
NAD#
NAD#
```

1645 and 1646 are RADIUS port for Authentication and Accounting.

NAD# **Show dot1x interface fastethernet 0/1 details**

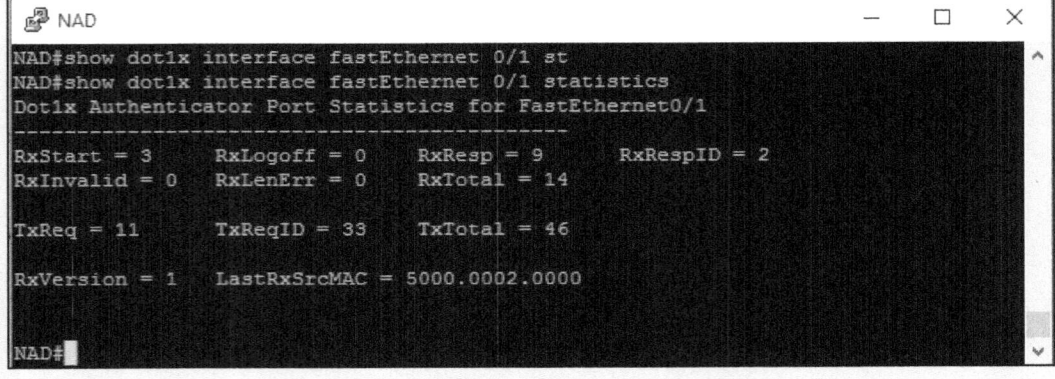

```
NAD                                                    —    □    ×
NAD#show dot1x interface fastEthernet 0/1 de
NAD#show dot1x interface fastEthernet 0/1 details

Dot1x Info for FastEthernet0/1
--------------------------------
PAE                    = AUTHENTICATOR
PortControl            = AUTO
ControlDirection       = Both
HostMode               = SINGLE_HOST
ReAuthentication       = Enabled
QuietPeriod            = 60
ServerTimeout          = 30
SuppTimeout            = 30
ReAuthPeriod           = 4000  (Locally configured)
ReAuthMax              = 2
MaxReq                 = 2
TxPeriod               = 60
RateLimitPeriod        = 0
Mac-Auth-Bypass        = Enabled

Dot1x Authenticator Client List
-------------------------------
Supplicant             = 5000.0002.0000
       Auth SM State   = AUTHENTICATED
       Auth BEND SM Stat = IDLE

Port Status            = AUTHORIZED
ReAuthPeriod           = 4000
ReAuthAction           = Reauthenticate
TimeToNextReauth       = 3560
Authentication Method  = Dot1x

NAD#
```

Supplicant MAC address is shown, Authentication status is authenticated, Port Status
is authorized and Authentication method is Dot1x.

NAD# **Show dot1x interface FastEthernet0/1 statistics**

```
NAD                                                    —    □    ×
NAD#show dot1x interface fastEthernet 0/1 st
NAD#show dot1x interface fastEthernet 0/1 statistics
Dot1x Authenticator Port Statistics for FastEthernet0/1
-------------------------------------------------------
RxStart = 3      RxLogoff = 0     RxResp = 9      RxRespID = 2
RxInvalid = 0    RxLenErr = 0     RxTotal = 14

TxReq = 11       TxReqID = 33     TxTotal = 46

RxVersion = 1    LastRxSrcMAC = 5000.0002.0000

NAD#
```

Showing packet count of dot1x for FastEthernet0/1 Authentication.

Ping from Client PC to other Destination for Testing Network Connectivity

```
Command Prompt                                                    _ | □ | X

Pinging 10.0.0.1 with 32 bytes of data:
Reply from 10.0.0.1: bytes=32 time=82ms TTL=126
Reply from 10.0.0.1: bytes=32 time=21ms TTL=126
Reply from 10.0.0.1: bytes=32 time=30ms TTL=126
Reply from 10.0.0.1: bytes=32 time=27ms TTL=126

Ping statistics for 10.0.0.1:
    Packets: Sent = 4, Received = 4, Lost = 0 (0% loss),
Approximate round trip times in milli-seconds:
    Minimum = 21ms, Maximum = 82ms, Average = 40ms

C:\Users\MANAGEMENT-STATION>ping 200.0.0.1

Pinging 200.0.0.1 with 32 bytes of data:
Request timed out.
Reply from 200.0.0.1: bytes=32 time=28ms TTL=62
Reply from 200.0.0.1: bytes=32 time=26ms TTL=62
Reply from 200.0.0.1: bytes=32 time=22ms TTL=62

Ping statistics for 200.0.0.1:
    Packets: Sent = 4, Received = 3, Lost = 1 (25% loss),
Approximate round trip times in milli-seconds:
    Minimum = 22ms, Maximum = 28ms, Average = 25ms

C:\Users\MANAGEMENT-STATION>_
```

802.1x Phasing

- **Monitor Mode:**

Monitor mode is the Phase 1 of 802.1x phasing. It works likes audit. Administrator uses this mode to verify that all devices are authenticating properly by using Logging data for verification. Authentication may be 802.1x or MAC authentication bypass (MAB). Monitor mode uses RADIUS accounting packets and Open Authentication and Multi Authentication feature to provide visibility to the administrator to monitor if a device which is authenticated successfully but failed due any misconfiguration. The administrator will be informed by logging so that issue can be resolved prior to moving to next phases

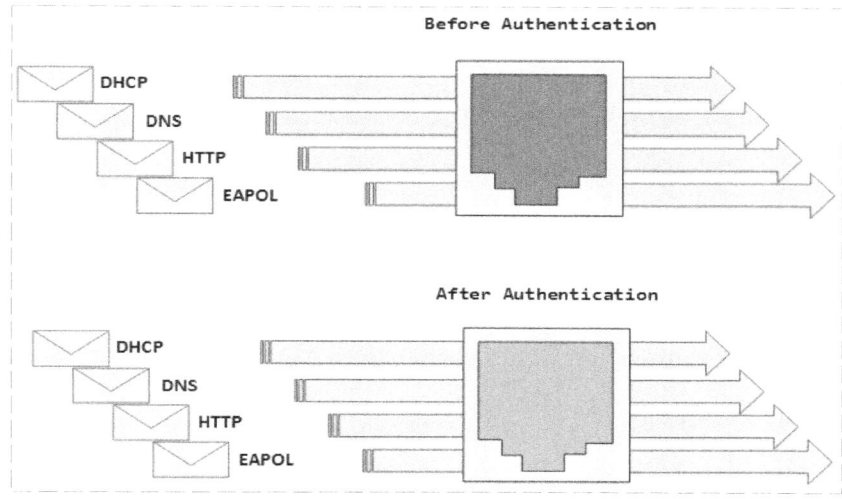

Figure 1-6. Monitor Mode

- **Low Impact Mode:**

In Low Impact Mode, Security is added over the framework built in Monitor mode by configuring ACL to the switch ports. These ACL restricts the port to very limited network access prior the authentication. When user or device is authenticated successfully, additional resources may have granted. In Low impact mode, host connected to the port may be allowed to use Dynamic Host Configuration Protocol (DHCP) and Domain Name System (DNS) and to route to the internet and blocked to use internal resources. After authentication, a downloadable ACL may allow all traffic.

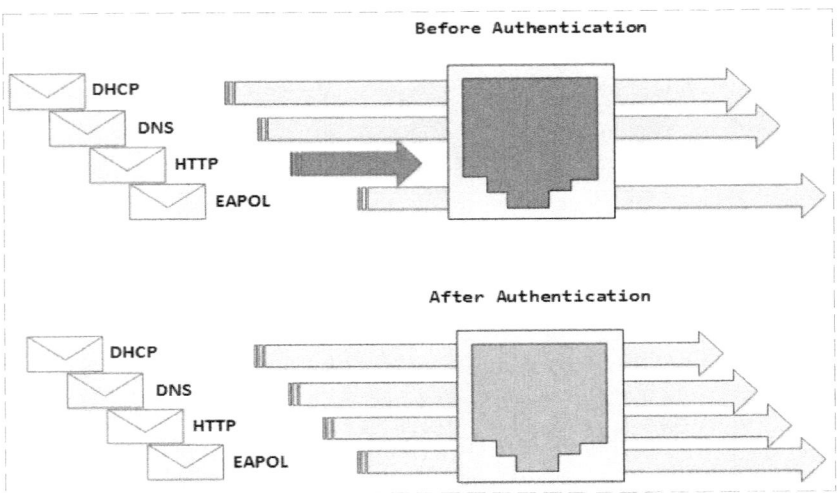

Figure 1-7. Low Impact Mode

- **Closed Mode:**

Closed mode is also lies in the 2nd phase. Closed mode is formerly called High Security mode. This mode is recommended mode for IT environment with experience in deployment of 802.1x. Difference between Closed mode and other modes that Interface command authentication open is not used hence any traffic before authentication will be dropped including DHCP, DNS, ARP etc.

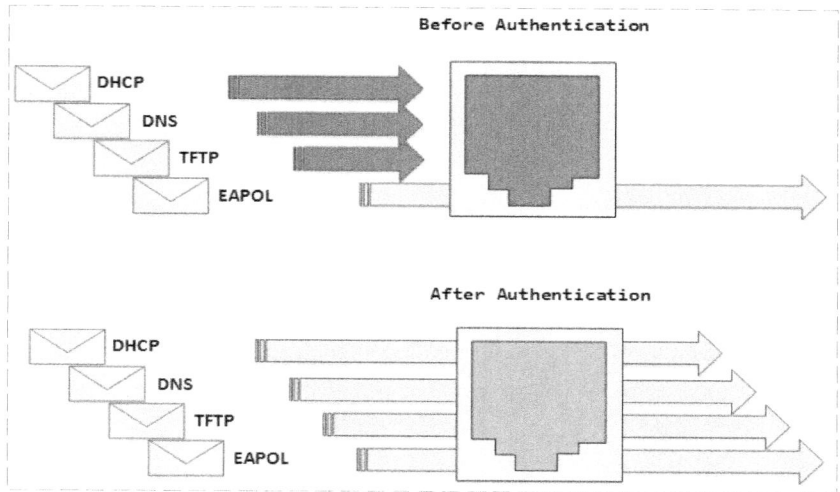

Figure 1-8. Closed Mode

MAC Authentication Bypass

MAB is termed as MAC authentication bypass, which allow you to control devices to access the network at layer 2. MAB is the endpoint authentication process in which Network access device is configured to authenticate Endpoint devices by using Authenticator (RADIUS) server. MAB ensures network visibility till the authentication process is completed. Port status at the end of the authentication process will be Authorized or Unauthorized depending upon the Condition if MAC address is successfully authenticated or not. This visibility may be helpful for audits, forensics, troubleshooting and Network statistics. By Using MAB, customized services can be delivered dynamically to the End point MAC addresses. Authenticated MAC address can be dynamically authorized for particular VLAN; specific ACL can also be configured. All dynamic authorization method that can be used for IEEE 802.1x authentication will also work with MAB. MAB can be implemented over the 802.1x supported devices as well as over the devices which do not support 802.1x authentication, MAB can be deployed as standalone authentication. As MAB is working over MAC address, it is independent of Usernames and passwords. MAC database must be configured, maintained and up to date for MAB authentication. It is not a strong authentication process because it can be overcome by MAC address spoofing. MAC authentication bypass is to be enabled on a port, which can dynamically enabled or disabled depending upon MAC authentication.

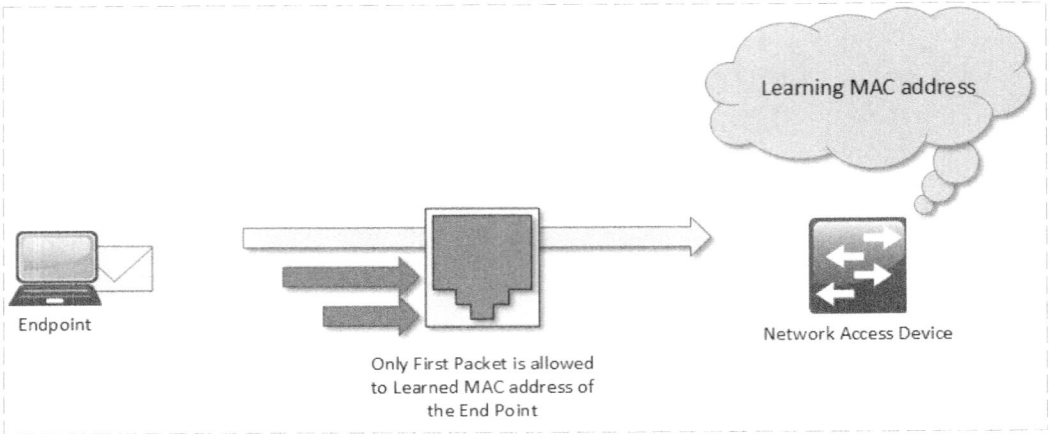

Figure 1-9. MAB

Session Initiation:

First of all, Switch Port begins the authentication session when it detects the link turn to up state. By initiating the authentication, the Switch sends Extensible Authentication Protocol (EAP) request identity message to the device or endpoint accessing the network. In case the switch does not receive a reply from the endpoint, it will retransmit the packet till maximum number of retries and IEEE 802.1x authentication is timeout and proceed to MAB.

MAC Address learning:

During MAC authentication Bypass process, Switch opens the port to detect single Packet for learning MAC address of the Endpoint. As it learns the MAC address of the source Authentication process proceeds further. In 802.1x authentication phase, only EAP packet is allowed. Hence, the Switch was unable to learn the MAC address. Switch can use Layer 2, Layer 3 with exception of bridging frames like CDP, LLDP, STP or DTP. As soon as switch learns MAC address, it will start discarding packet again and send the access-request packet to the RADIUS server

Authentication session:

Access-Request packets are Password Authentication Protocol (PAP) by default. This request includes the Source MAC address of the Endpoint in three attributes: Attribute 1, Attribute 2 and Attribute 31, which are Username, Password and Calling Station ID respectively. MAC address is the same in all of these attributes. Authentication server (RADIUS) may use different attribute for authentication. Some Server may use Attribute 31 while other uses Attribute 1 and 2. As MAB uses PAP protocol and attribute Username and password as authentication, MAB requests are differentiated by setting attribute 6 (Service type) to attribute 10 (call-check) in a MAB access request.

RADIUS Attribute	Format	Example
1 (Username)	12 hexadecimal digits, all lowercase, and no punctuation	aabbccdd0011
2 (Password)	Same as the username but encrypted	\xf2\xb8\x9c\x9c\x13\xdd#
31 (Calling-Station-Id)	6 groups of 2 hexadecimal digits, all uppercase, and separated by hyphens	AA-BB-CC-DD-00-11

Table 4. MAC address format in RADIUS attributes

Single-Host Mode

If the port of Network access device is configured as single-host mode, only a single MAC or IP address can be authenticated (by any method) configured on a port. If a different or multiple MAC addresses are detected on the port after an endpoint has authenticated with MAB, then a security violation will be triggered on the port. This is the default behaviour.

Configuring Host-Mode

```
Router(config)# interface [Interface-name]
Router(config-if)# dot1x host-mode ?
  multi-auth    Multiple Authentication Mode
  multi-host    Multiple Host Mode
  single-host   Single Host Mode
Router(config-if)# dot1x host-mode single-host
Router(config-if)# end
```

Multi-domain Authentication Host Mode

Multi-domain authentication was specifically designed to address the requirements of IP telephony or voice VLAN. When multi-domain authentication is configured, two endpoints are allowed on the port, one in the voice VLAN and one in the data VLAN. Either, both, or none of the endpoints can be authenticated with MAB. Additional MAC addresses will trigger a security violation.

Multi-Authentication Host Mode

If the port is configured for multi-authentication (multi-auth) host mode, then multiple endpoints can be authenticated in the data VLAN. Each new MAC address that appears on the port will be separately authenticated. Any, all, or none of the

endpoints can be authenticated with MAB. Multi-auth host mode can be used for bridged virtual environments or to support hubs.

Multi-host Mode

Unlike multi-auth host mode, which authenticates every MAC address, multi host mode authenticates the first MAC address and then allows an unlimited number of other MAC addresses. Because of the security implications of multi host mode, multi-auth host mode typically is a better choice than multi host mode.

Lab 1.2: MAC Authentication Bypass (MAB)
Case Study:

In an organization, Administrator deploying MAC Authentication Bypass. Router is used as Network Access Device (NAD). Endpoint PCs including Switch is considered in Endpoint Devices. Requirement of the Lab is to configure MAB Authentication with. Cisco ISE Internal Datastore can be used for Endpoint registry.

Topology Diagram:

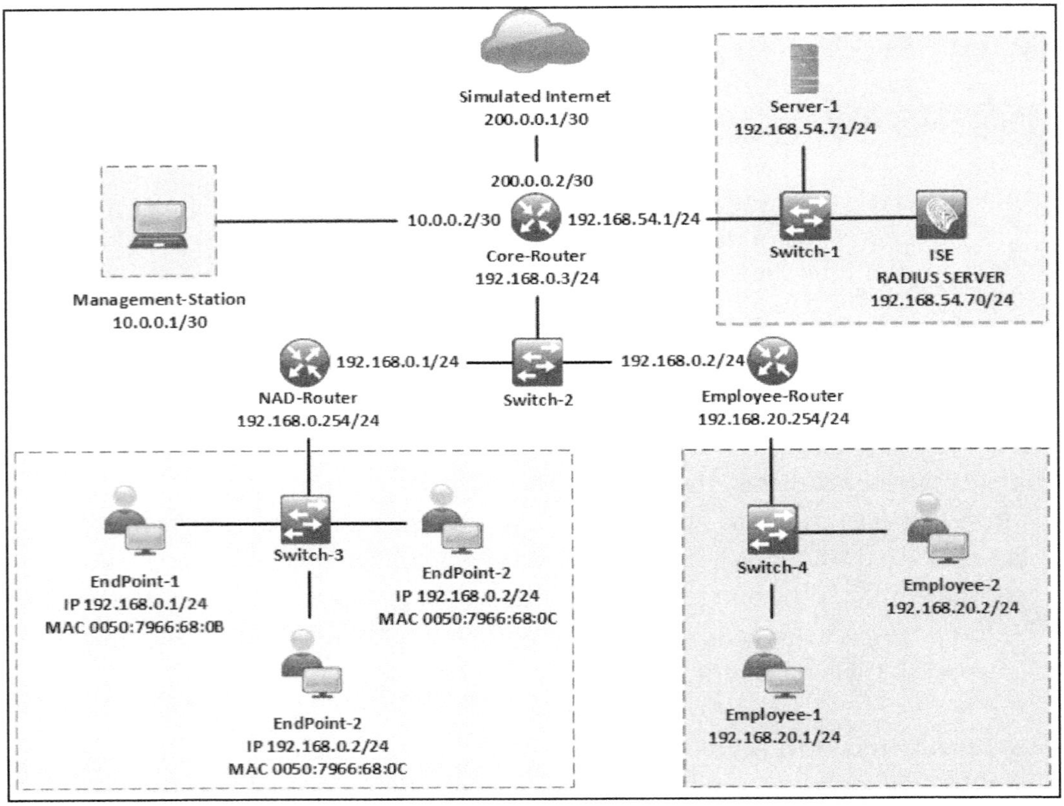

Core-Router Configuration

Router(config)#hostname Core-Router
Core-Router(config)#interface FastEthernet 0/0
Core-Router(config-if)#ip add 192.168.54.1 255.255.255.0
Core-Router(config-if)#no sh
Core-Router(config-if)#ex
*Mar 1 00:11:23.391: %LINK-3-UPDOWN: Interface FastEthernet0/0, changed state to up
*Mar 1 00:11:24.391: %LINEPROTO-5-UPDOWN: Line protocol on Interface FastEthernet0/0, changed state to up

Core-Router(config)#Interface FastEthernet 0/1
Core-Router(config-if)#ip add 10.0.0.2 255.255.255.252
Core-Router(config-if)#no sh
Core-Router(config-if)#ex
*Mar 1 00:11:48.143: %LINK-3-UPDOWN: Interface FastEthernet0/1, changed state to up
*Mar 1 00:11:49.143: %LINEPROTO-5-UPDOWN: Line protocol on Interface FastEthernet0/1, changed state to up

Core-Router(config)#Interface FastEthernet 1/0
Core-Router(config-if)#ip add 200.0.0.2 255.255.255.252
Core-Router(config-if)#no sh
Core-Router(config-if)#ex
*Mar 1 00:12:15.455: %LINK-3-UPDOWN: Interface FastEthernet1/0, changed state to up
*Mar 1 00:12:16.455: %LINEPROTO-5-UPDOWN: Line protocol on Interface FastEthernet1/0, changed state to up

Core-Router(config)#Interface FastEthernet 2/0
Core-Router(config-if)#ip add 192.168.10.3 255.255.255.0
Core-Router(config-if)#no sh
Core-Router(config-if)#ex
*Mar 1 00:12:43.687: %LINK-3-UPDOWN: Interface FastEthernet2/0, changed state to up
*Mar 1 00:12:44.687: %LINEPROTO-5-UPDOWN: Line protocol on Interface FastEthernet2/0, changed state to up

*Mar 1 00:12:52.451: %CDP-4-DUPLEX_MISMATCH: duplex mismatch discovered on FastEthernet2/0 (not half duplex), with Switch Ethernet0/0 (half duplex).

Core-Router(config)#no cdp run
*Mar 1 00:13:35.487: %LINK-3-UPDOWN: Interface FastEthernet2/0, changed state to up
*Mar 1 00:13:36.487: %LINEPROTO-5-UPDOWN: Line protocol on Interface FastEthernet2/0, changed state to up

Core-Router(config)#router ospf 10
Core-Router(config-router)#network 192.168.54.0 0.0.0.255 area 0
Core-Router(config-router)#network 10.0.0.0 0.0.0.3 area 0

Core-Router(config-router)#network 200.0.0.0 0.0.0.3 area 0
Core-Router(config-router)#network 192.168.10.0 0.0.0.255 area 0
Core-Router(config-router)#ex
Core-Router(config)#
*Mar 1 00:14:39.039: %OSPF-5-ADJCHG: Process 10, Nbr 192.168.10.1 on FastEthernet2/0 from LOADING to FULL, Loading Done

Employee-Router Configuration

Router(config)#hostname Employee-Router
Employee-Router(config)#interface FastEthernet 0/0
Employee-Router(config-if)#ip add 192.168.10.2 255.255.255.0
Employee-Router(config-if)#no sh
Employee-Router(config-if)#ex
Employee-Router(config)#
*Mar 1 00:12:49.559: %LINK-3-UPDOWN: Interface FastEthernet0/0, changed state to up
*Mar 1 00:12:50.559: %LINEPROTO-5-UPDOWN: Line protocol on Interface FastEthernet0/0, changed state to up

Employee-Router(config)#interface FastEthernet 0/1
Employee-Router(config-if)#ip add 192.168.20.254 255.255.255.0
Employee-Router(config-if)#no sh
Employee-Router(config-if)#ex
*Mar 1 00:13:15.127: %LINK-3-UPDOWN: Interface FastEthernet0/1, changed state to up
*Mar 1 00:13:16.127: %LINEPROTO-5-UPDOWN: Line protocol on Interface FastEthernet0/1, changed state to up

Employee-Router(config)#router ospf 10
Employee-Router(config-router)#network 192.168.20.0 0.0.0.255 area 0
Employee-Router(config-router)#network 192.168.10.0 0.0.0.255 area 0
Employee-Router(config-router)#ex
*Mar 1 00:13:44.191: %OSPF-5-ADJCHG: Process 10, Nbr 192.168.10.1 on FastEthernet0/0 from LOADING to FULL, Loading Done
*Mar 1 00:13:44.195: %OSPF-5-ADJCHG: Process 10, Nbr 200.0.0.2 on FastEthernet0/0 from LOADING to FULL, Loading Done

NAD Router Configuration:

Router(config)#hostname NAD-Router
NAD-Router(config)#interface FastEthernet 0/0
NAD-Router(config-if)#ip add 192.168.10.1 255.255.255.0
NAD-Router(config-if)#no sh
NAD-Router(config-if)#ex

```
*Mar  1 00:05:37.719: %LINK-3-UPDOWN: Interface FastEthernet0/0, changed state to up
*Mar  1 00:05:38.719: %LINEPROTO-5-UPDOWN: Line protocol on Interface FastEthernet0/0, changed
state to up


NAD-Router(config)#interface FastEthernet 0/1
NAD-Router(config-if)#ip add 192.168.0.254 255.255.255.0
NAD-Router(config-if)#no sh
NAD-Router(config-if)#ex
*Mar  1 00:06:05.619: %LINK-3-UPDOWN: Interface FastEthernet0/1, changed state to up
*Mar  1 00:06:06.619: %LINEPROTO-5-UPDOWN: Line protocol on Interface FastEthernet0/1, changed
state to up


NAD-Router(config)#router ospf 10
NAD-Router(config-router)#network 192.168.0.0 0.0.0.255 area 0
NAD-Router(config-router)#network 192.168.10.0 0.0.0.255 area 0
NAD-Router(config-router)#network 1.1.1.1 0.0.0.0 area 0
NAD-Router(config-router)#ex


NAD-Router(config)#interface loopback 0
*Mar  1 00:07:52.731: %LINEPROTO-5-UPDOWN: Line protocol on Interface Loopback0, changed state
to up
NAD-Router(config-if)#ip add 1.1.1.1 255.255.255.255
NAD-Router(config-if)#ex
NAD-Router(config)#


NAD-Router(config)#aaa new-model
NAD-Router(config)#aaa authentication dot1x default group radius
NAD-Router(config)#dot1x system-auth-control
NAD-Router(config)#ip radius source-interface loopback 0
NAD-Router(config)#radius-server host 192.168.54.70
NAD-Router(config)#radius-server key cisco123


NAD-Router(config)#interface Fastethernet 0/1
NAD-Router(config-if)#dot1x port-control auto
NAD-Router(config-if)#dot1x pae authenticator
NAD-Router(config-if)#dot1x reauthentication
NAD-Router(config-if)#dot1x timeout tx-period 60
NAD-Router(config-if)#dot1x timeout reauth-period 4000
NAD-Router(config-if)#ex
```

Switch-3 Configuration:

Switch-3(config)# interface Ethernet 0/0
 Switch-3(config-if)#switchport mode access
Switch-3(config-if)# dot1x pae supplicant

Collection MAC Addresses

Go to Endpoint PC-1 and issue the command show IP

```
Endpoint-1                                    —    □    ×

VPCS> show ip

NAME          : VPCS[1]
IP/MASK       : 192.168.0.1/24
GATEWAY       : 192.168.0.254
DNS           :
MAC           : 00:50:79:66:68:0b
LPORT         : 20000
RHOST:PORT    : 127.0.0.1:30000
MTU           : 1500

VPCS>
```

Go to Endpoint PC-2 and issue the command show IP

```
Endpoint-2                                    —    □    ×

VPCS> show ip

NAME          : VPCS[1]
IP/MASK       : 192.168.0.2/24
GATEWAY       : 192.168.0.254
DNS           :
MAC           : 00:50:79:66:68:0c
LPORT         : 20000
RHOST:PORT    : 127.0.0.1:30000
MTU           : 1500

VPCS>
```

Go to Endpoint PC-3 and issue the command show IP

```
Endpoint-3                                    —    □    ×

VPCS> show ip

NAME          : VPCS[1]
IP/MASK       : 192.168.0.3/24
GATEWAY       : 192.168.0.254
DNS           :
MAC           : 00:50:79:66:68:0d
LPORT         : 20000
RHOST:PORT    : 127.0.0.1:30000
MTU           : 1500

VPCS>
```

Go to Switch-3and issue the command show Interface Ethernet 0/0

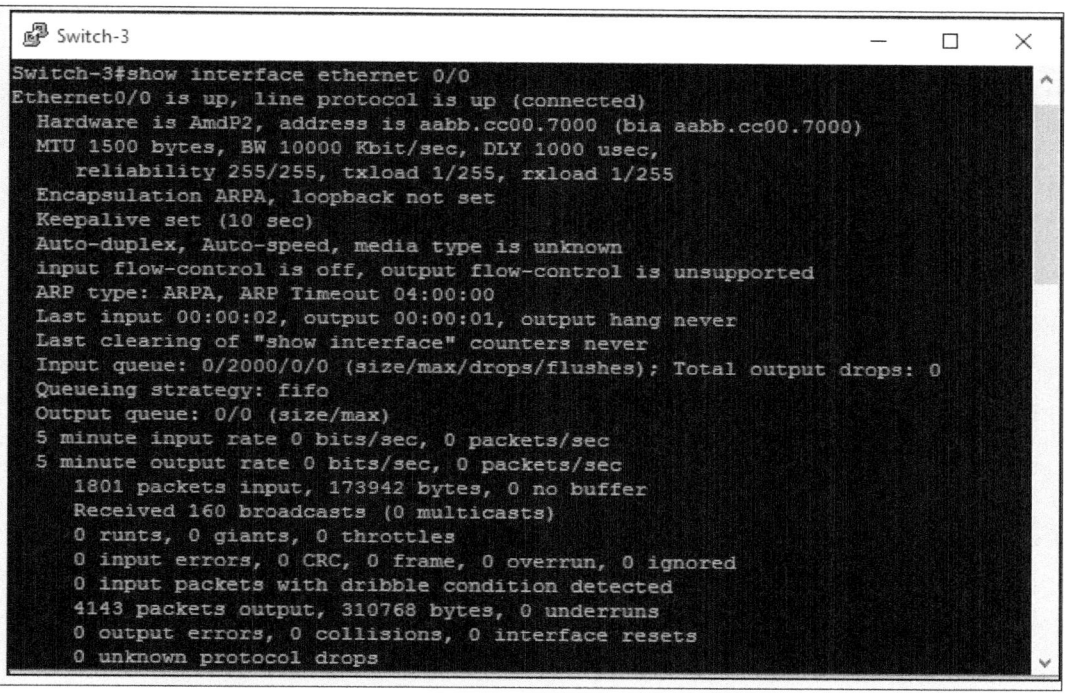

Configuring Cisco ISE

Go to the Management-Station and check if IP Address is properly configured. If not,
Set the IP address to 10.0.0.1 /30 and gateway 10.0.0.2 as shown in the figure below

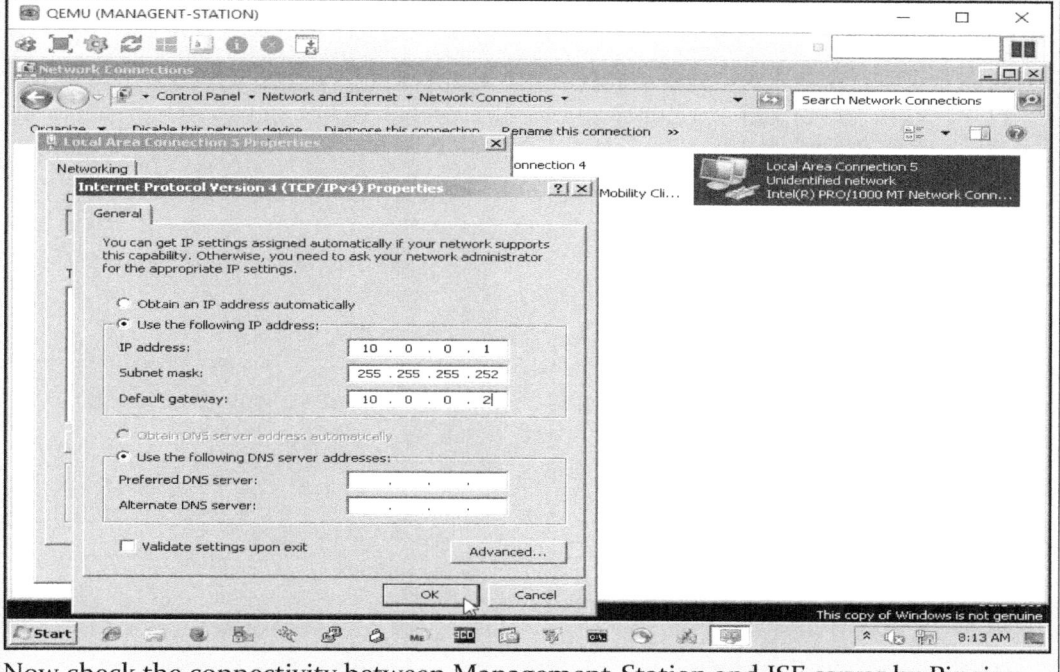

Now check the connectivity between Management-Station and ISE server by Pinging.

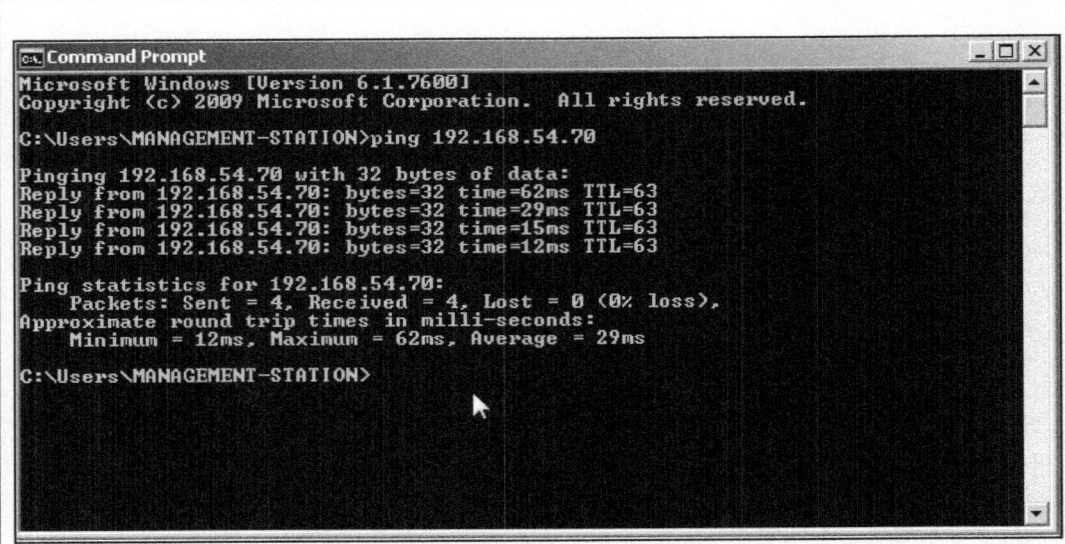

Now go to Internet Explorer and go to URL https://192.168.54.70

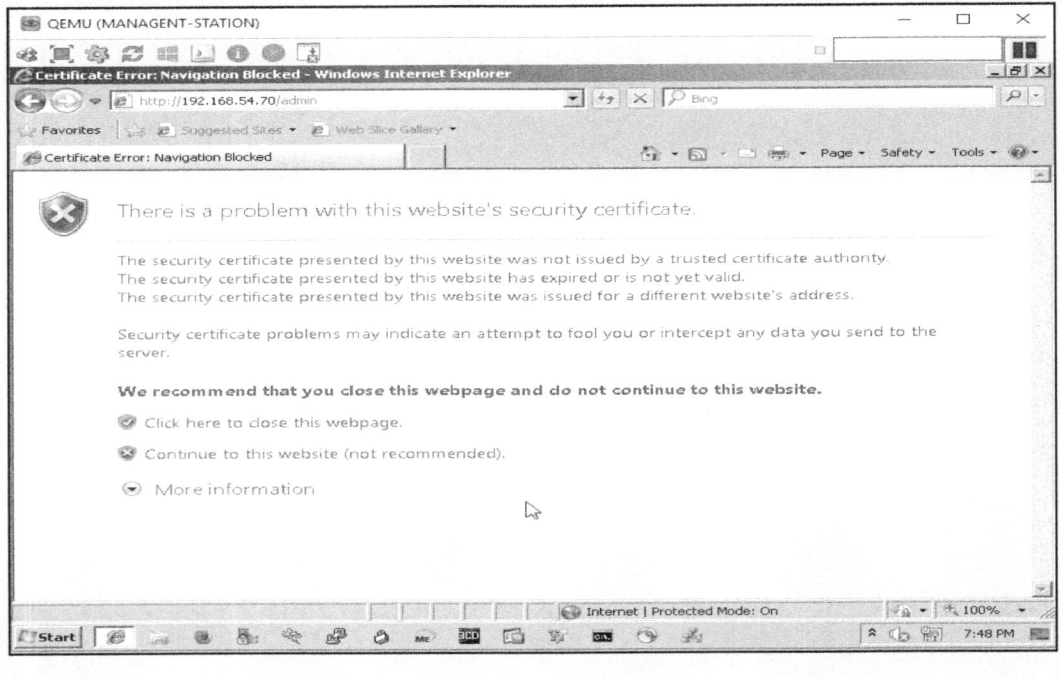

Click on **Continue to this Website**

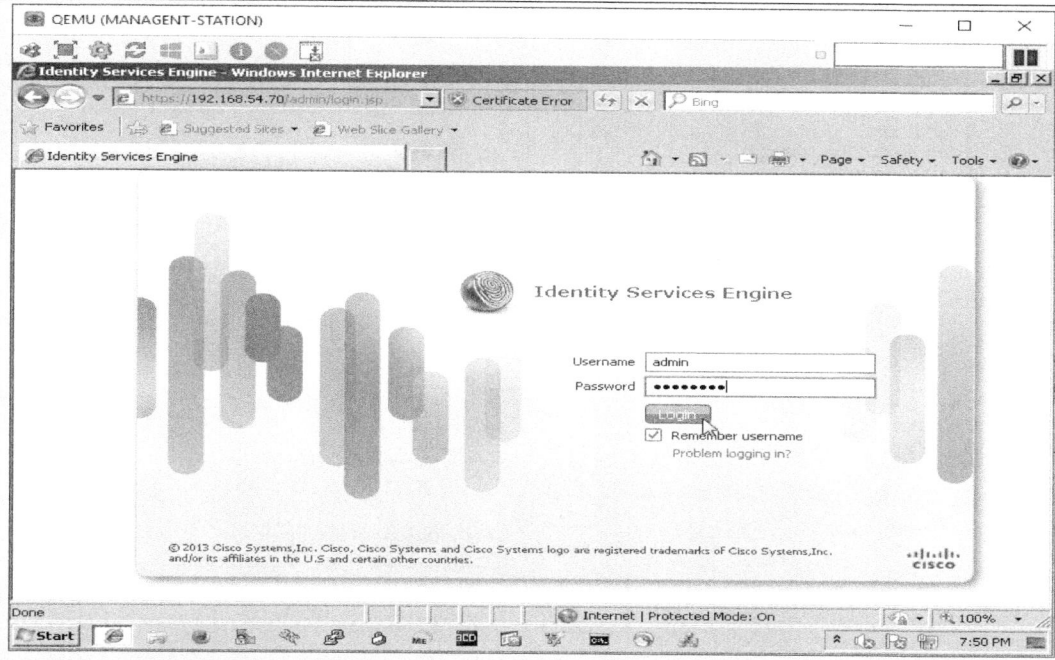

Username : admin

Password : Cisco123

After Successful Login, Go to **Administration > Network Resources > Network Devices** to add the Device (NAD-Router), which will request to authenticate Dot1x Client as shown below.

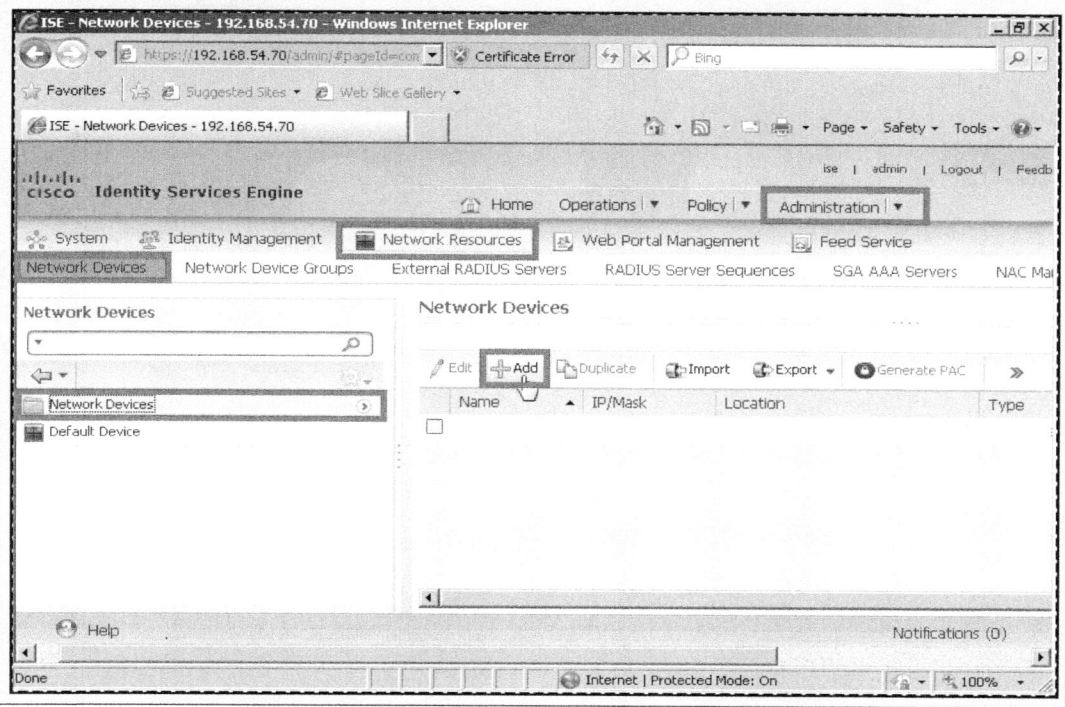

Click on Add button to add Device

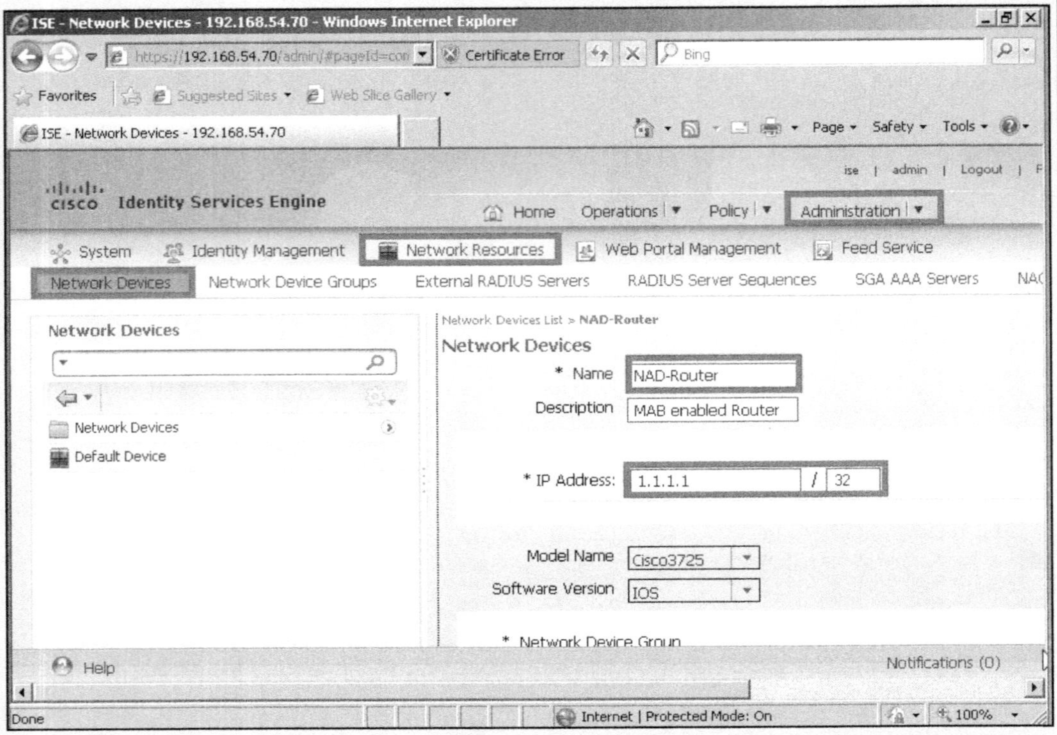

Configure NAME of the device, IP address configured as Source-Interface on NAD.

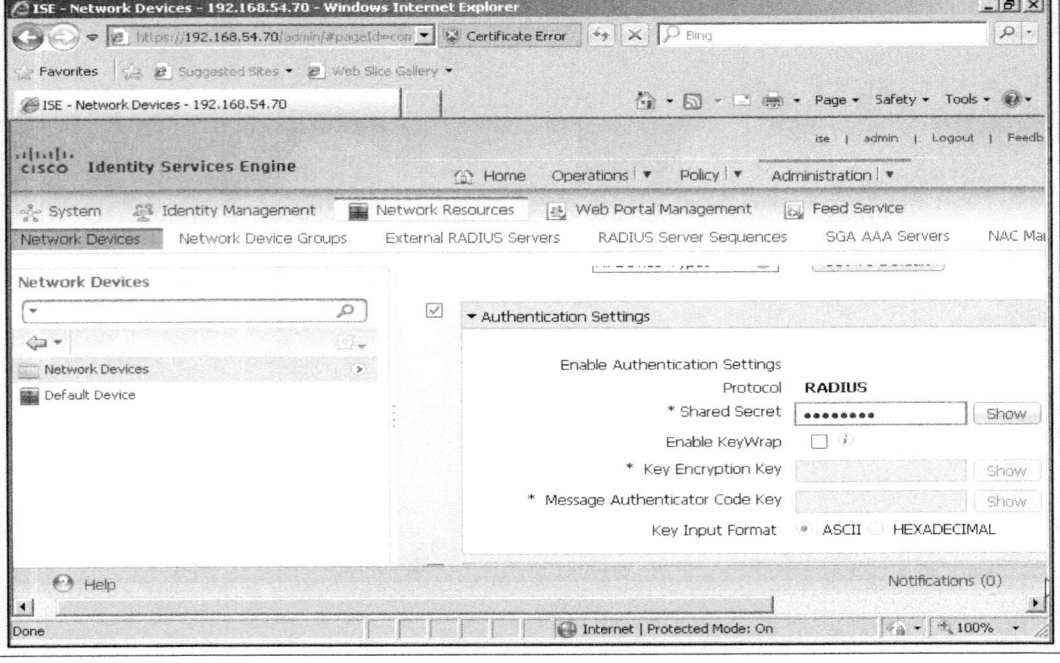

Scroll down to set Authentication settings. Set Password configured as Server key on NAD device " **cisco123**" and save settings.

Go to **Administration** > **Identity Management** > **Identities** > **Endpoint** and Add MAC Addresses of All Endpoints as shown in figure below

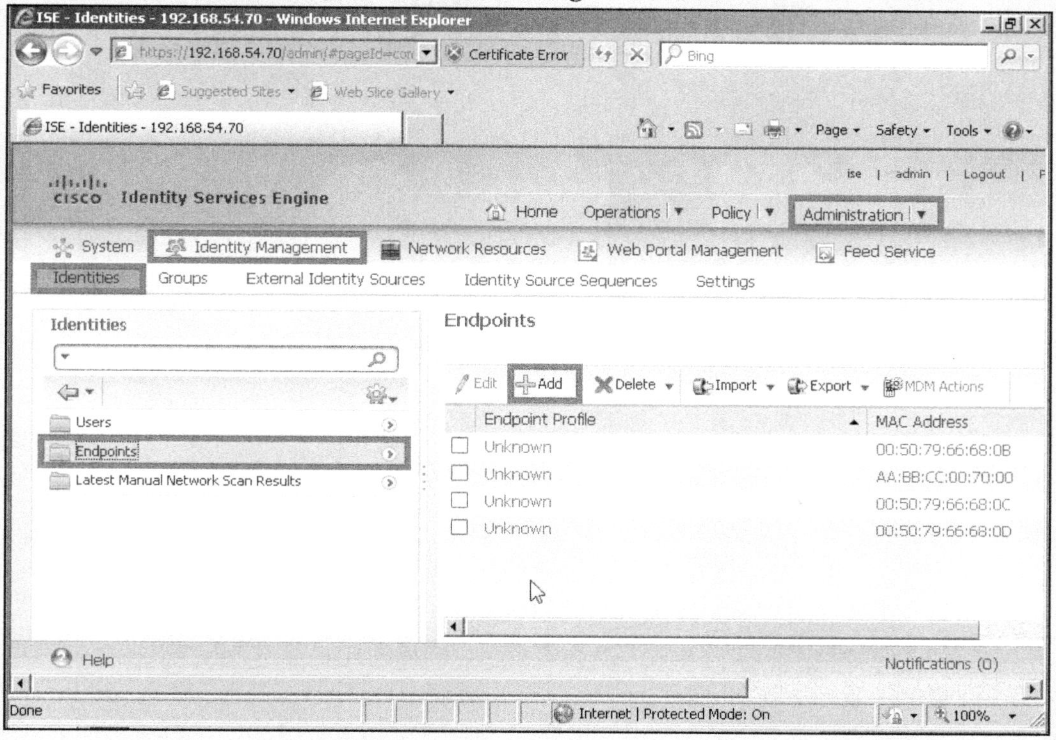

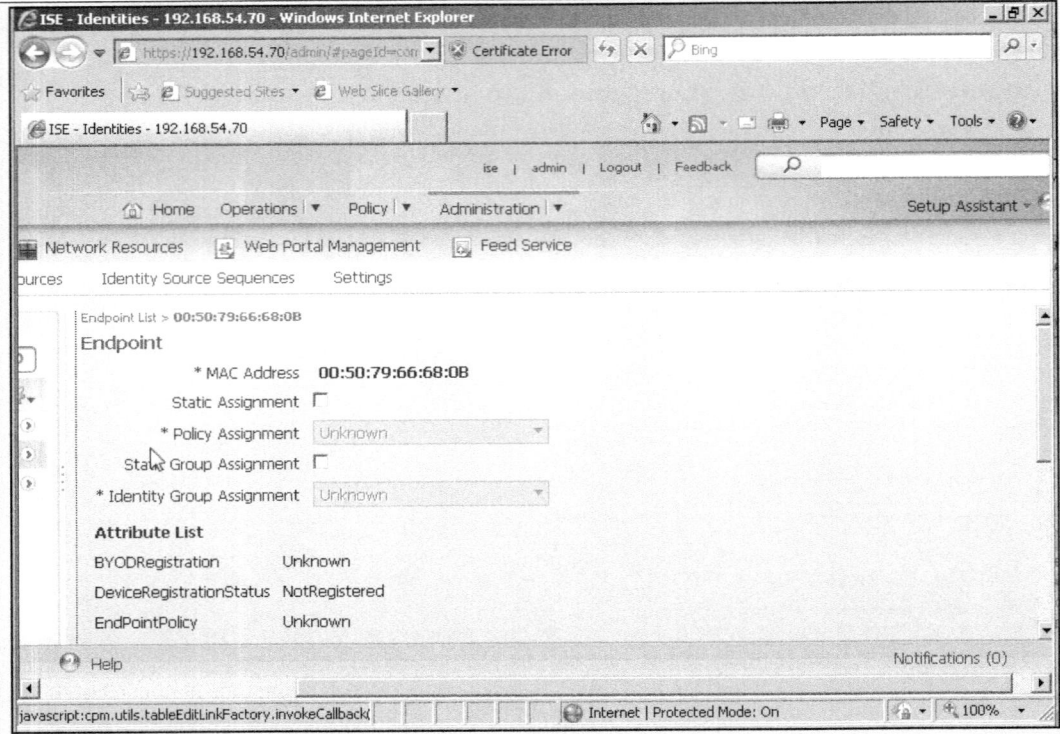

MAC Address Configuration of Endpoint should look like this.

Go to **Policy** > **Authorization** and Create a New Authorization policy for MAB

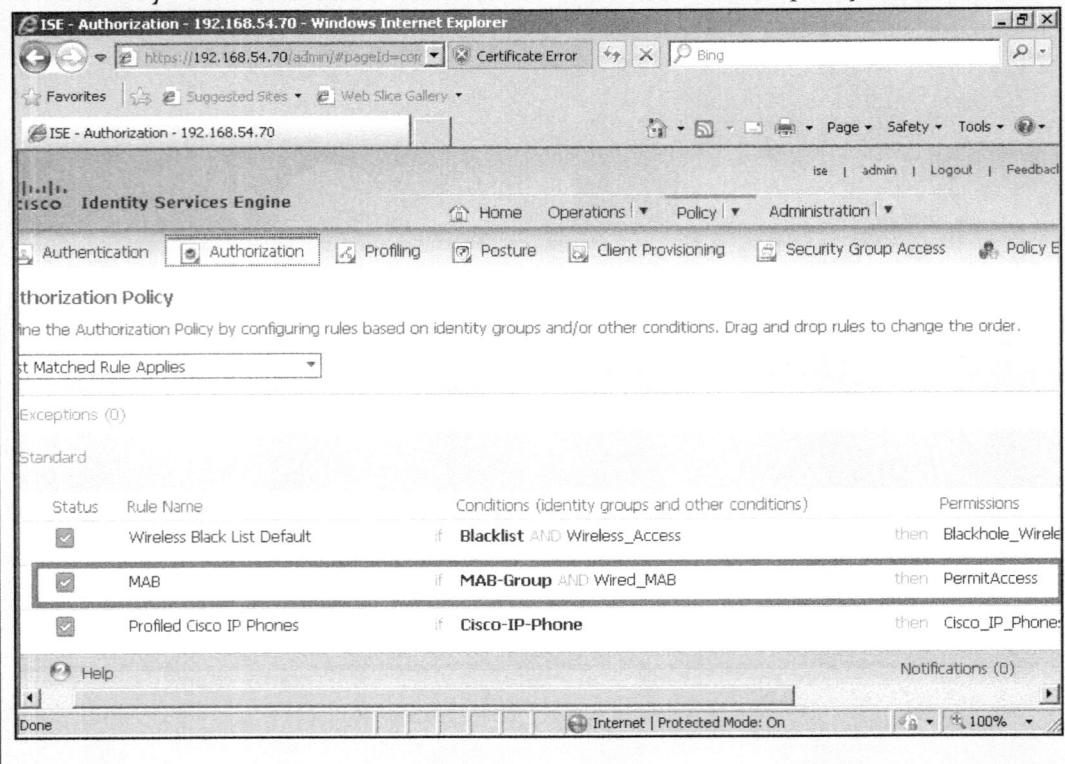

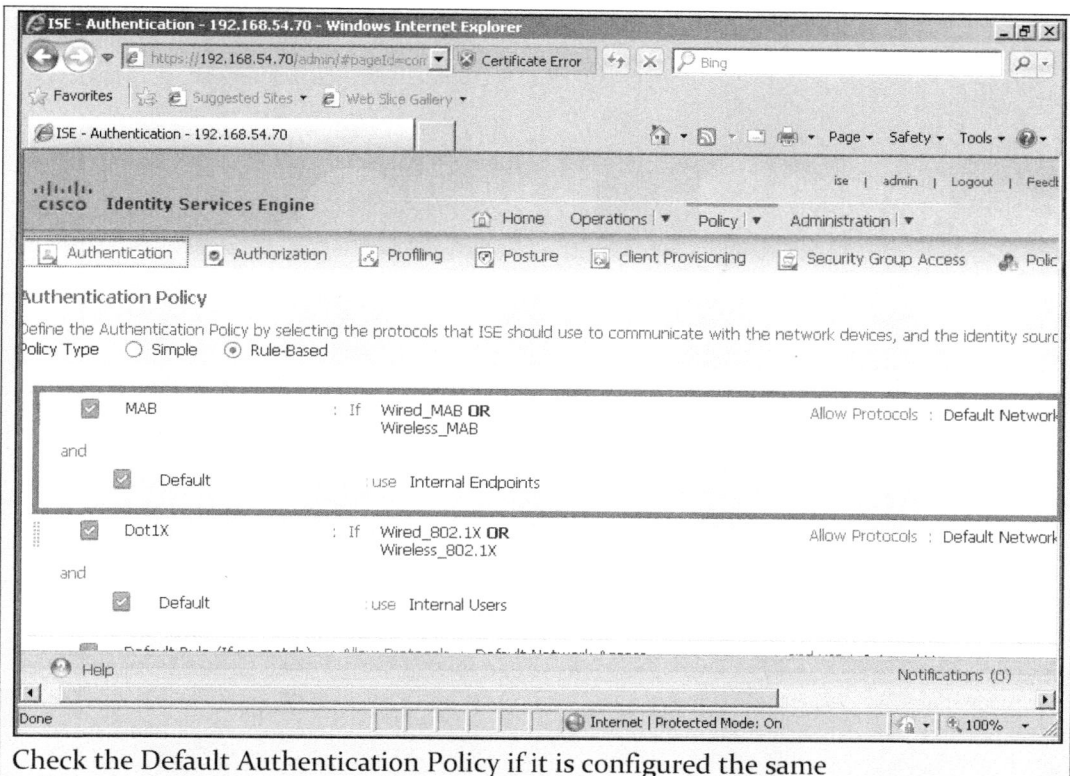

Check the Default Authentication Policy if it is configured the same

Verification:
Go to Cisco ISE Operation > Authentication

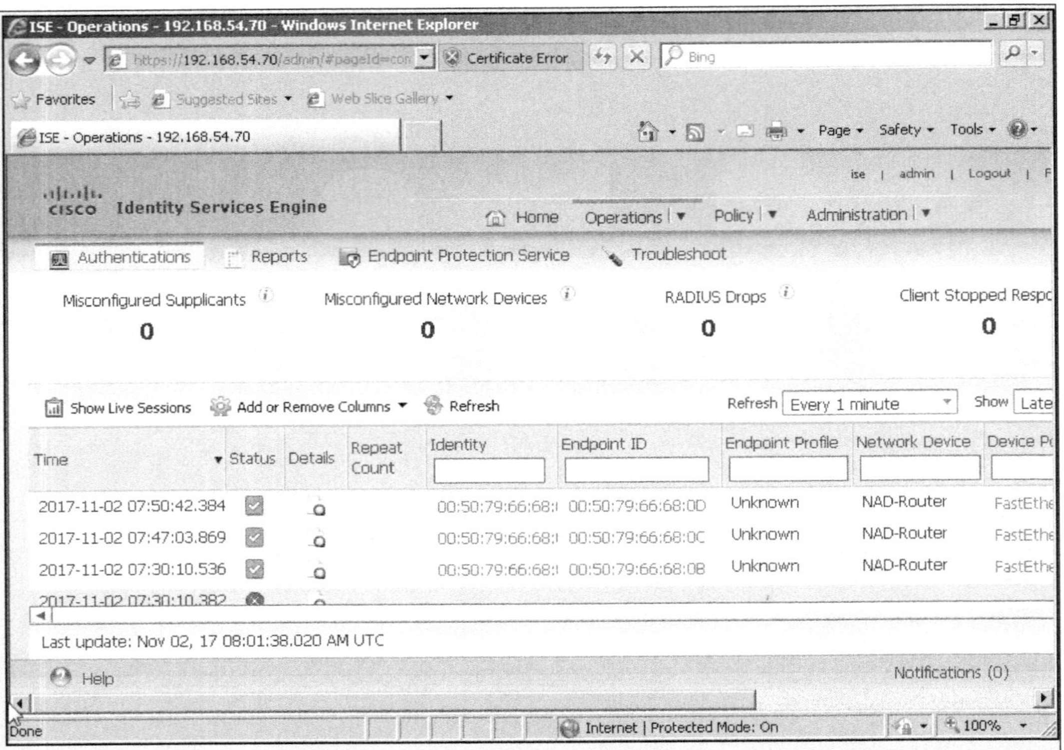

EndPoint ID **00:50:79:66:68:0D** , **00:50:79:66:68:0C** , **00:50:79:66:68:0B** and **AA:BB:CC:00:70:00** are authenticated with Network Device **NAD-Router** through interface **fastethernet 0/1.**

Cisco ISE Dashboard showing 4 Successful Authentications.

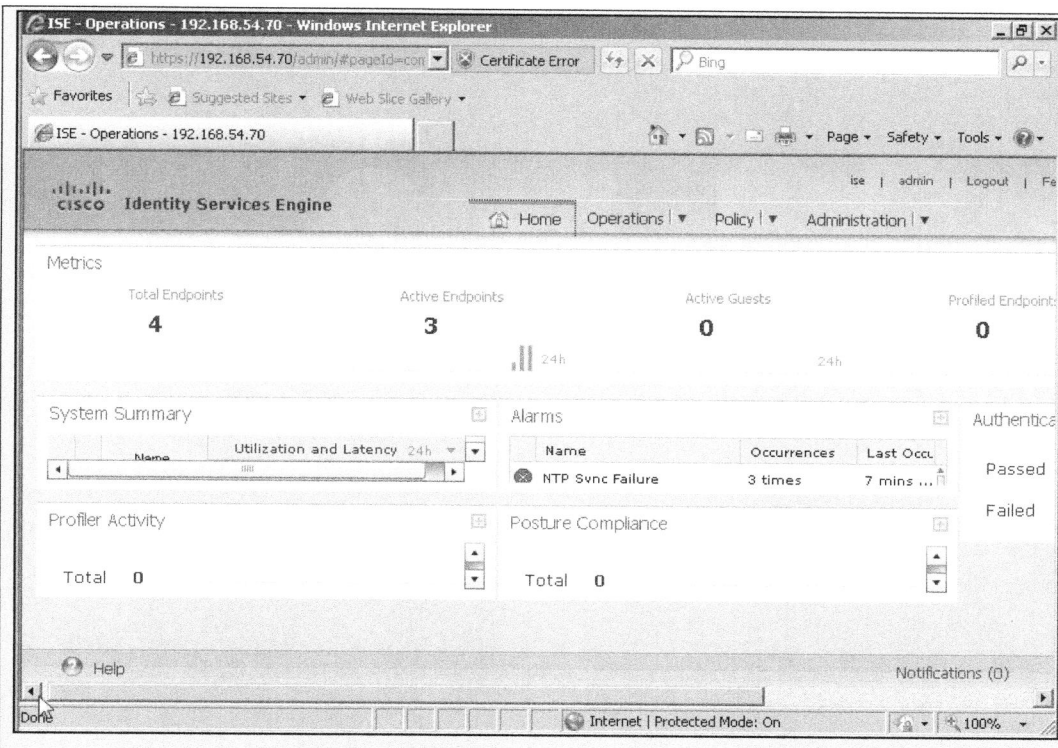

Ping from Endpoint-1 to Simulated Internet Address for Checking Layer3 connectivity.

NAD-Router#**show dot1x interface fastEthernet 0/1 details**

On Interface Fast Ethernet 0/1, configured as Authenticator, and MAC Authentication is enabled. Supplicant 0050:7966:680d which is MAC address of EndPoint-3 is authenticated, Port Status is authorized and Authentication method is MAB.

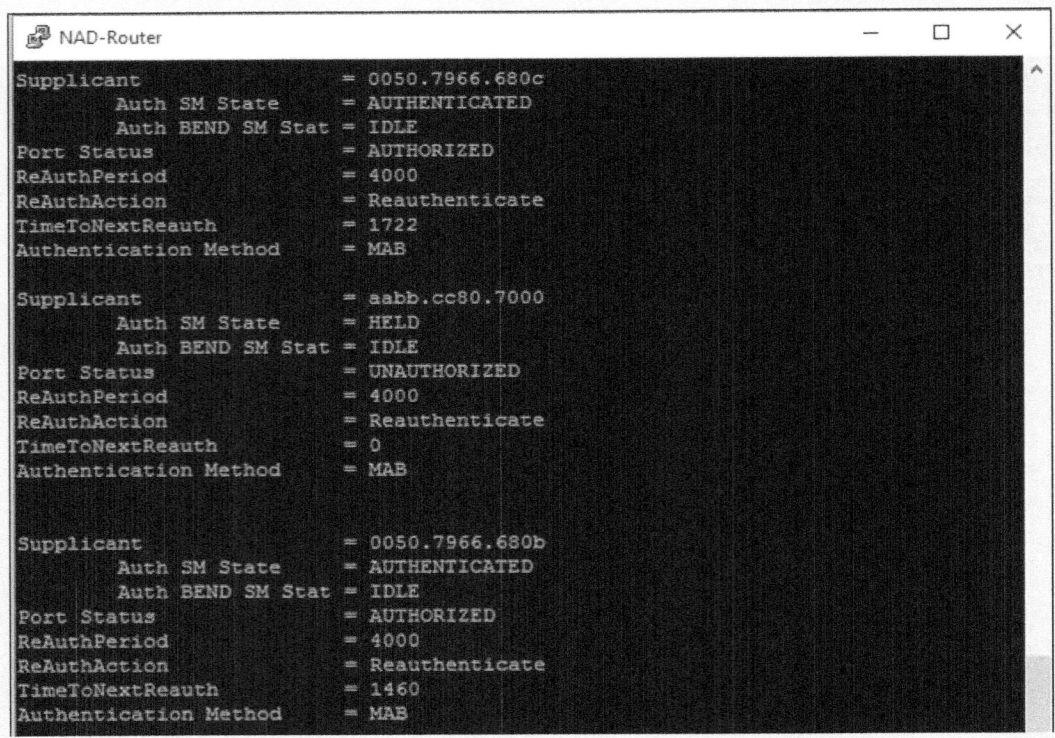

```
NAD-Router                                                    —    □    ×

NAD-Router#show dot1x interface fastEthernet 0/1 de
NAD-Router#show dot1x interface fastEthernet 0/1 details

Dot1x Info for FastEthernet0/1
-----------------------------------
PAE                      = AUTHENTICATOR
PortControl              = AUTO
ControlDirection         = Both
HostMode                 = MULTI_AUTH
ReAuthentication         = Enabled
QuietPeriod              = 60
ServerTimeout            = 30
SuppTimeout              = 30
ReAuthPeriod             = 4000 (Locally configured)
ReAuthMax                = 2
MaxReq                   = 2
TxPeriod                 = 60
RateLimitPeriod          = 0
Mac-Auth-Bypass          = Enabled


Dot1x Authenticator Client List
-----------------------------------
Supplicant               = 0050.7966.680d
      Auth SM State      = AUTHENTICATED
      Auth BEND SM Stat  = IDLE


Port Status              = AUTHORIZED
ReAuthPeriod             = 4000
ReAuthAction             = Reauthenticate
TimeToNextReauth         = 1921
Authentication Method    = MAB
```

```
NAD-Router                                                    —    □    ×

Supplicant               = 0050.7966.680c
      Auth SM State      = AUTHENTICATED
      Auth BEND SM Stat  = IDLE
Port Status              = AUTHORIZED
ReAuthPeriod             = 4000
ReAuthAction             = Reauthenticate
TimeToNextReauth         = 1722
Authentication Method    = MAB

Supplicant               = aabb.cc80.7000
      Auth SM State      = HELD
      Auth BEND SM Stat  = IDLE
Port Status              = UNAUTHORIZED
ReAuthPeriod             = 4000
ReAuthAction             = Reauthenticate
TimeToNextReauth         = 0
Authentication Method    = MAB


Supplicant               = 0050.7966.680b
      Auth SM State      = AUTHENTICATED
      Auth BEND SM Stat  = IDLE
Port Status              = AUTHORIZED
ReAuthPeriod             = 4000
ReAuthAction             = Reauthenticate
TimeToNextReauth         = 1460
Authentication Method    = MAB
```

Supplicant 0050:7966:680C which is MAC address of EndPoint-2 is authenticated, Port Status is authorized and Authentication method is MAB. Similarly, Supplicant 0050:7966:680B which is MAC address of EndPoint-1 and Supplicant AABB:CC80:7000 is MAC address of Switch-3 which are authenticated, Port Status is authorized and Authentication method is MAB.

Network Authorization Enforcement

Downlaodable Access Control List (dACL)

Downloadable Access Control List dACLs are the strong tools for Network Administrators to limit the access dynamically as user access the network. By using downloadable ACL, users can be restricted according to the related policies. These Downloadable ACLs can be assigned to different groups as well as individual users. The main advantage of this downloadable ACL is that it has to be configured on authentication server only, and can be downloaded on multiple devices in a network as it provides single point of configuration. Changes and modification will also have done on a single device instead of modifying the configuration on all devices. dACL is related to the authentication process. As a User or device is authenticated, dACL related the Policy configured with that authentication information applies to the Endpoint. For Example, a User is configured over authentication server to be permitted for HTTP access only. When User establishes the connection, it will first have authenticated. As the user is authenticated, server will check for the policies attached to this authentication process. dACL will be configured for the user to permit HTTP access only. User will only access HTTP.

Configuring Downloadable ACL

- Click Policy, and click Policy Elements.
- Click Results.
- Expand Authorization, and click Downloadable ACLs.
- Click the Add button in order to create a new downloadable ACL.
- In the Name field, enter a name for the DACL. This example uses DACL.

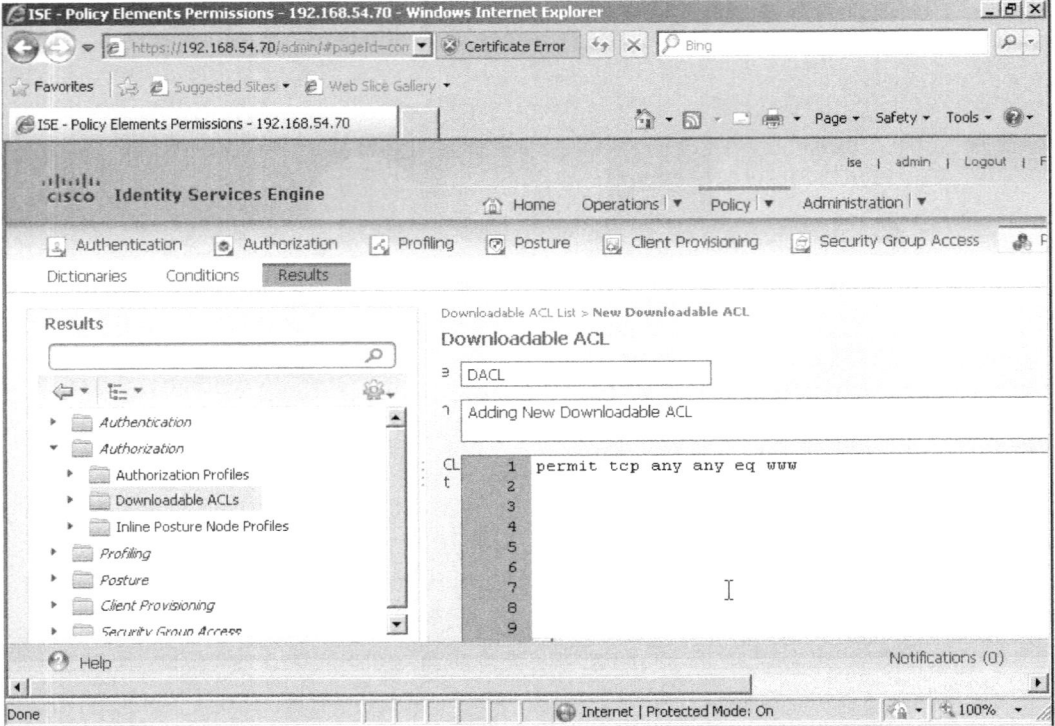

Figure 1-10. Configuring Downloadable ACL

Dynamic VLAN

VLAN can be assigned statically as well as dynamically. In Static VLAN assignment, Port is configured in a specific VLAN independent of MAC address or user connected through that port. In Dynamic assignment of VLAN, VLAN Membership Policy Server (VMPS) act as a Centralized server for the assignment of VLANs to the port dynamically depending on the MAC address of the Endpoint device connect through that Port. If the Endpoint switched from one port to another port of the access switch, Older port will automatically remove from configured VLAN and New port will automatically have assigned to that VLAN. VMPS use UDP port as a transport to listen VLAN Query Protocol (VQP). When VMPS server receives the request, it searches for the match in its database for the MAC address to VLAN mapping.

In case VLAN is configured on the port, VMPS sends VLAN name to the Client device, else it sends access denied response if it is not in secure mode. If server is in secure mode, it turns the port down. In access-denied response, Switch blocks the traffic coming from that port.

There are three modes of VMPS server

1. Open Mode

If VLAN is allowed on the port, VLAN name is sent as response to the client, else access denied response is send. If VLAN does not match against the condition and fall-back VLAN is configured, fall-back VLAN name is send as response to the client. If fall-back is not configured, Access-denied response is send to the client.

2. Secure Mode

In secure mode, Port-shutdown response is sent instead of Access-denied. For Example if VLAN in the database does not match, the port is shutdown.

3. Multiple Mode

Multiple host (MAC addresses) can also be configured on a port, if they are all assigned to same VLAN. In this case, if link goes down, port will become unassigned and will be reassigned when link turn up.

This example shows how to define the primary and secondary VMPS servers:

```
Switch# configure terminal
Enter configuration commands, one per line. End with CNTL/Z.
Switch(config)# vmps server 192.168.1.100 primary
Switch(config)# vmps server 192.168.1.101
Switch(config)# end
```

This example shows how to configure a dynamic access port and then verify the entry:

```
Switch# configure terminal
Enter configuration commands, one per line. End with CNTL/Z.
Switch(config)# interface fa1/1
Switch(config-if)# switchport mode access
Switch(config-if)# switchport access vlan dynamic
Switch(config-if)# end
```

Troubleshooting commands for VMPS are

```
Switch# show vmps
Switch# show vmps statistics
Switch# show interface [Interface] switchport
```

Security Group Access (SGA)

SGA stands for Security Group Access (SGA). SGA security solution in which a Cloud or group of trusted device within a network by using Device and Users identity information. Each device in a SGA group or cloud is verified and authenticated by its adjacent peers or neighbours. This authentication communication is secured, encrypted. Integrity checks and path replay protection make it more secure. SGA packets are tagged for identification and proper encryption. This SGA packet tag is called Security Group Tag (SGT).

Some of the key features of Security Group Access are as follows:

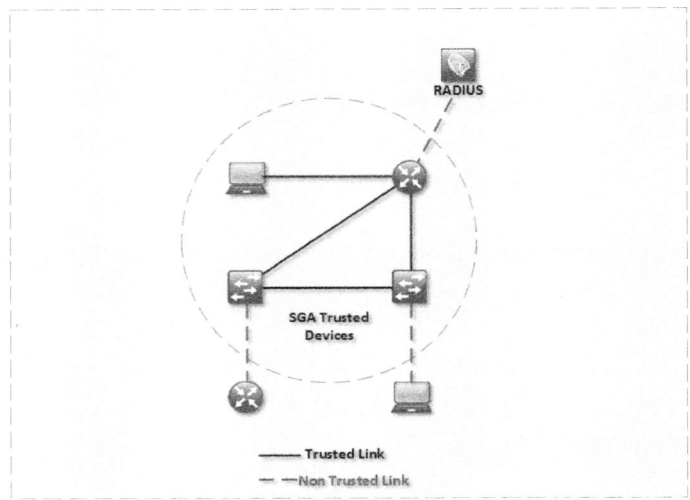

Figure 1-11. SGA

- **Network Device Admission Control (NDAC):**

In a trusted Cloud of Authenticated network devices, each device of SGA is authenticated for its credentials by its peer devices. Network device admission control NDAC uses 802.1x Authentication. As Extensible Authentication protocol method, EAP-FAST (Extensible Authentication Protocol-Flexible Authentication via Secure Tunnelling) is used.

- **Endpoint Admission Control (EAC):**

As an authentication process for the user or endpoint to access the SGA trusted network cloud, following authentication can be used
1. IEEE 802.1x Port-Based Authentication
2. MAC authentication Bypass (MAB)
3. Web Authentication (WebAuth)

- **Security Group (SG)**

Creating Groups of Users, Endpoints, device and resources that will share Access Control Policies.

- **Security Group Tags (SGT)**

A 16-bit Unique Security Group Number is assigned which is global in a SGA Domain. This SGT number is automatically generated.

- **Security Group Access Control List (SGACL)**

Administrator can permit and deny resources, control the network access, limit and restrict the Security group by using Access control list related to the security groups.

Change of Authorization (CoA)

Change of Authorization (CoA) is a process for changing the attributes, which are related to the Authentication, Authorization and Accounting (AAA). This is the feature of RADIUS server. When an Endpoint is authenticated, after some time a user is changed or a new user connected just after previous user get disconnected. Policy change for the user or user group is called as Change of Authorization (CoA). In this CoA process, re-authentication is initialized and new policy is applied. Request of Change of Authorization (CoA) is send by External Server with Administrative access to the authenticator server, which causes dynamically reconfiguration of session, authorization and accounting. Change of Authorization request allows session identification, re-authentication of hosts and termination of sessions.

There are two possible responses of the Change of Authorization (CoA) request, which are: -

1. CoA acknowledgment (ACK) [CoA-ACK]
2. CoA non-acknowledgment (NAK) [CoA-NAK]

CoA acknowledgment (ACK) [CoA-ACK]

If an authorization state is changed successfully, a positive acknowledgment (ACK) is sent. The attributes returned within a CoA ACK can vary based on the CoA Request.

CoA non-acknowledgment (NAK) [CoA-NAK]

A negative acknowledgment (NAK) indicates a failure to change the authorization state and can include attributes that indicate the reason for the failure.

Session Re-authentication:

Re-authentication of session will check for device response for the session, session identification attribute requested for. if 802.1x is authenticated currently, device will respond with Extensible Authentication Protocol over Lan (EAPol). In case of MAB authentication, device will send access request to the server. If session is under authentication, device terminates the authentication and restart authentication.

Session Termination

CoA Disconnect-Request end the session. Host port is not disabled during this termination. CoA disconnect request locate the desired session. If session is located, session is terminated and device reply with Disconnect-Ack message. If session is not located, device is returned with Disconnect-NAK message. This session termination request is session oriented hence contain session identification attributes.

CoA Request Bounce Port:

When more than one host are connected through a port, and VLAN change occur. this will affect all of the host causing DHCP renegotiation. If a device (Such as printer) which do not detect the change of authentication port is connected through that port, CoA Request Bounce port disable the port and re-enable it (Port-Bounce) and return with CoA-ACK message

Command for Configuring CoA

Switch(config)# **aaa server radius dynamic-author**

Enters dynamic authorization local server configuration mode and specifies a RADIUS client from which a device accepts Change of Authorization (CoA) and disconnect requests. Configures the device as a AAA server to facilitate interaction with an external policy server.

Commands for troubleshooting CoA

Command	Purpose
debug aaa coa	Displays debug information for CoA processing.
debug aaa pod	Displays debug messages related to packet of disconnect (POD) packets.
debug radius	Displays information associated with RADIUS.
show aaa attributes protocol radius	Displays the mapping between an authentication, authorization, and accounting (AAA) attribute number and the corresponding AAA attribute name.

Table 5. CoA Monitoring and Troubleshooting commands

Mind Map

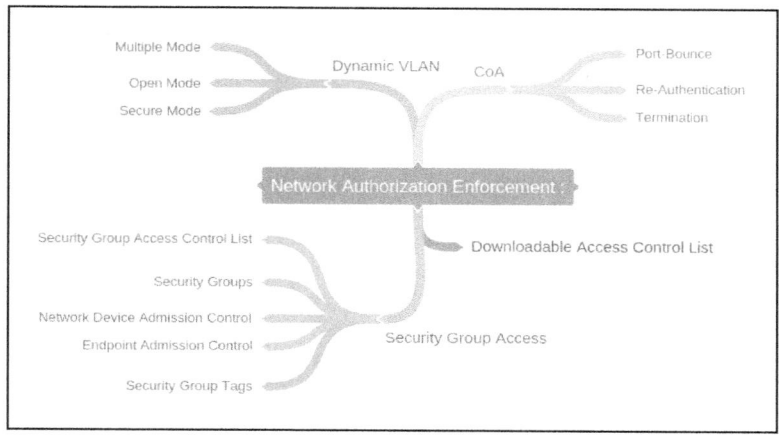

Central Web Authorization

Central Web Authentication is the process in which web- based authentication and the authentication server RADIUS does authorization. In Central Web Authentication, Web based authentication is redirected when a client accessing the network is failed to authenticate via 802.1x or MAC authentication bypass. Central Web Authentication offers a central web authenticating device i.e. RADIUS server which provides authentication and authorization using Web portal. When Client is failed to authenticate via Dot1x or MAB, Client is redirected to Web Portal where it can log in on the guest portal. Authorization profile configured on the Authentication server will authorize this guest login. Major advantages of Central Web Authentication are, it configures along with dot1x and MAB authentication. A Central device sends attributes for web redirection instead of Local Web authentication. In the process of Central Web Authentication, when client failed to authenticate via dot1x or MAB, and logs in via redirection to Web Portal, Change of Authorization CoA can bounce the port for new authentication so that Server will learn the user authenticated by Webauth and apply the attribute like dynamic VLAN assignment or dACL.

Creating Authorization Profile for Central Web Authorization
- Click Policy, and click Policy Elements.
- Click Results.
- Expand Authorization, and click Authorization profile.
- Click the Add button in order to create a new authorization profile for central webauth.
- In the Name field, enter a name for the profile.
- Choose ACCESS_ACCEPT from the Access Type drop-down list.
- Check the Web Authentication check box, and choose Centralized from the drop-down list.
- In the ACL field, enter the name of the ACL on the switch that defines the traffic to be redirected.

- Choose Default from the Redirect drop-down list.
- Check the DACL Name checkbox, and choose DACL from the drop-down list if you decide to use a DACL instead of a static port ACL on the switch.

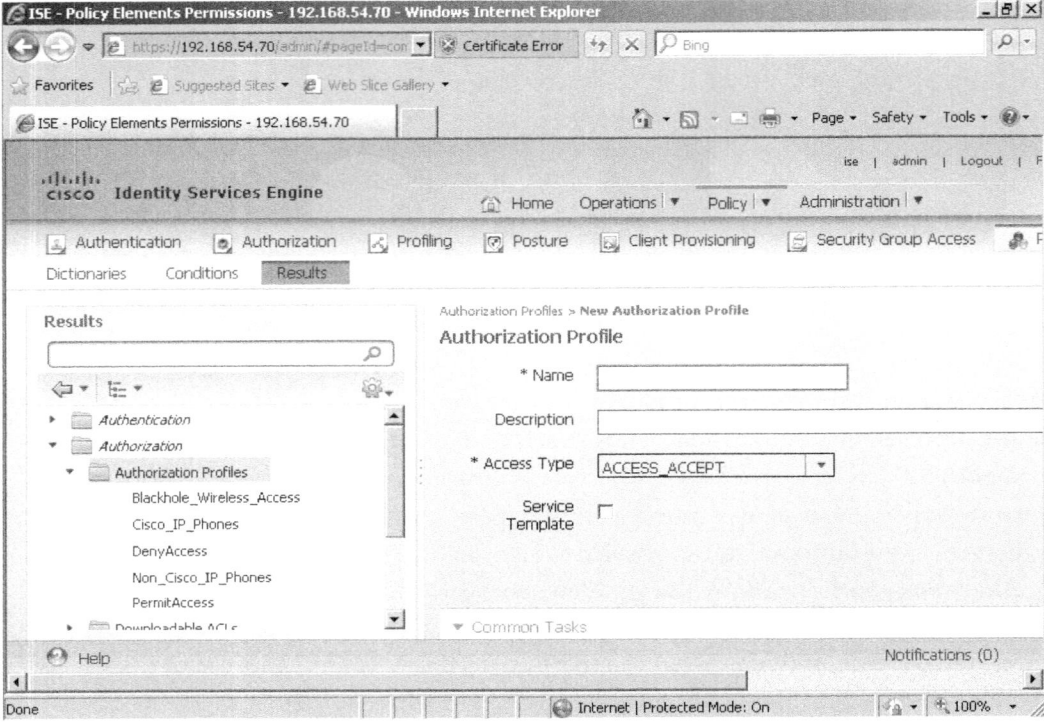

Figure 1-12. Authorization Profile Configuration

Profiling

Profiling of Endpoint feature is very important in authentication and authorization of Network access devices. Profile function collects the data of Endpoint devices accessing the network, identifies the device connected to the network and its location. Depending upon the Endpoint profile, Authentication server permits the access of the resources. Profiling can facilitate the authentication using 802.1x Port-based Authentication, MAC Authentication Bypass (MAB) as well as Network Admission Control (NAC).

Profiling service can identify, locate, and ensure the access of all endpoints connected or connecting to the network. This profiling is regardless of endpoints device type. Profiling collects the attribute and classifies these endpoints into groups with respect to the profile configured, and stores them in database with their matched profile.

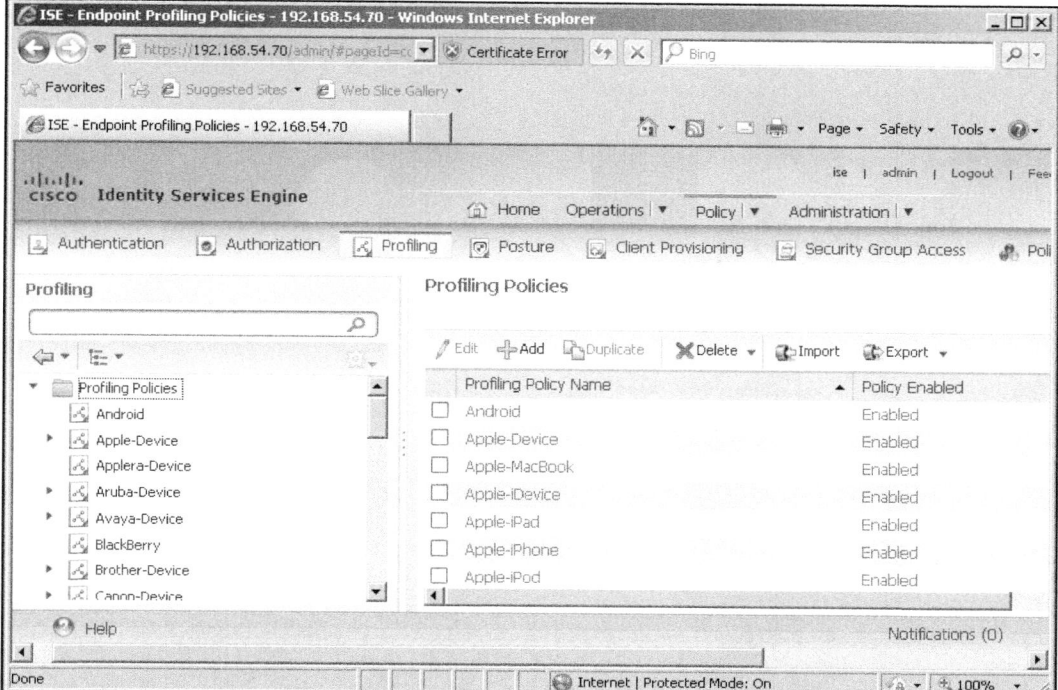

Figure 1-13 Default Profiling Policies

By the help of Network Probe, Profile service collects an attribute or number of attributes of any endpoint allowing to create update or modify the profile in the database. Some network probes are listed below

- IP Address and MAC Address Binding
- NetFlow Probe
- DHCP Probe
- DHCP SPAN Probe
- HTTP Probe
- HTTP SPAN Probe
- RADIUS Probe
- Network Scan (NMAP) Probe
- DNS Probe
- SNMP Query Probe
- SNMP Trap Probe

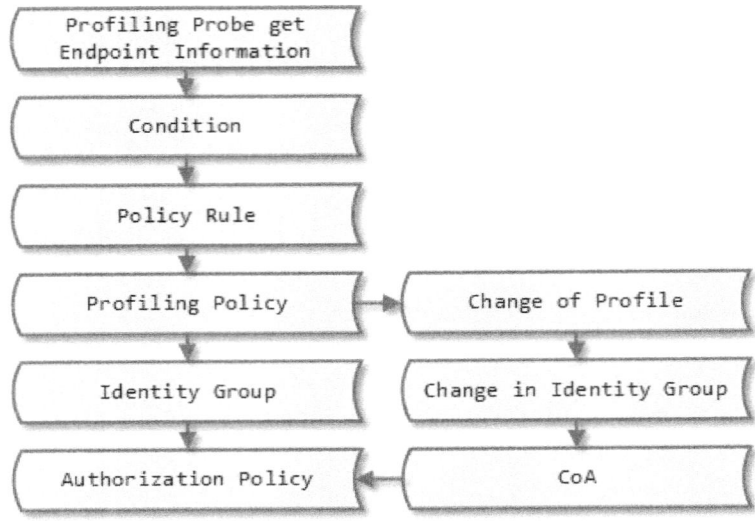

Figure 1-14. Profiling Flow Chart

Guest Services

Guest Service feature allow the new users or end points trying to access the network. Using Guest Service, a guest account is created by the user through Guest port and then these endpoints accessing through guest portal able to access the resources as they are allowed depending on downloadable access control list dACL in the Network Access Device (NAD). Guest user or visitors are redirected to the HTTP or HTTPS guest portal to access the network.

Any user with privilege can create temporary guest user account and sponsor it. As any User can create guest user account hence Guest service authenticates the sponsor as well. Sponsors are the creator of guest user accounts. Logs and statistics are stored during the process of user account creation to the network access of guest user. These logs and reports can be used for security auditing and reporting.

When a guest user first access the network, User must be redirected to HTTP or HTTPS guest portal (using limited Access) so that it can create guest user account and get access to the network. For this purpose, Wireless LAN Controller (WLC) or Network Access Device (NAD) guest user is connected through should be enabled and support HTTP or HTTPS portal Login.

To use web-based authentication, you must enable the HTTP server within the switch. You can enable the server for either HTTP or HTTPS. To do so, use the following commands

```
ip http server
ip http secure-server
```

Configuring Sponsor Group Policy

1. Choose Administration > Guest Management > Sponsor Group Policy.
2. Click Actions to select either Insert New Rule Above or Insert New Rule Below.

    A new policy entry appears in the position you designated in the Sponsor Group Policy window.

3. Enter values for the following sponsor policy fields:

    - **Rule Name**—Enter a name for the new policy.
    - Identity Groups—Choose a name for the identity group associated with the policy. Click + ("plus" sign) to display a drop-down list of group choices, or choose any for the policy for this identity group to include all users.
    - **Other Conditions**—Choose the types of conditions or attributes for the identity group associated with the policy. Click + next to Condition(s) to display the following list of condition and attribute choices that you can configure:
    - **Select Existing Condition from the Library**—This lets you select a Condition Name option from the pull-down list (Simple Conditions, Compound Conditions, or Time and Date Conditions) as needed.
    - **Create new condition (Advanced option)**—This displays a list of dictionaries that contain specific attributes related to the dictionary type.
    - **Sponsor Group**—Choose the sponsor group to associate with this sponsor group policy. Click + next to Sponsor Group to display a drop-down list of sponsor group choices. Select a group option.

4. Click Save to save your changes to the Cisco ISE system database and create this new sponsor group policy.

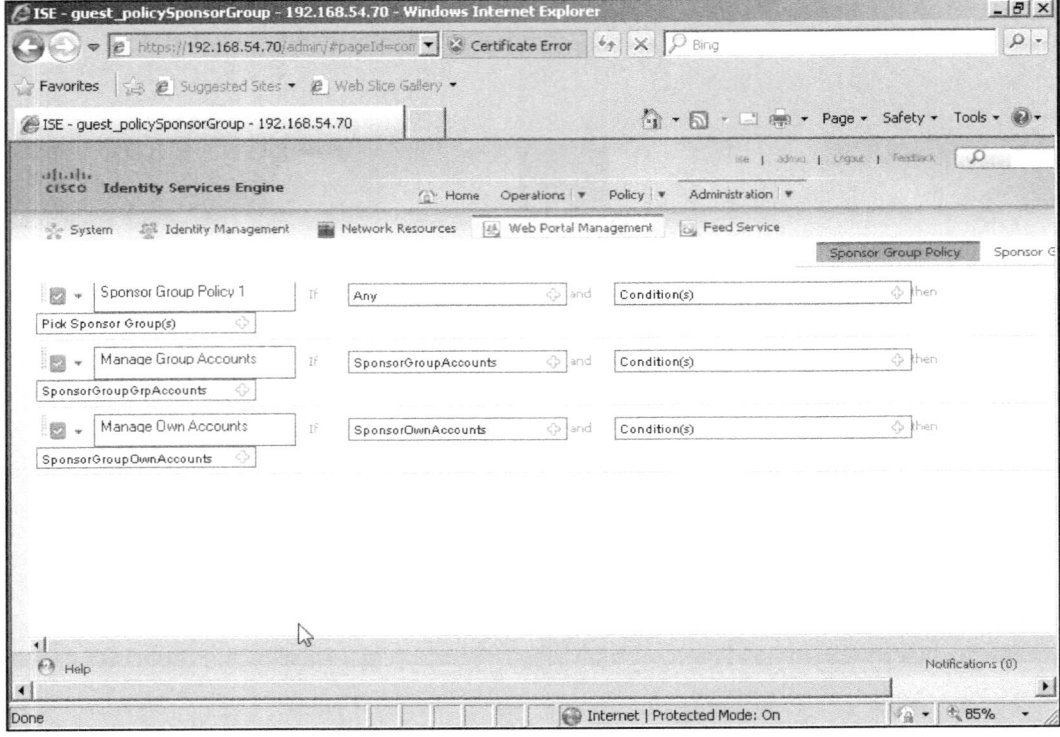

Figure 1-15. Sponsor group Policy

The Cisco ISE Guest Services support the following scenarios:

- Wireless LAN Controller with Local WebAuth
- Wired NAD with Central WebAuth
- Wired NAD with Local Web Auth

Lab 1.3: Implementing Registered and Self Registered Guest Services using Central Web Authentication over Cisco ISE

Case Study: Implementing a secure access on a network of reputed company for the registered guest users as well as new guest users visiting the company every day. In this lab Central Web Authentication is implemented using Guest Services feature of Cisco ISE.

Prerequisites:
Cisco ISE features including Profiling, Posturing, Central Web Authentication, Guest Services are supported by these devices.

- Catalyst 2960/3560/3750 Series, 12.2(55) SE
- Catalyst 3560/3750 Series, 15.0(2) SE
- Catalyst 4500 Series, IOS-XE 3.3.0/15.1(1) SG
- Catalyst 6500 Series, 12.2(33) SXJ and others.

Due to Cisco Bug in Switches, use recommended switches for this lab. Due to hardware limitation this lab cannot be performed on our vRacks platform.

Topology Diagram:

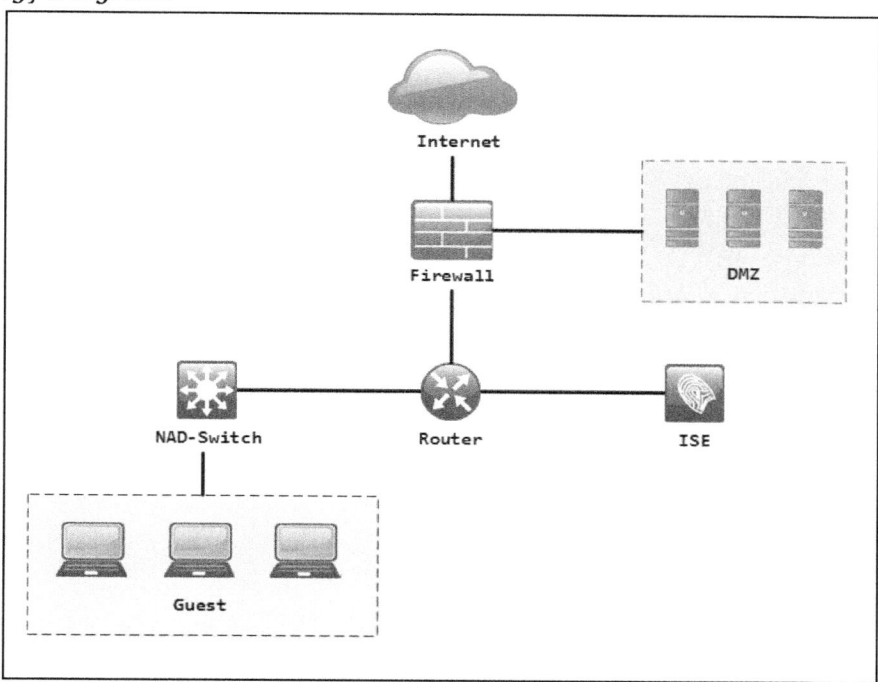

Configuring Network Access Device

Switch(config)# hostname SW1
SW1(config)# username admin password 0 admin

SW1(config)# aaa new-model
SW1(config)# aaa authentication login default local
SW1(config)# aaa authentication dot1x default group radius
SW1(config)# aaa authorization exec default none
SW1(config)# aaa authorization network default group radius

SW1(config)# aaa server radius dynamic-author
SW1(config-locsvr-da-radius)# client 10.10.50.30 server-key cisco

SW1(config)# dot1x system-auth-control
SW1(config)# dot1x critical eapol

SW1(config)# interface Ethernet 1/0
SW1(config-if)# switchport access vlan 1
SW1(config-if)# switchport mode access
SW1(config-if)# authentication open

```
SW1(config-if)# authentication order mab webauth
SW1(config-if)# authentication priority mab webauth
SW1(config-if)# authentication port-control auto
SW1(config-if)# mab
SW1(config-if)# spanning-tree portfast

SW1(config)# interface vlan 1
SW1(config-if)# ip address 10.10.50.254 255.255.255.0
SW1(config-if)# no shutdown

SW1(config)# ip http server
SW1(config)# ip http secure-server

SW1(config)# ip access-list extended redirect
SW1(config-ext-nacl)# permit ip any host 172.16.3.100
SW1(config-ext-nacl)# permit tcp any any eq www
SW1(config-ext-nacl)# permit tcp any any eq 443
SW1(config-ext-nacl)# permit tcp any any eq 8443
SW1(config-ext-nacl)# deny   ip any any

SW1(config)# radius-server host 10.10.50.30 auth-port 1645 acct-port 1646 key cisco
SW1(config)# radius-server vsa send accounting
SW1(config)# radius-server vsa send authentication
```

Configuring Cisco ISE

Go to **Cisco ISE** > **Administration** > **Network Resources** > **Network Devices** > **Add**

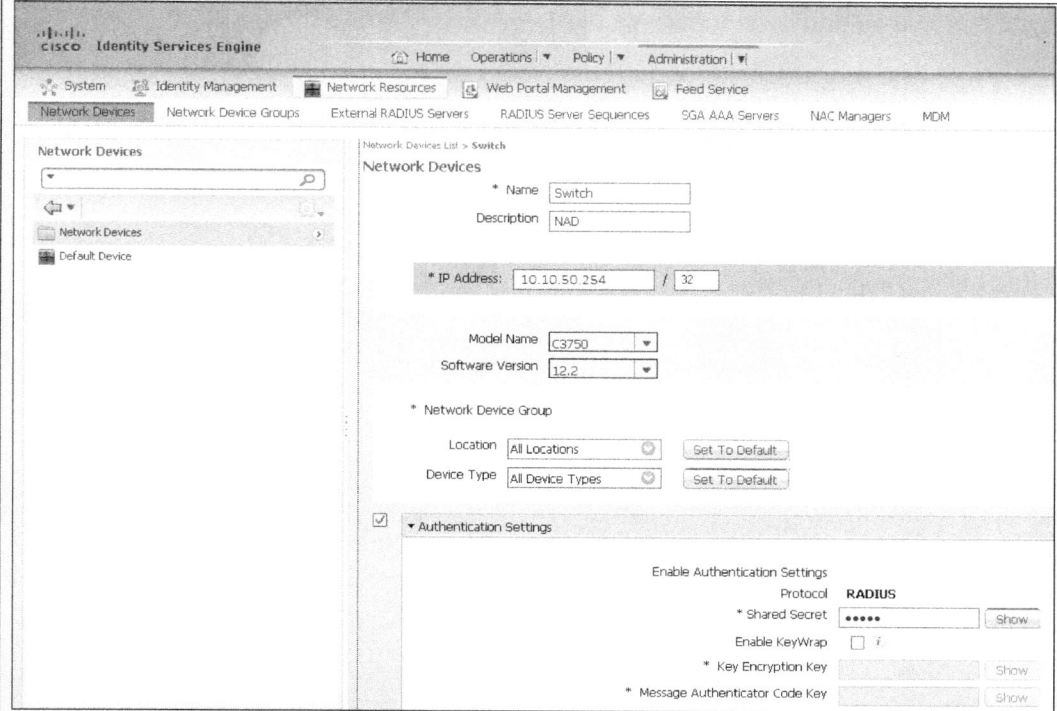

Configure the Name of NAD device, IP address of Source Interface for Radius configured on Switch i.e. 1.1.1.1/32 and Authentication password cisco.

Go to **Policy > Authentication**

Select the MAB Authentication rule and edit. In the attribute Internal Endpoint, select the option if user not found to continue.

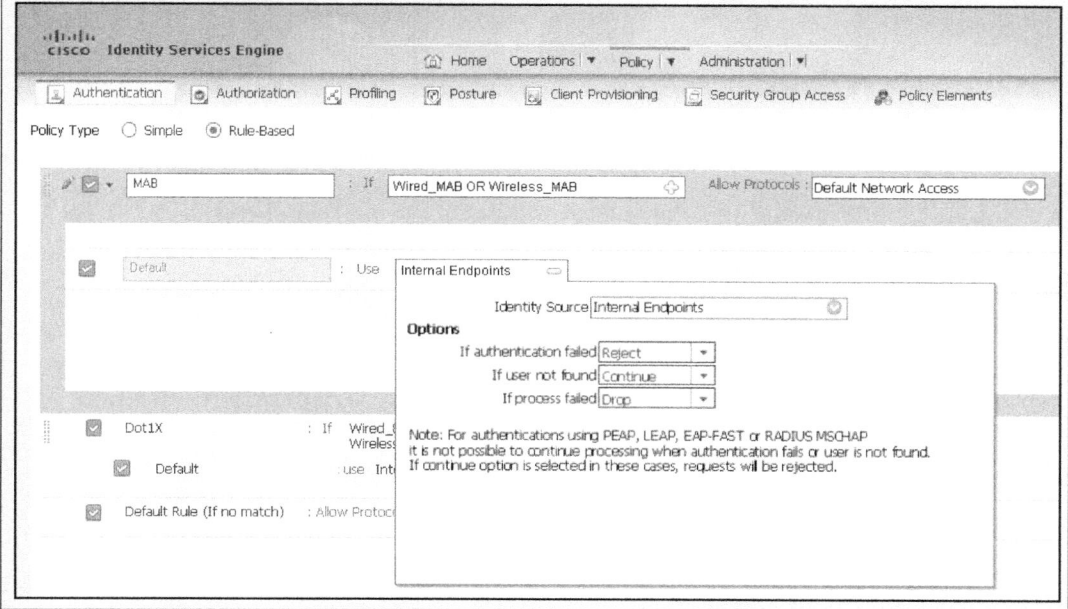

Go to **Policy** > **Policy Element** > **Results** > **Authorization** > **Downloadable ACL** > **Add**

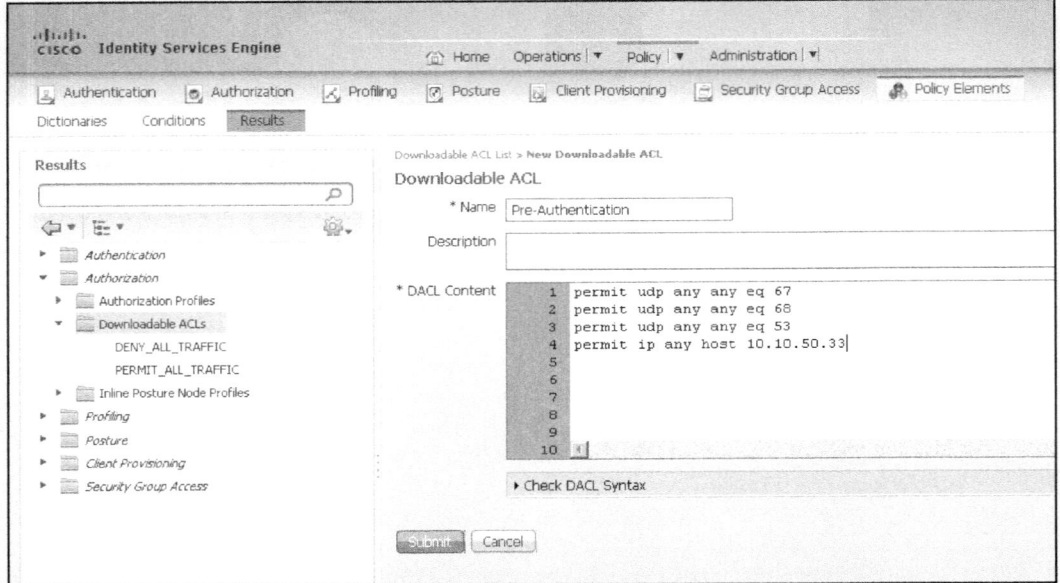

"**Pre-Authentication**" ACL is configured to restrict user to limited access.

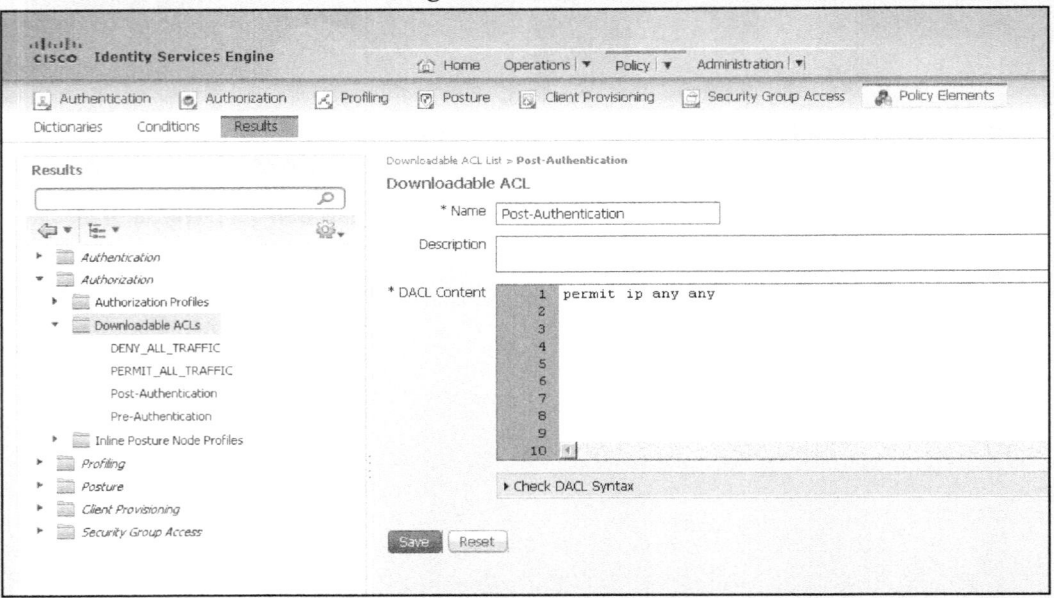

"**Post-Authentication**" ACl is configured for Permit access after authentication

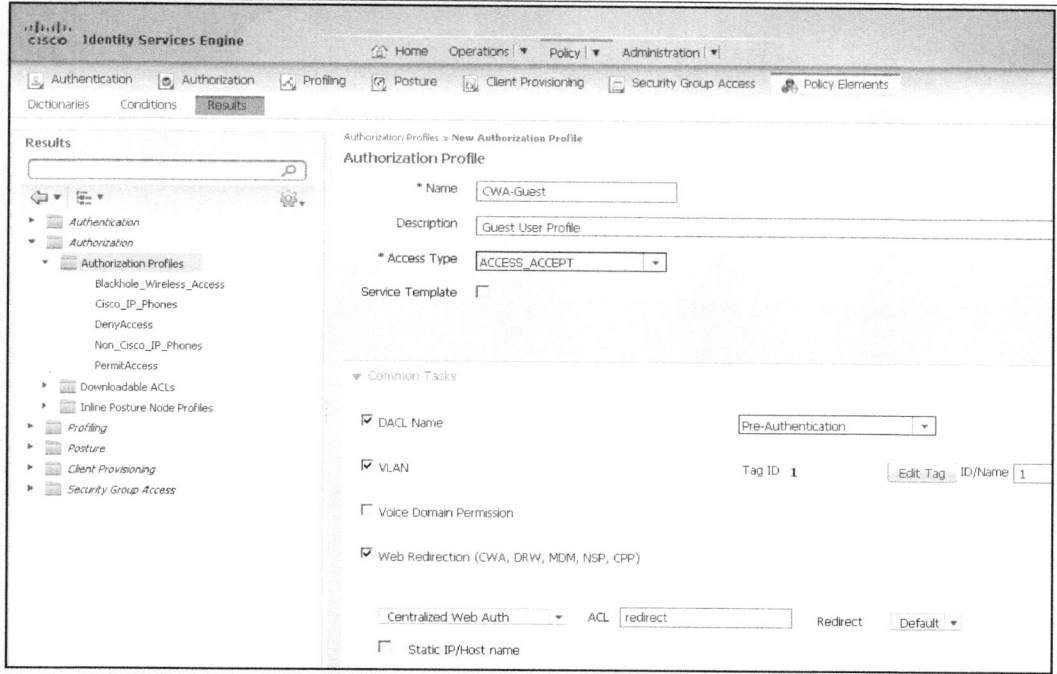

Go to **Policy > Policy Element > Results > Authorization > Authorization Profile > Add** and configure the following attributes as shown.

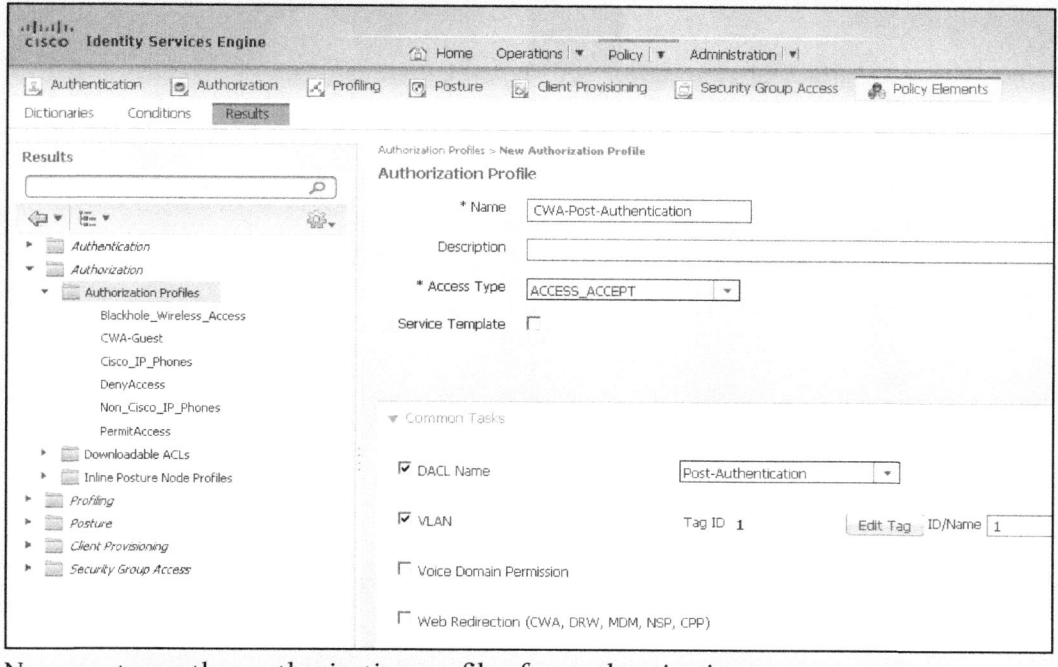

Now create another authorization profile after authentication process.

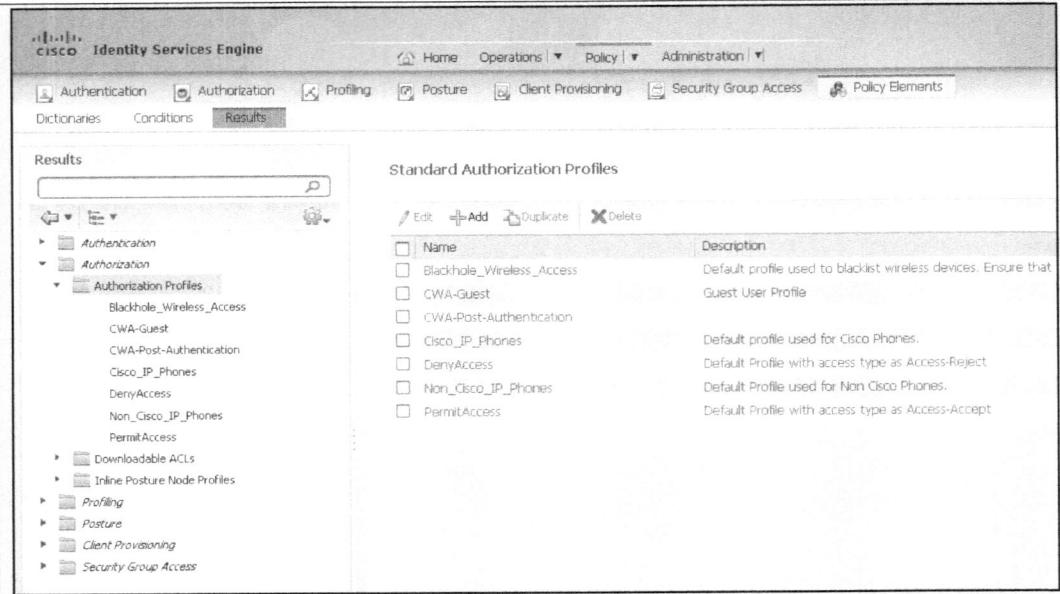

After configuration, configured Authorization profiles **CWA-Guest** and **CWA-Post-Authentication** will be shown

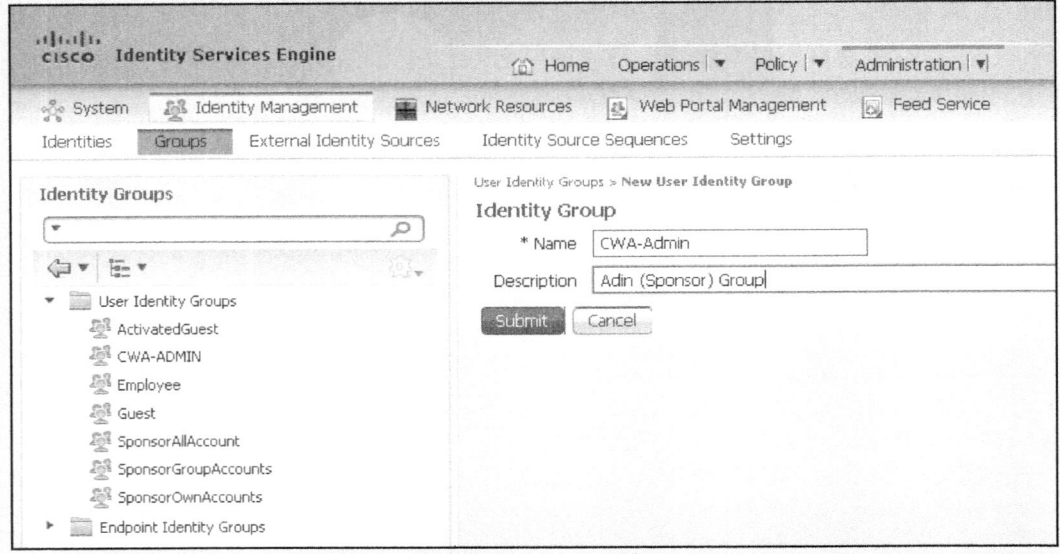

Create an identity group **CWA-ADMIN** for admin user who can sponsor guest users.

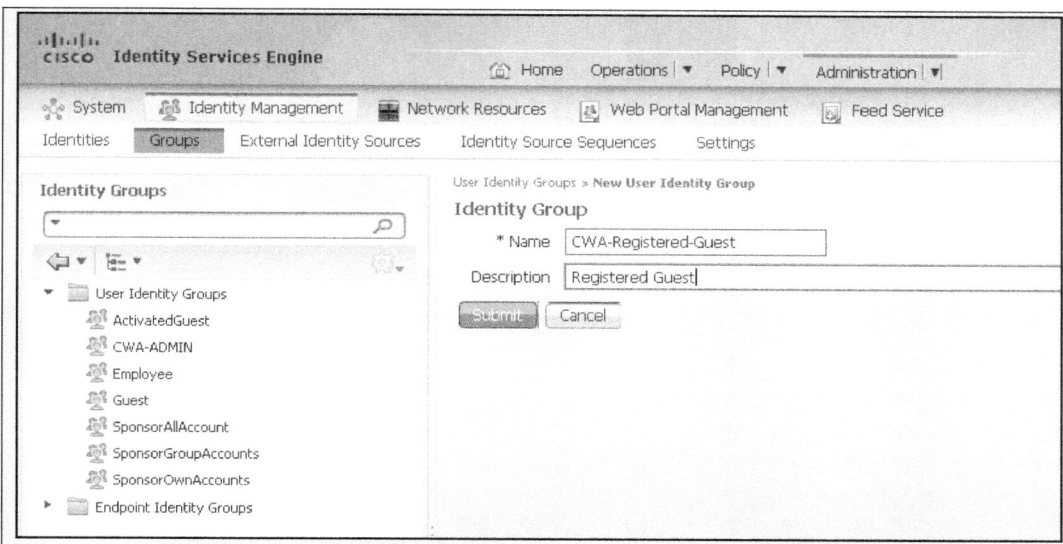

Create an identity group **CWA-Registered-Guest** group for Admin created Guest Users.

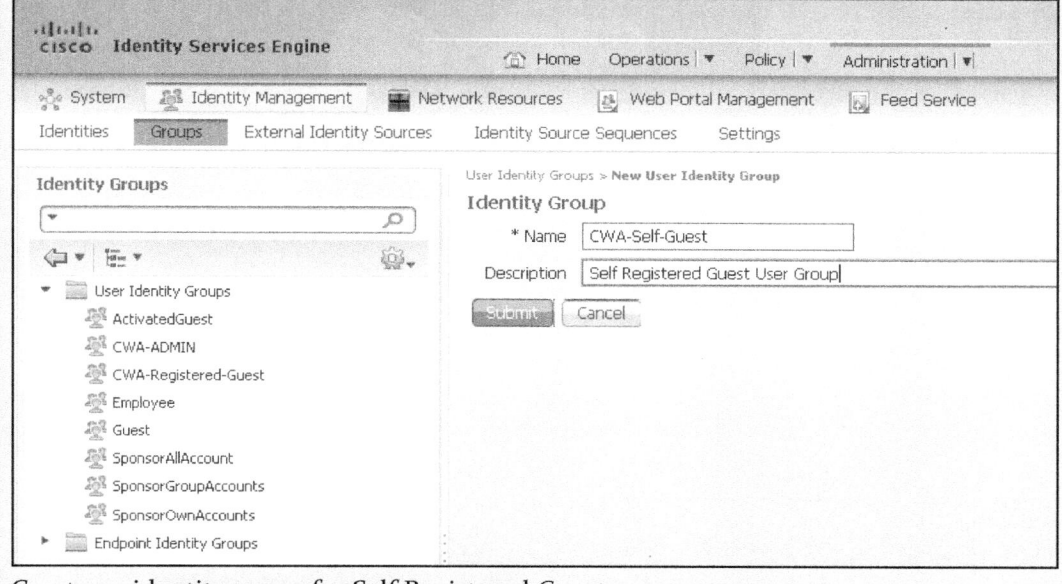

Create an identity group for Self Registered Guest users.

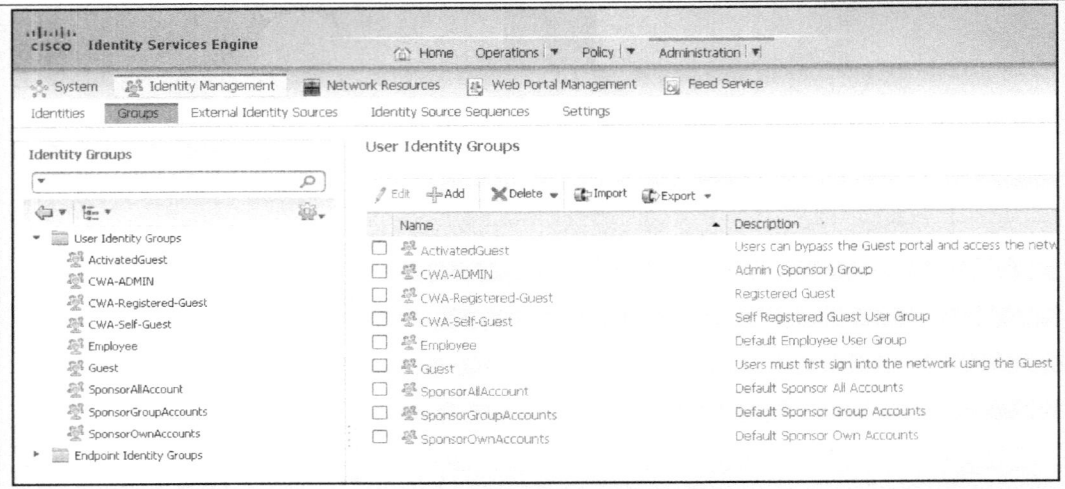

All three created groups as well as default groups are shown.

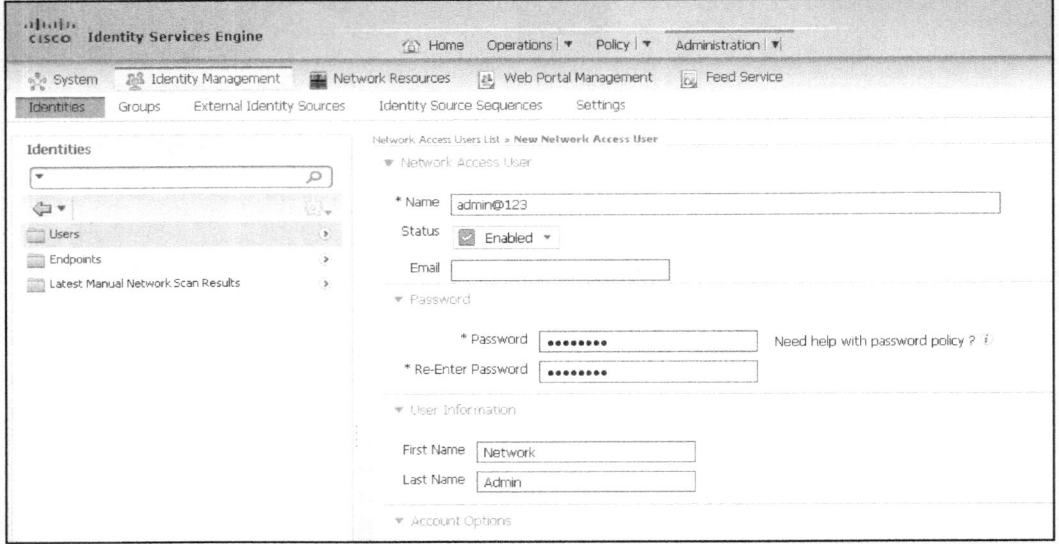

Create an admin user, set password and select the identity group as **CWA-ADMIN**

Name: admin@123

Password: Cisco123

IdentityGroup: CWA-ADMIN

Go to Policy > Authorization and add a new rule

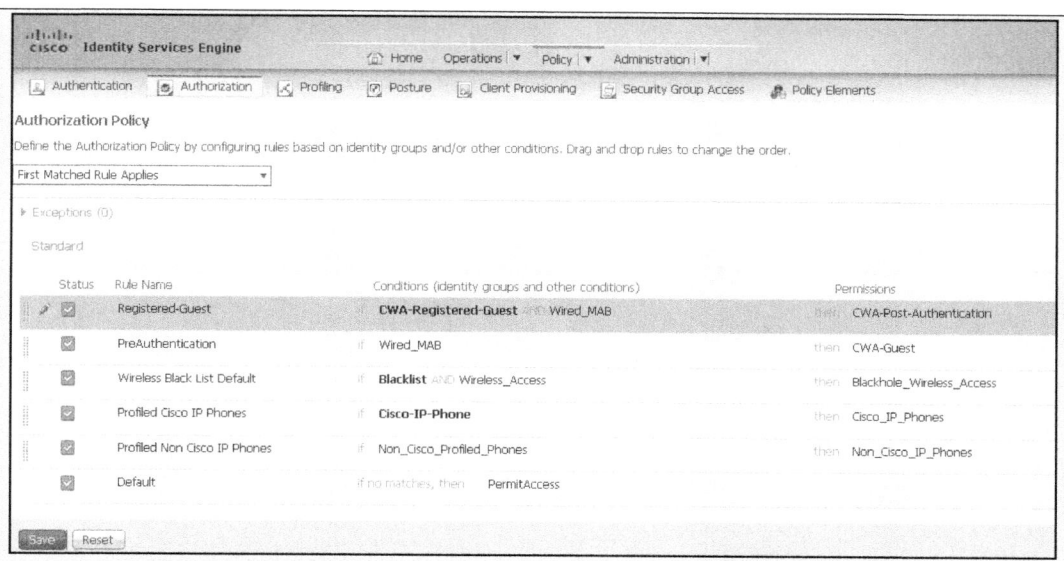

Configure new rule as Registered-Guest and apply the same attribute as shown

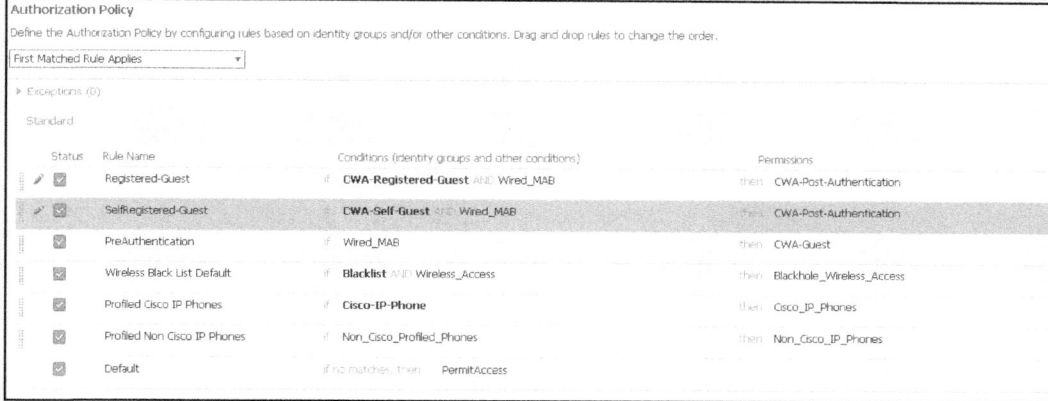

Similarly add new Rule as Self Registered-Guest and apply the attribute as shown

Verification:

Now turn the PC on and Open web browser and access any URL, you will be redirected to this portal

https://<ISE IP Address>:8443/Guestportal

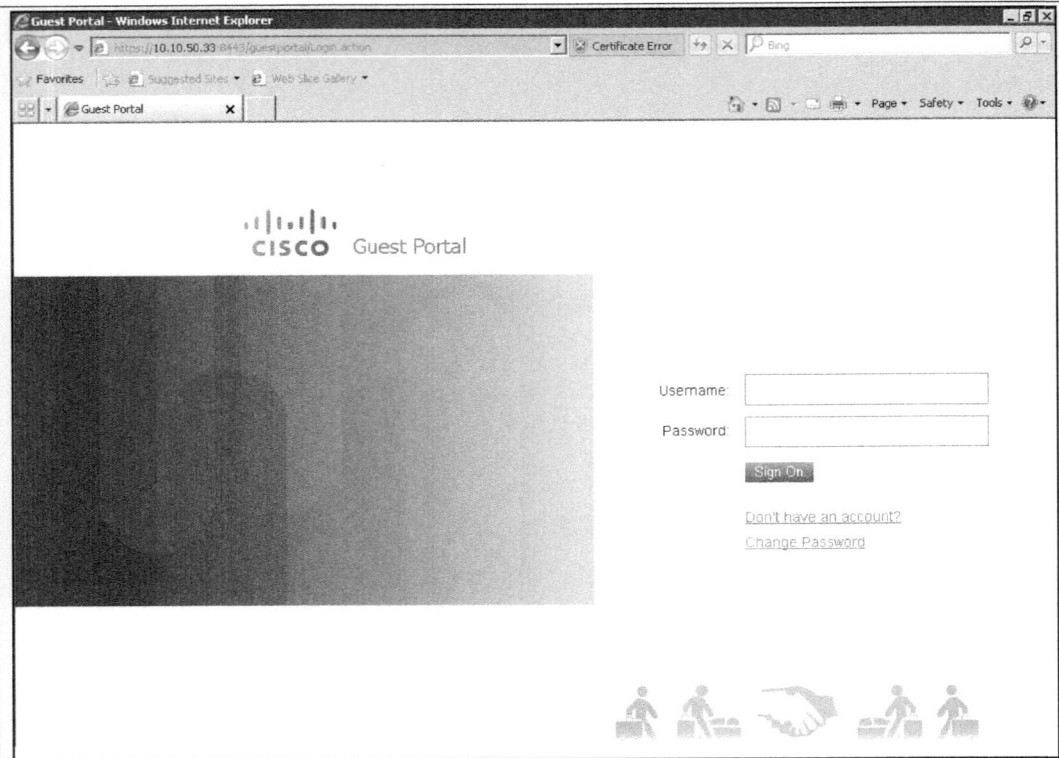

If user is admin created, Guest will have Username add password delivered by Email or SMS from Admin. If User is new, Click on Don't have account Option.

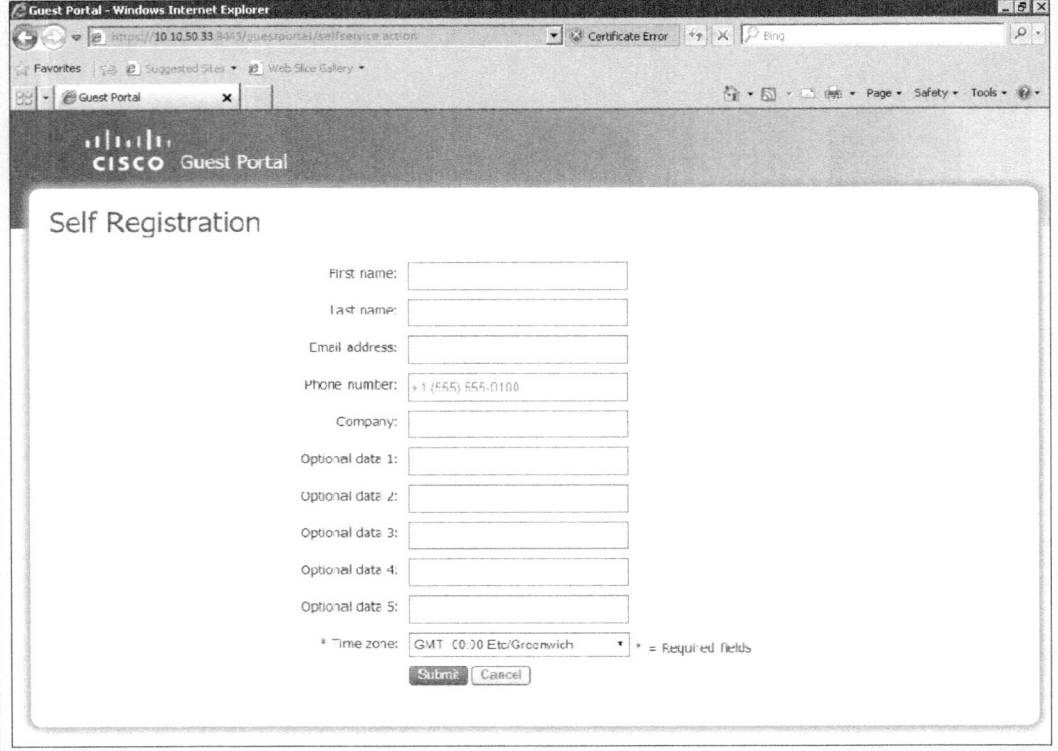

Submit the attributes to get username and password

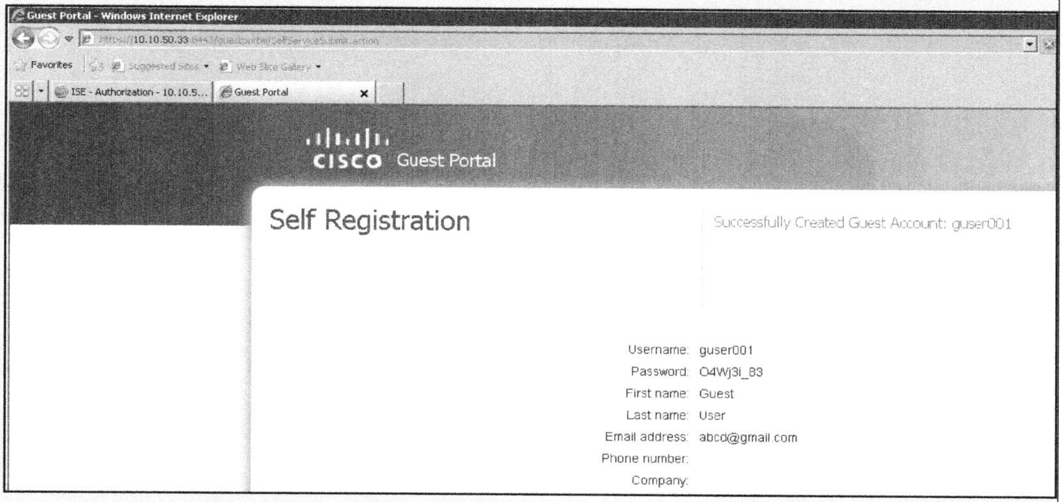

Here are the attributes for the new user.
Username: guser001
Password: O4Wj3i_83

Click Ok button below, you will be redirected again

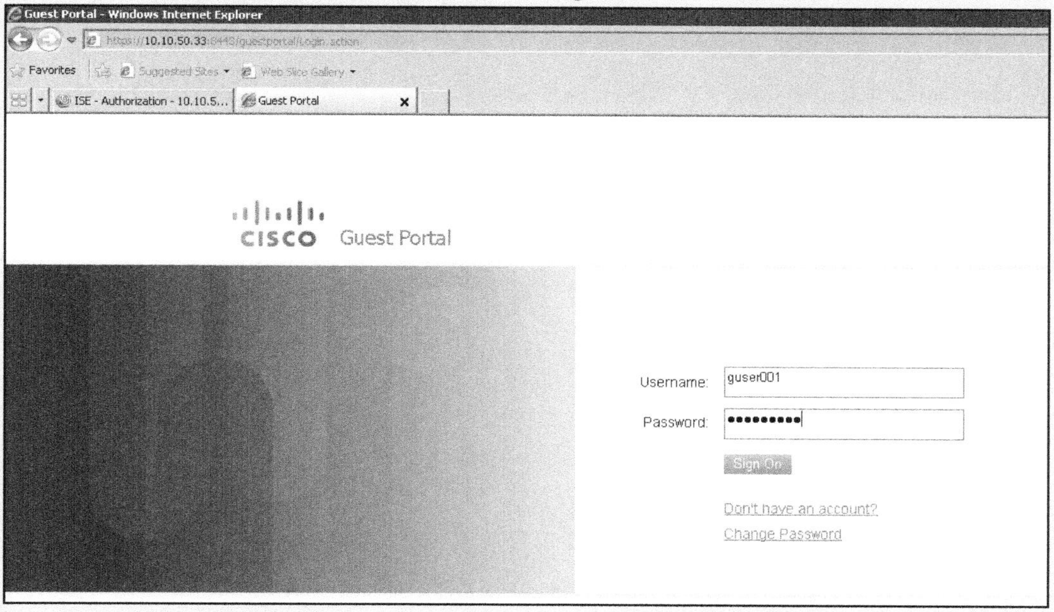

Submit your credentials.
Username: guser001
Password: O4Wj3i_83

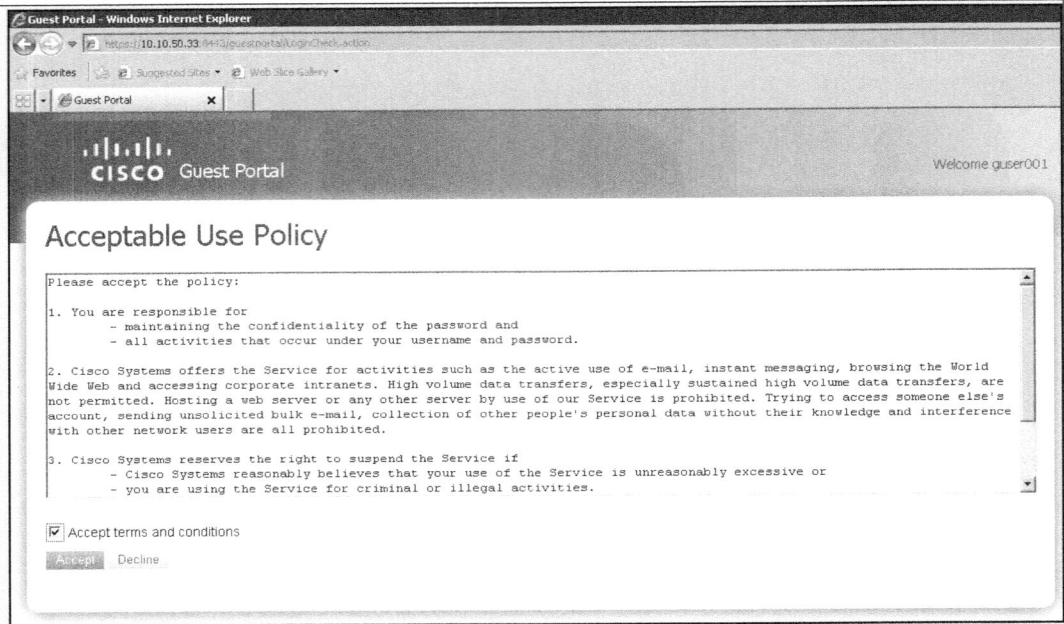

Accept the policy

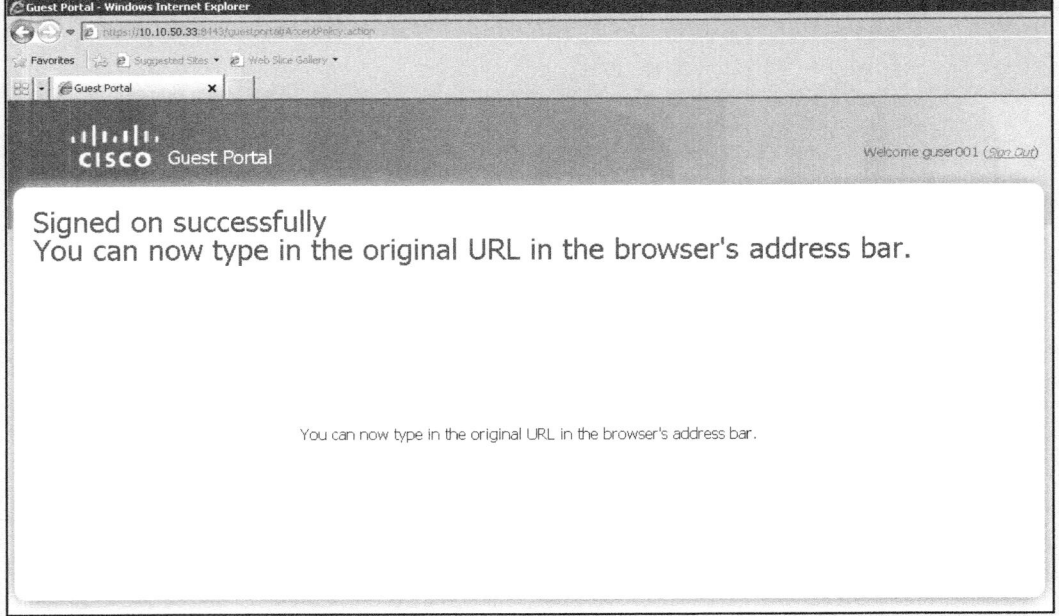

You are successfully authenticated and authorized.

Posturing

Posture service collects the attributes from the Endpoint to the Authentication server in order to learn about the health, Security or Trust level of the Endpoint device. These Attributes may be related to device type of the Endpoint, Operating System as well as Security Application that could be any Antivirus, Endpoint Firewall or Scanning software. In Posture Validation Process, certain set of rules is applied over Posture data for assessment depending upon the level of trust of the Endpoint device.

For enforcing the security policies, Client interaction with Posturing feature is either by using Network Admission Control (NAC) or AnyConnect ISE Posture Agent. Process running on ISE must support Clear disconnection of user at the time of termination because ISE Posture agent does not support Windows Fast User Switching with Native Supplicant. In Windows Fast User Switching with native Supplicant, there is no clear disconnection of older user. Hence recommended is to disable Windows Fast User switching.

Components of Posture Service
Posture Service basic components are
1. Posture Administration Services
2. Posture Run-time Services

Posture Administrative Services:
If the Posturing feature is enabled and configured on Cisco ISE, Administrative Service of Posturing provides back-end support for the conditions and actions, which are related to posturing. These Posturing conditions and remediation actions are associated with authorization policies configured. Posture Administrative services feature required Apex Licence to be installed in Cisco ISE, otherwise Administrative services feature of Posturing will not be available.

Posture Run-Time Services:
Posture Run - Time Service is used for encapsulation of communication in between Client Endpoint and Cisco ISE server. In Posture Run-Time Service, Process is initialized with Discovery phase by sending Discovery packets from Client end to the ISE server. As an Endpoint authenticated by 802.1x Port-based Authentication, Client attempts to connect the server by sending Discovery packets. These discovery packets are sent to HTTP port 80 and HTTPS port 8905 for communication. After discovery phase, if Acceptable User policy is configured and accepted, Posture Phase is initialized. Cisco ISE server send token to the client. In this token Agent GUID, User policy status and other information are present. Using this Posture Token Endpoint is allowed is reconnect the network without Posturing process. Format used in Posturing phase is NEA PB/PA (RFC5792) for communication.

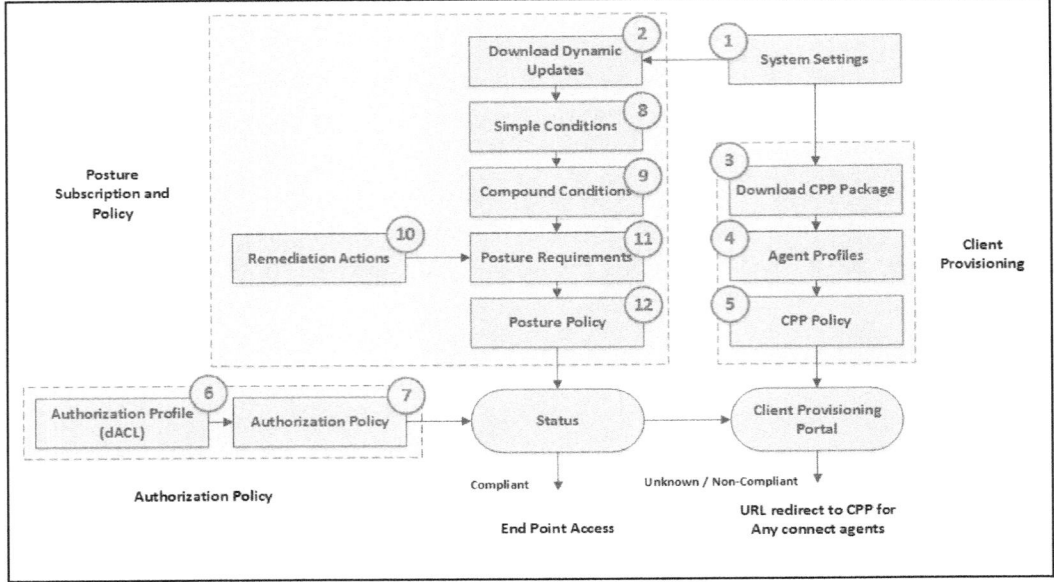

Figure 1-16. Posturing

Licensing and Deployment:
To enable Posture services, you have to install license on Cisco Identity Service Engine (ISE). Cisco provides three licenses for Cisco ISE.

- Base License
- Plus License
- Apex License

Only Apex license will entertain Posture Service that means to run Posturing feature, Cisco ISE must be installed with Apex License. Posture Service can serve single node as well as multiple nodes. Posturing can be deployed in Standalone environment (Single node) in which single node is configured or in distributed Environment (Multiple nodes) for monitoring, troubleshooting, Administration services and Policy run-time services.

Enabling Posture Session Service

- Enable session services in Cisco ISE and install the advanced license package.
- If you have more than one node that is registered in a distributed deployment, all the nodes that you have registered appear in the Deployment Nodes page, apart from the primary node. You can configure each node as a Cisco ISE node (Administration, Policy Service, and Monitoring personas).
- The posture service only runs on Cisco ISE nodes that assume the Policy Service persona and does not run on Cisco ISE nodes that assume the administration and monitoring personas in a distributed deployment.

1. Choose Administration > System > Deployment > Deployment.

2. Choose a Cisco ISE node from the Deployment Nodes page.

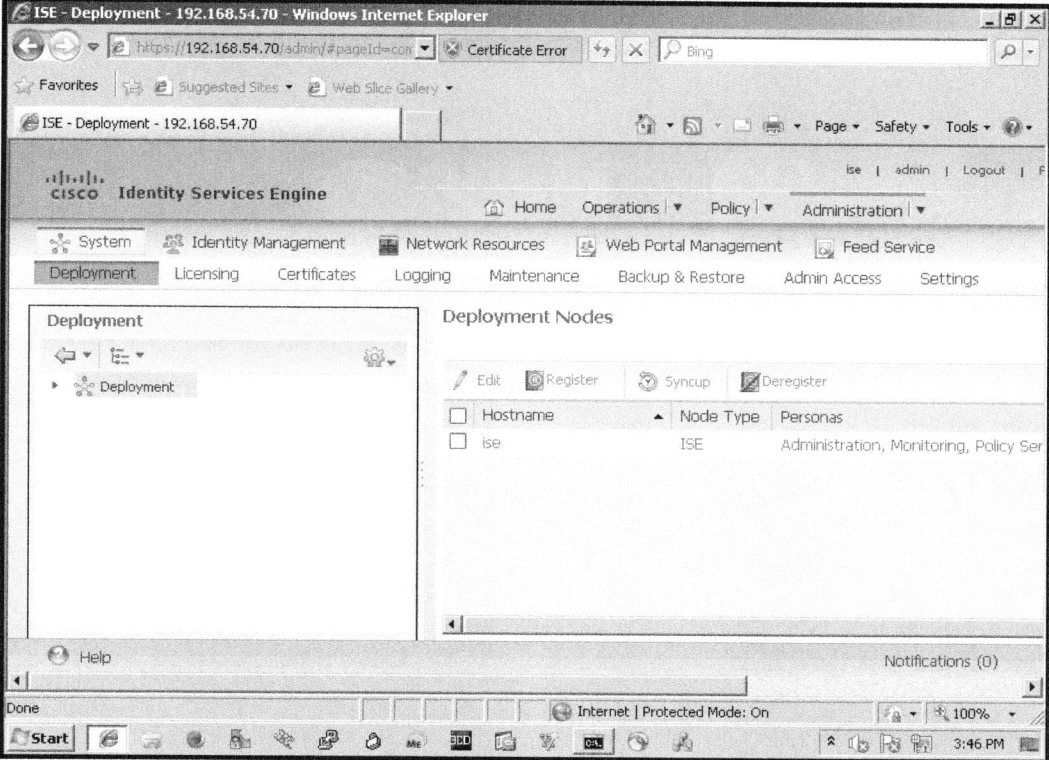

Figure 1-17. ISE Posture Service

3. Click Edit.
4. On the General settings tab, check the Policy Service check box,
   If the Policy Service check box is unchecked, both the session services and the profiling service check boxes are disabled.
5. Check the Enable Session Services check box, for the Policy Service persona to run the Network Access, Posture, Guest, and Client Provisioning session services. To stop the session services, uncheck the check box.
6. Click Save.

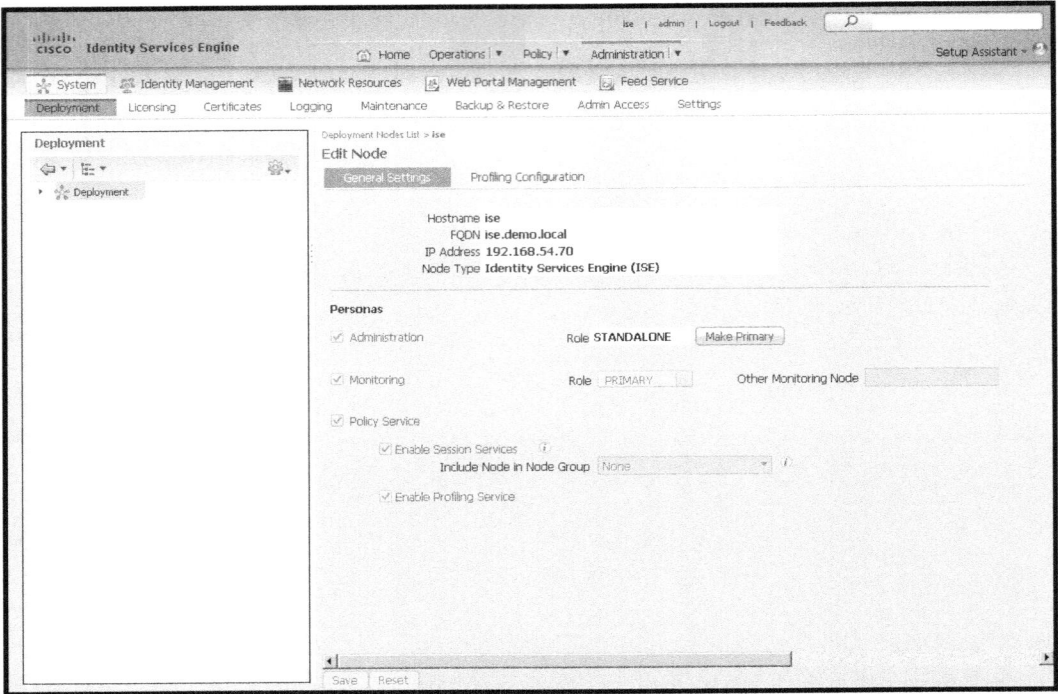

Figure 1-18. Enabling ISE Posture Service

Run the Posture Assessment Report

You can run the Posture Detail Assessment report to generate a detailed status of compliance of the clients against the posture policies that are used during posture assessment.

1. Choose Operations > Reports > ISE Reports > Endpoints and Users > Posture Detail Assessment.
2. Click the Time Range drop-down arrow and select the specific time period.
3. Click Run to view the summary of all the endpoints that logged on for a selected period of time.

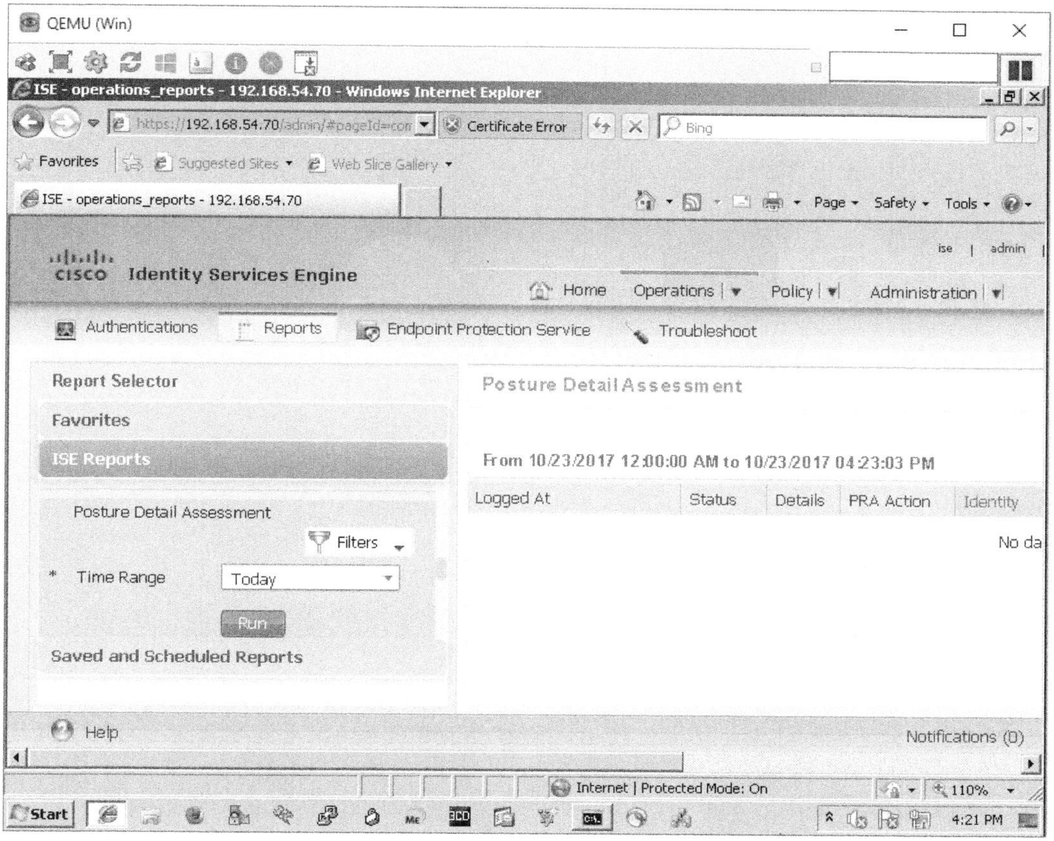

Figure 1-19. ISE Posture Assessment

Simple Posture Conditions

1. File Conditions
A condition that checks the existence of a file, the date of a file, and the versions of a file on the client.

2. Registry Conditions
A condition that checks for the existence of a registry key or the value of the registry key on the client.

3. Application Conditions
A condition that checks if an application (process) is running or not running on the client.

4. Service Conditions
A condition that checks if a service is running or not running on the client.

5. Dictionary Conditions
A condition that checks a dictionary attribute with a value.

Compound Posture Conditions

1. Compound Conditions

Contains one or more simple conditions, or compound conditions of the type File, Registry, Application, or Service condition

2. Antivirus Compound Conditions

Contains one or more AV conditions, or AV compound conditions

3. Antispyware Compound Conditions

Contains one or more AS conditions, or AS compound conditions

4. Dictionary Compound Conditions

Contains one or more dictionary simple conditions or dictionary compound conditions

Token	Description
Healthy	The endpoint device complies with the currently required credentials so you do not have to restrict this device.
Checkup	The endpoint device is within the policy but does not have the latest security software; update recommended. Use to proactively remediate a host to the Healthy state.
Transition	The endpoint device is in the process of having its posture checked and is given interim access pending a result from a full posture validation. Applicable during host boot where all services may not be running or while audit results are not yet available.
Quarantine	The endpoint device is out of policy and needs to be restricted to a remediation network. The device is not actively placing a threat on other hosts; but is susceptible to attack or infection and should be updated as soon as possible.
Infected	The endpoint device is an active threat to other hosts; network access should be severely restricted and placed into remediation or totally denied all network access.
Unknown	The posture credentials of the endpoint device cannot be determined. Quarantine the host and audit, or remediate until a definitive posture can be determined.

Table 6. Posturing Token Discription

Configuring Cisco ISE for Posture Services:

Before configuring Cisco ISE for Posture Service, make sure you have configured the Network Access Device with Dot1x Authentication. Authentication process is running

however you can either Authenticate the endpoint device using dot1x or MAB or configured continue to access if user not found on ISE database.

- Go to **https://www.cisco.com/web/secure/pmbu/posture-offline.html** .
- Save the posture-offline.zip file to your local system. This file is used to update the operating system information, checks, rules, and antivirus and antispyware support charts for Windows and Macintosh operating systems.
- Access the Cisco ISE administrator user interface and choose **Administration > System > Settings > Posture.**
- Click the arrow to view the settings for posture.
- Choose Updates . The Posture Updates page appears.
- From the Posture Updates page, choose the Offline option.
- From the File to update field, click Browse to locate the single archive file (posture-offline.zip) from the local folder on your system.

Cisco ISE Configuration:

To update Cisco ISE, go to Administration > System > Settings > Posture > Updates and select Web for Online automatic update or Offline for manual update.

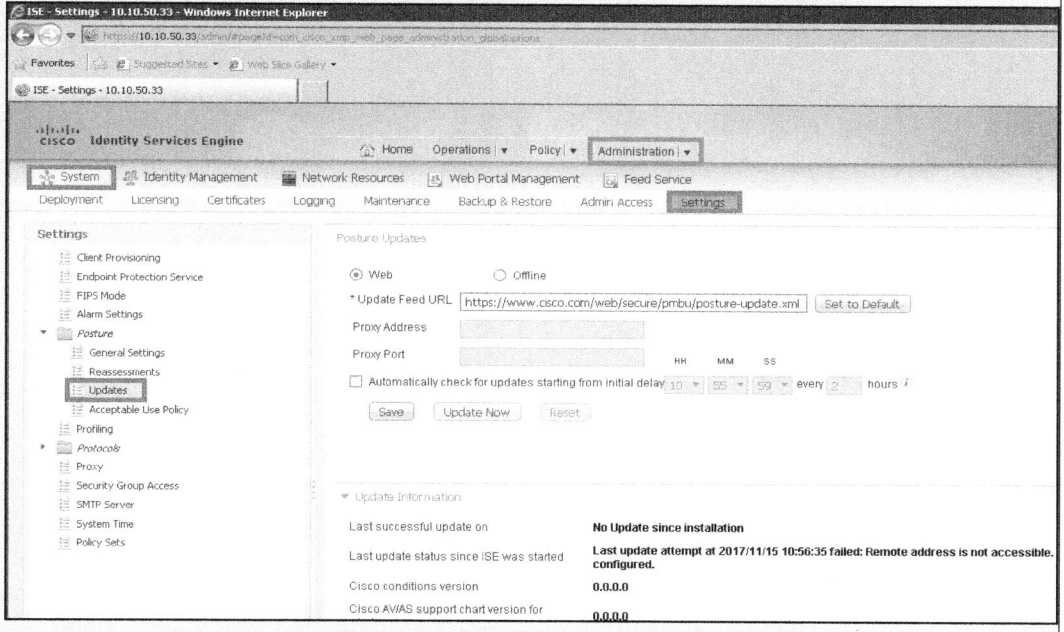

Figure 1-20. Cisco ISE Posture Update

For online update Cisco ISE must be connected with Internet and DNS must be responsive. Setup Proxy address and Proxy port if required and Click Update now. For frequent automatic update Check the checkbox for automatic update.

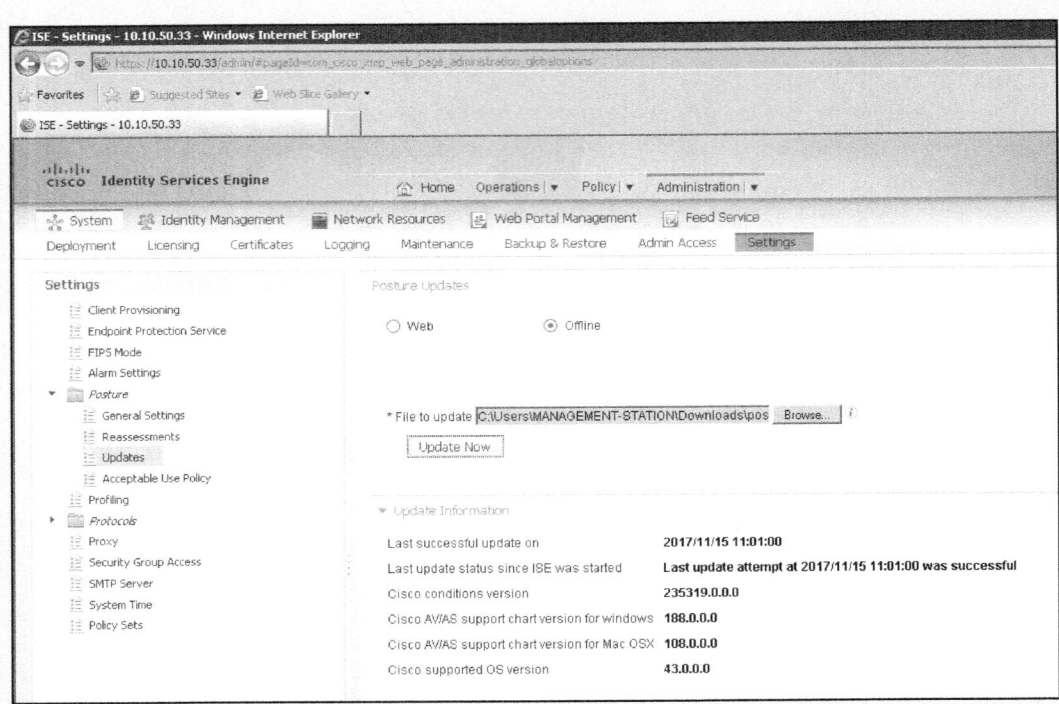

Figure 1-21. Cisco ISE Posture Update

Updating Manually by selecting file from directory.

Now go to **Policy > Policy Elements > Results > Client Provisioning > Resources > Add > Agent Resources from Cisco Site**

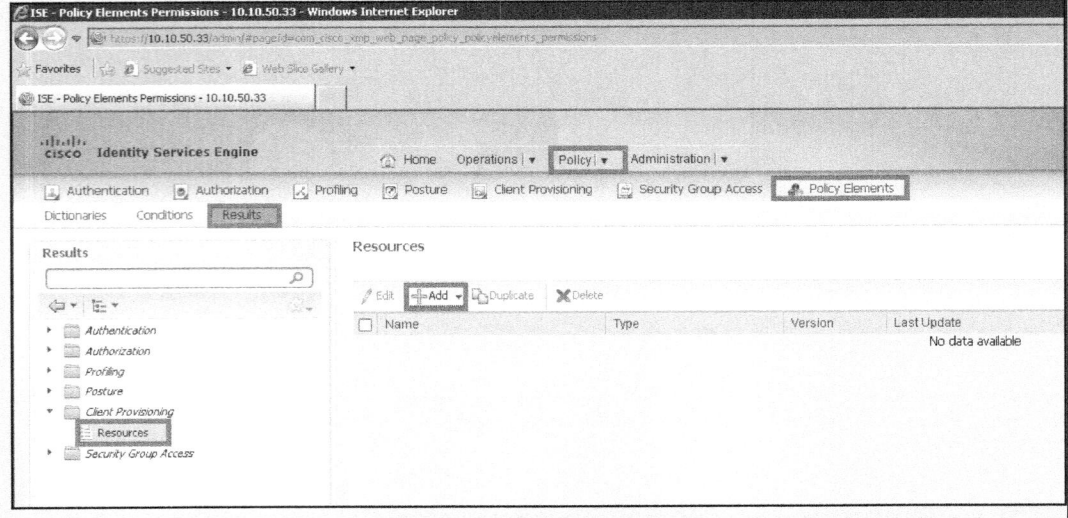

Figure 1-22. Cisco ISE Client provisioning Resources

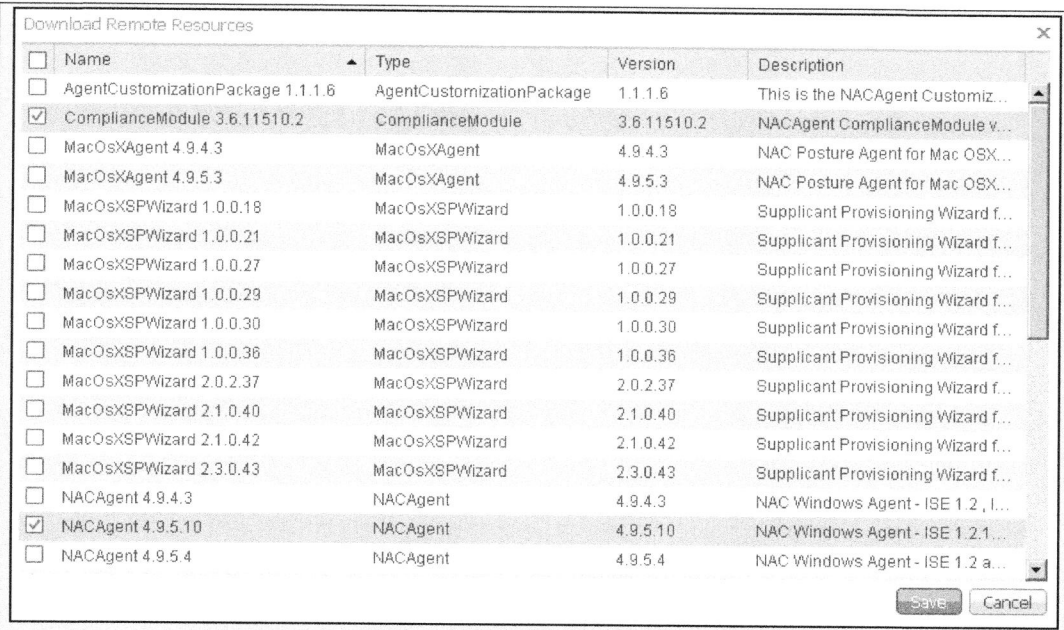

Figure 1-23. Cisco ISE Client provisioning Resources

Download the shown **NACAgent4.9.5.10**(Latest Version) and **Compliance Module 3.6.11510.2.**

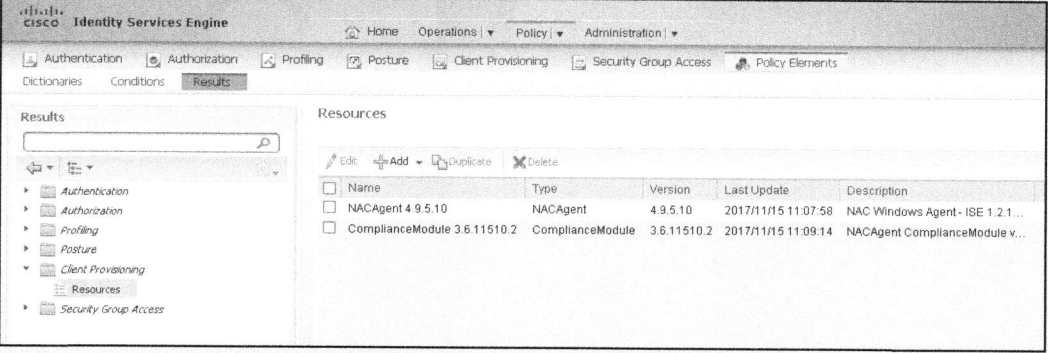

Figure 1-24. Cisco ISE Client provisioning Resources

Final Configuration of Client Provisioning Resources.

Now click Add button and Create Posture Agent Profile by Selecting **ISE Posture Agent Profile**

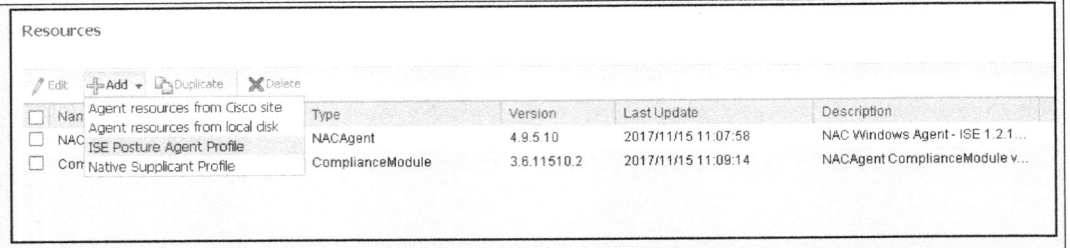

Figure 1-25. Cisco ISE Posture Agent Profile

Following Page will show, just name the Posture Profile. You can modify the attribute as required. In our case, use default settings and save it.

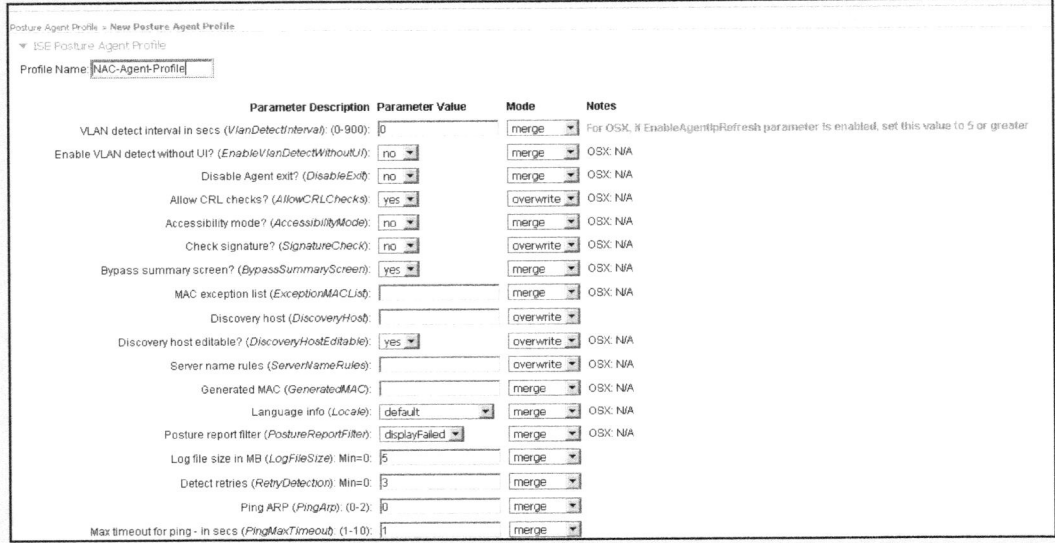

Figure 1-26. Cisco ISE Posture Agent Profile

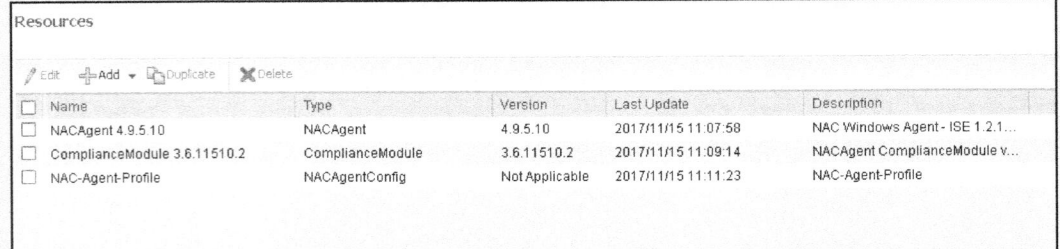

Figure 1-27. Cisco ISE Posture Agent Profile

Final Configuration of Client Provisioning Resources section. Now to Create Client Provisioning Policy, Go to **Policy** > **Client Provisioning**

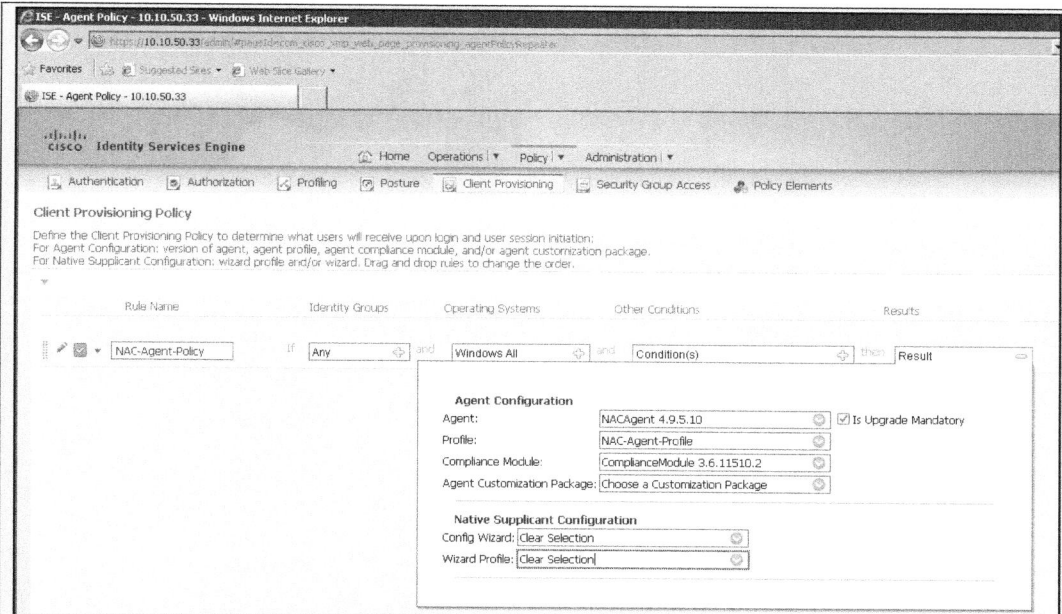

Figure 1-28. Cisco ISE Client provisioning Policy

Configure a new Policy, Rule name **NAC-Agent-Profile**, Identity group **Any**, Operating System **Windows** and Set the attributes of Result that are Agent as **NACAgent4.9.5.10**, Profile as **NAC-Agent-Profile**, Compliance Module as **ComplianceModule3.6.11510.2**.

Now Go to **Policy > Policy Element > Conditions > Posture > File Condition**

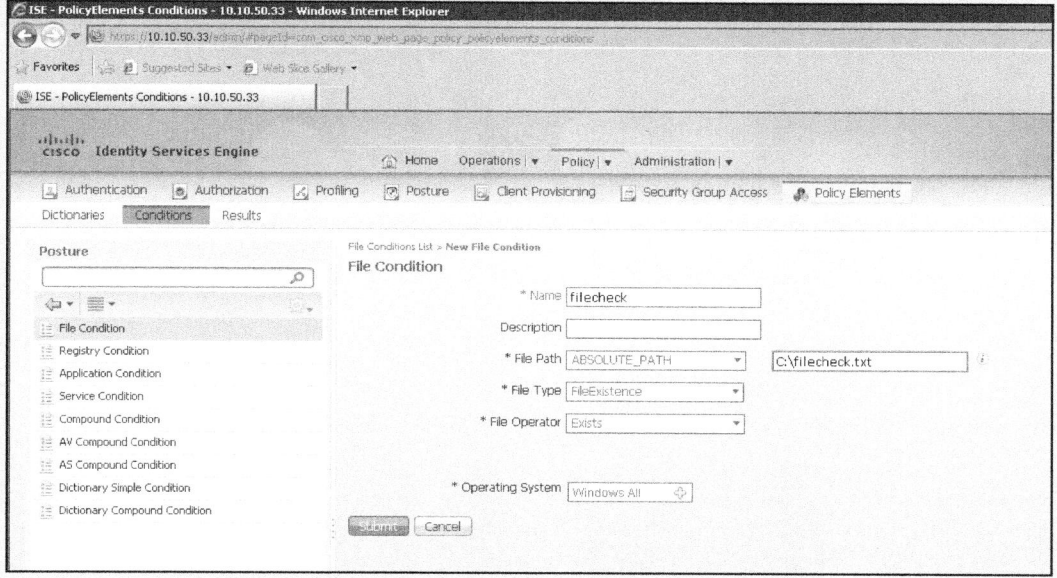

Figure 1-29. Cisco ISE Posture File condition

Here we are adding a condition to check for File in C directory of Endpoint Client.

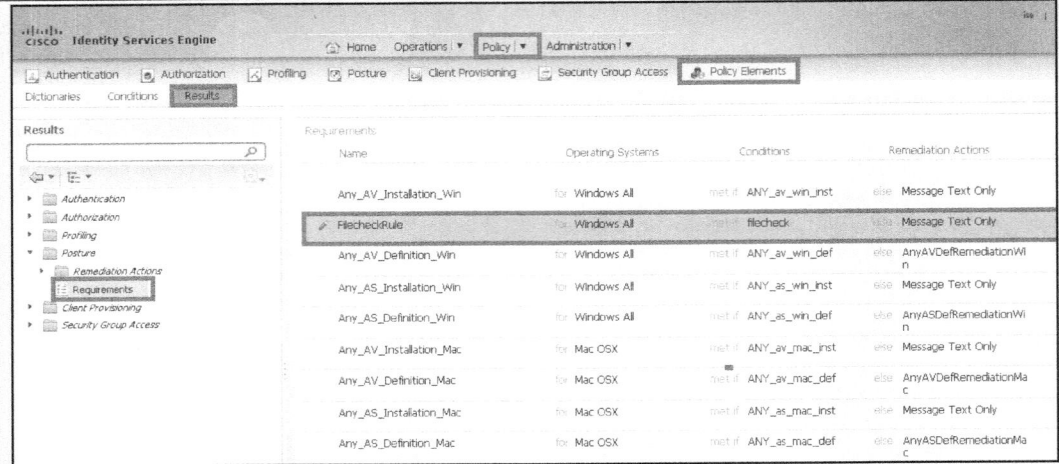

Figure 1-30. Cisco ISE Posture requirement

Now add this filecheck condition into posture requirement. Go to **Policy > Policy Element > Results > Posture > Requirements** and set the requirement as shown.

Now Go to **Policy > Posture** to create Policy for Posture.

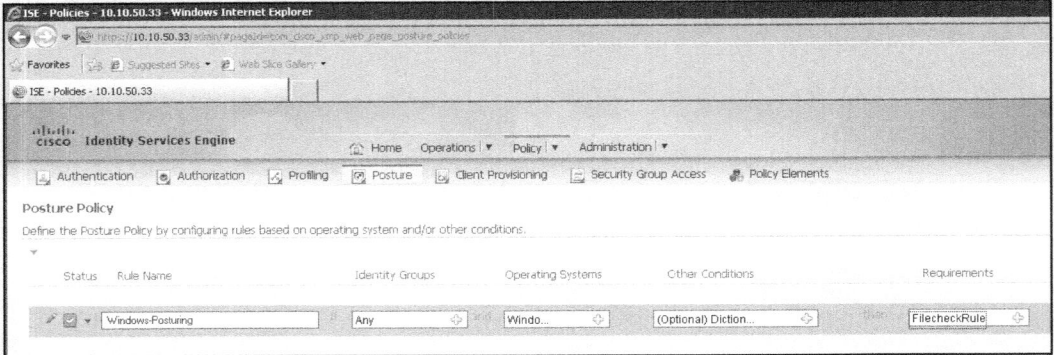

Figure 1-31. Cisco ISE Posture Policy

Create a Posture Policy in which Any User authenticating will be inspected for Windows Operating System and File Check Requirement.

Go to **Policy > Policy Element > Results > Authorization > Authorization Profile** to create redirection profile to Client Provisioning Portal.

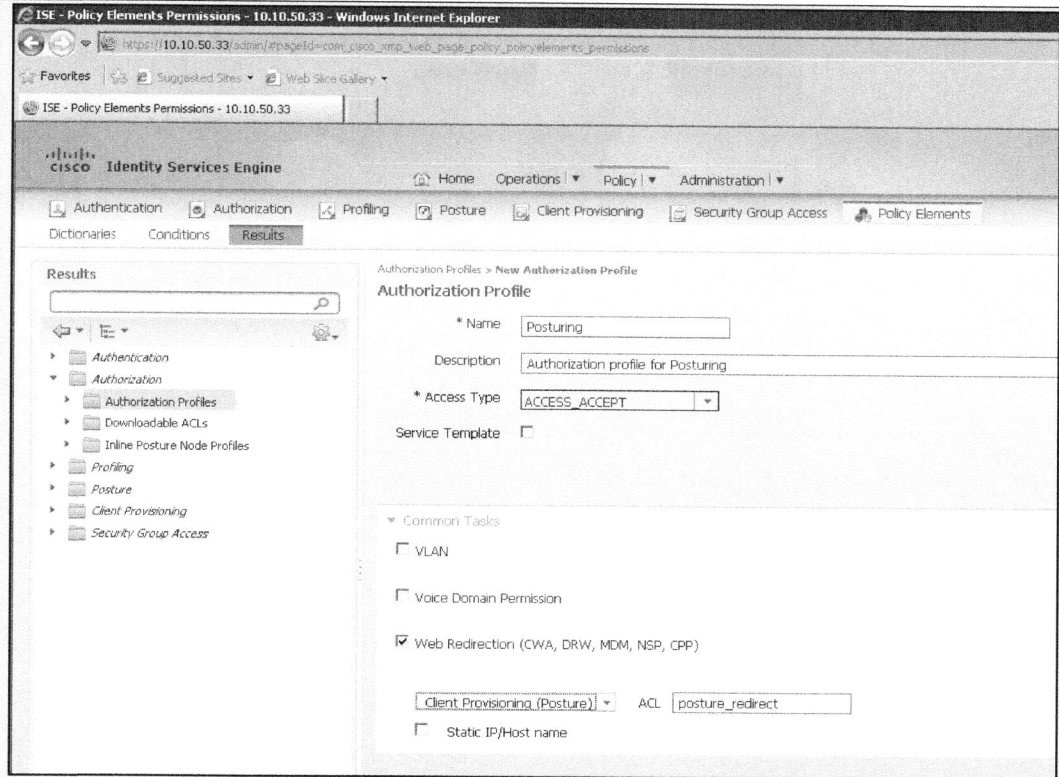

Figure 1-32. Cisco ISE Authorization Profile for Posture

Name the Authorization Profile, Check the Web Redirection box, Select Client Provisioning (Posture) and Select the type the redirection ACL name configured on NAD Switch.

Go to **Policy** > **Authorization** and Create rule

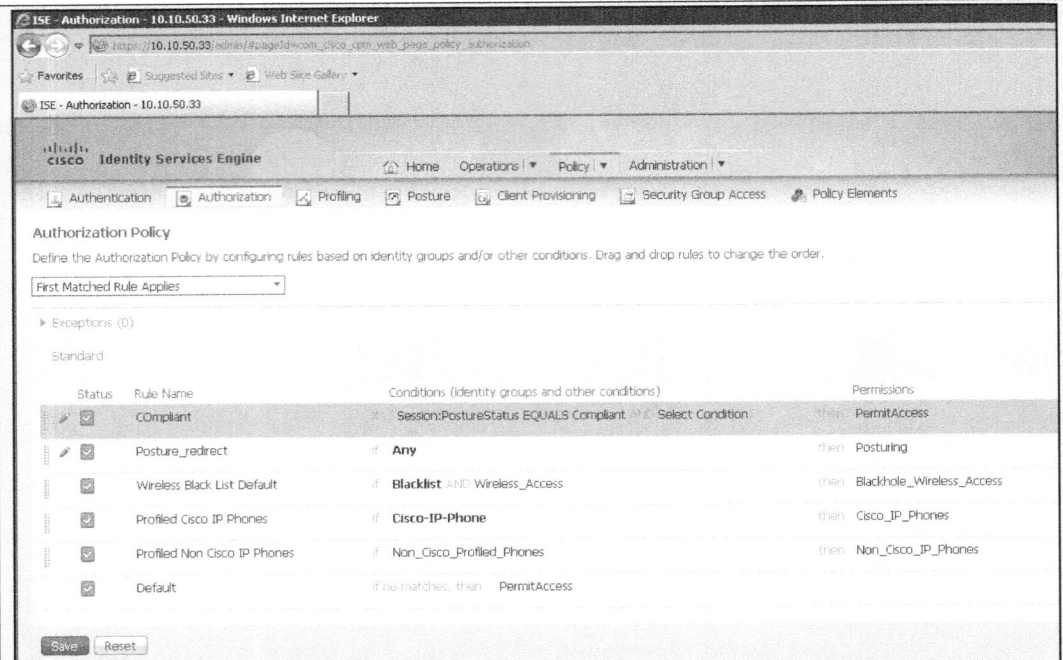

Figure 1-33. Cisco ISE Authorization Policy

Create two rules, Posture_redirect for Redirection of Client to Provisioning Portal, another for client compliant with the conditions. If Client is compliant first rule will match and Access will be permitted. If not, second rule will redirect them to Portal.

Verification:

Go to Client PC and Open the web browser.

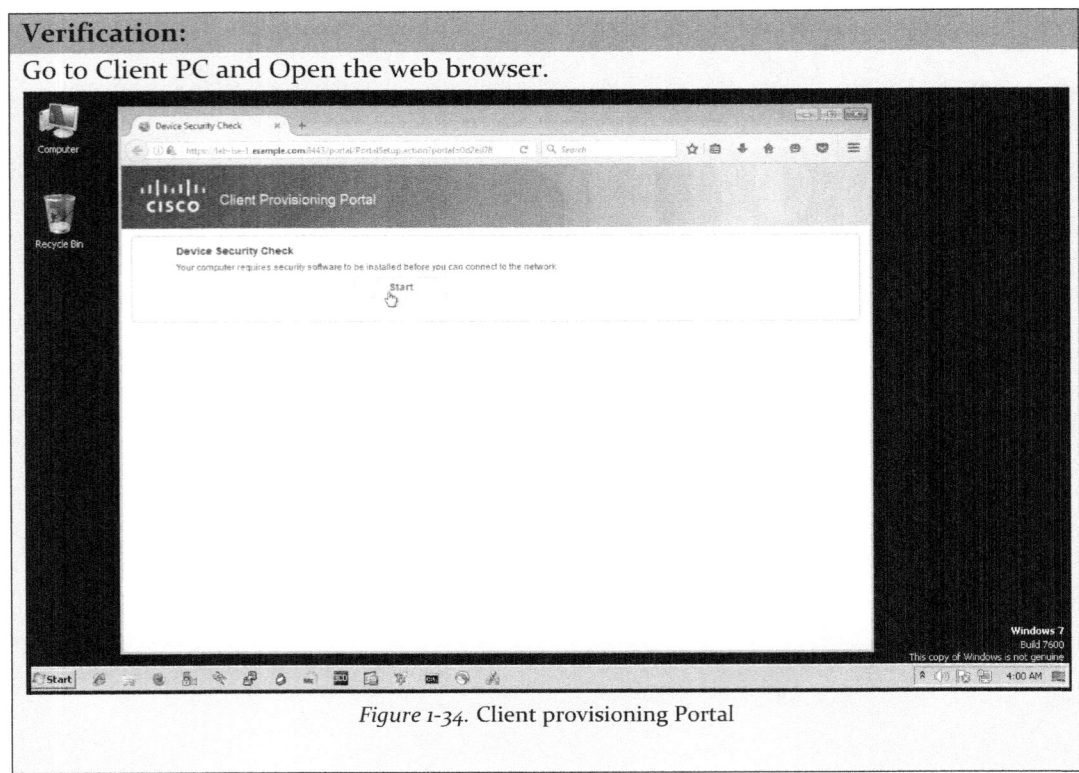

Figure 1-34. Client provisioning Portal

You will be redirected to Client provisioning Portal page, and Device security check will start inspection.

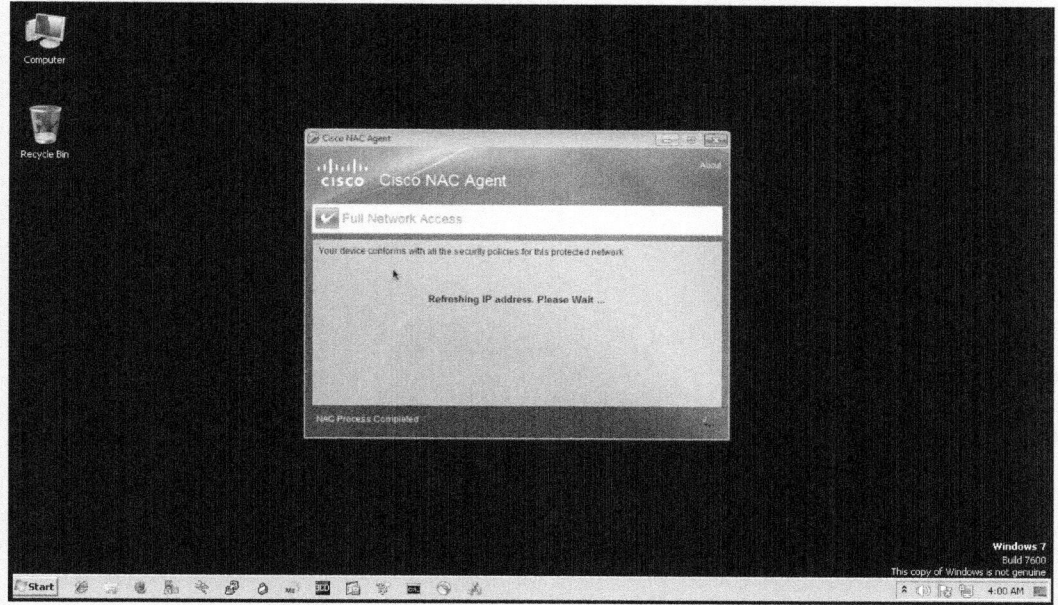

Figure 1-35. Cisco NAC Agent

NAC Agent will be downloaded automatically. After running the NAC Agent application, It will check for conditions. Once client is successfully meets all conditions, Access will be permitted.

Bring Your Own Device (BYOD) Access

Introduction:

Every organization in this world is rapidly growing their working environment and production. For growing their organization, they need to provide more flexible and efficient work place to their employees. Mobility is one of the most required options in today's world. One can connect and access the network from any remote location securely. This saves his time and efficiency and productivity of an organization. As Mobility is a beneficial option for an organization, there are also some challenges that are attached with for Administrator. These challenges include Authentication, Authorization, Secure access and secure communication. Another challenges are to provide support to mobile devices, Monitoring and provide security. The number of mobile devices is significantly increasing day by day. Client accessing from Smartphones, tablets, Home PCs and Laptops are the great challenge.

Bring your Own Devices

Laptops, Smartphones and Tablets are replacing typical PCs in every organization. These devices are becoming more efficient with faster computing, integration and ability to connect with advanced technologies. Employees and Client and Users use

these devices for their personal and professional work. One client may also access through multiple device to the company's network.

Bring your Own Device started with allowing the endpoint, with limited access to the network. But now a day, Clients and Employees are using their own devices, to access network resources to do their job. In case of BYOD access, Network administrator must have to secure the Corporate data for un authorized access as well as Mobile Device Management (MDM) becomes more important with BYOD access.

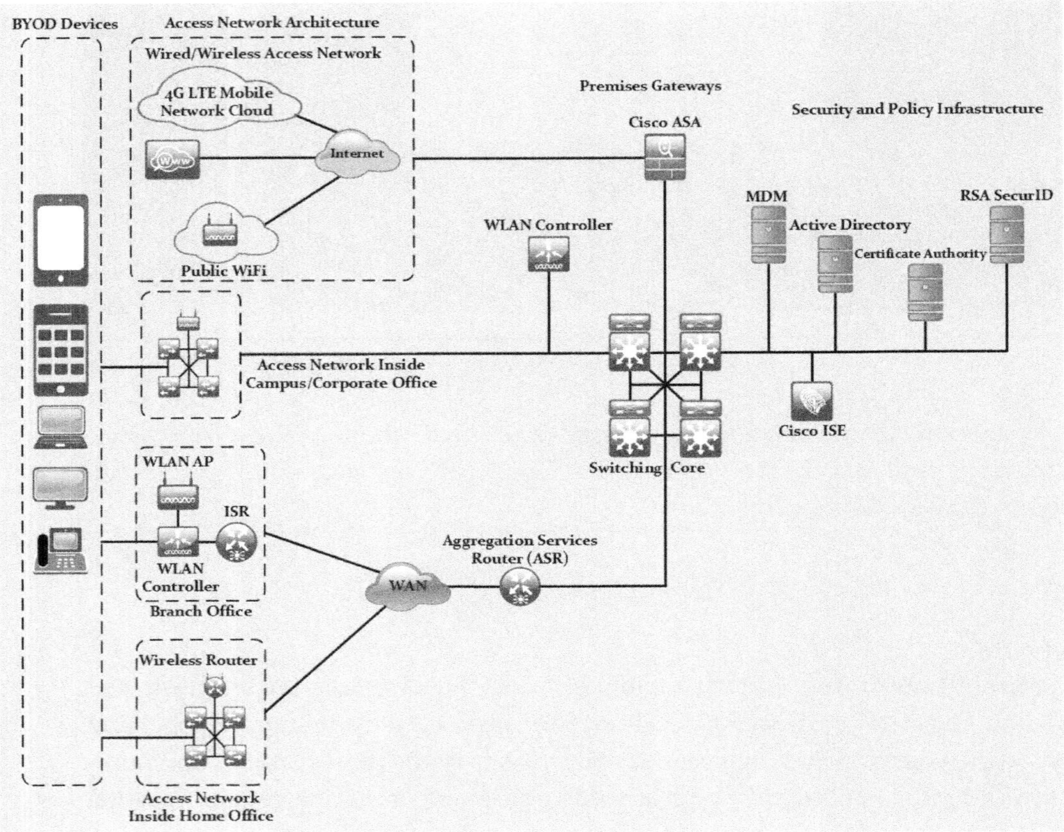

Figure 1-36. BYOD high-level architecture

Mobility Device Management

Mobility Device Management MDM ensures that the device is locked and remotely wiped if it is lost, stolen or when the employee is restricted to access in case of termination. Cisco Meraki provides the unified management, Over-the-air centralized management, monitoring and diagnostics of Macs, PCs, Androids, iPads and the other network devices over the centralized dashboard. By Using Mobile Device Management Location of the BYOD device, information of hardware and software, recent location as well as remotely locking, blocking and wiping the device. Following are some of the functions provided by MDM:

- Enforcing a device to be locked after certain login failure attempts.
- Enforcement of strong password polices for all BYOD devices.
- MDM can detect any attempt of hacking BYOD devices and then limiting the network access of these affected devices.
- Enforcing confidentiality by using encryption as per organization's policy.
- Administration and implementation of *Data Loss Prevention (DLP)* for BYOD devices. It helps to prevent any kind of data loss due end user's carelessness.

Mobile Application Management (MAM)

Mobile Application Management (MAM) provides controlling and monitoring at the application level. It is responsible for provisioning and controlling access to the application used in an organization for Bring your own Device (BYOD) i.e. smartphones and tablet computers.

Mobile Application Management (MAM) differs from Mobile Device Management (MDM), which focuses on controlling the entire device and requires that users enrol their device and install a service agent.

Enterprise Mobility management (EMM)

Enterprise Mobility management (EMM) suites include a MAM function, EMM suites require a device management profile in order to enable application management capabilities.

Elements of BYOD Policy:

1. Type of Access:

Employee connecting to Company's network from its own device is allowed to access voluntarily or it is mandatory to access from BYOD device. It depends upon the need and nature of business of an organization.

2. Who Can Access:

If all employees are allowed to access from their device or selected employees are permitted. If an organization has temporary employees what does the policy says about them.

3. Supported Devices:

In Bring your Own Device (BYOD) what type of devices are allowed to access the network resource and company's data and which devices are not allowed and restricted to access.

4. Defined Security Requirements

List clearly defined security policies for BYOD

Device Registering:

In the process of BYOD Device Registration, following are the key steps that includes the process of registration.

- Endpoint User trying to connect the device is prompted for credentials. These credentials are Username and Password.
- As the user submit Active Directory Username and Password, Extensible authentication protocol (EAP) login request is sent to Wireless LAN Controller (WLC) which forward this request to RADIUS server.
- RADIUS Server will respond with authorization result with URL-Redirection to NSP Portal.
- User access the NSP Portal from Web browser and register his device.
- When user register the device, BYOD registration flag is set for the identity of Endpoint, Endpoint device is registered to Registered Devices identity group and a CA certificate is sent to the device.

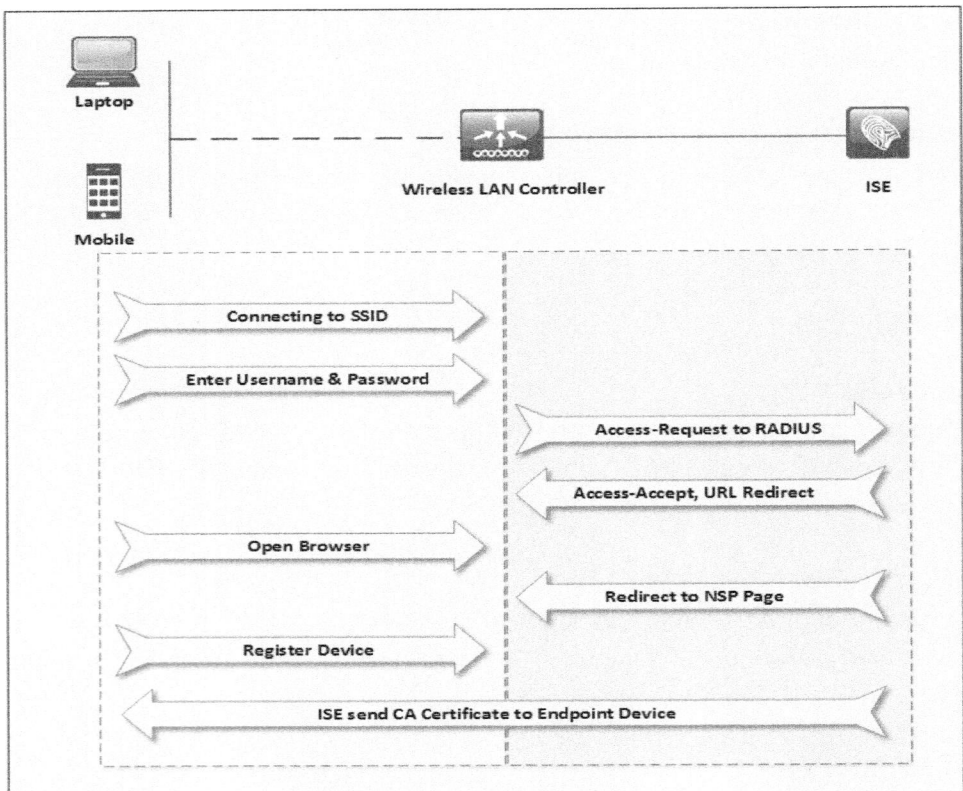

Figure 1-37. Device Registering

Personal Device Portals

Cisco Identity Service Engine (ISE) provides multiple web-based portals to support BYOD. These portals do not involve in the guest or sponsor portals.

1. Blacklist Portal

Black list portal contains information of those personal devices which are "blacklisted" and restricted to access the network.

2. Client Provisioning Portals

Client Provisioning Portal forces employees to download a posture agent on their devices that checks for compliance.

3. BYOD Portals

Using BYOD Portal, employees can register their devices using Native Supplicant Provisioning.

4. MDM Portals

MDM Portal enable employees to enrol their devices with an external Mobile Device Management (MDM) system.

5. My Devices Portals

My Device Portal enable employees to add and register devices, including those that do not support native supplicant provisioning.

My Device Portal

My Device Portal can be redirected from Server or user can access the portal directly. If a user has registered the device using BYOD Portal or My Device Portal, Device can be managed using My Device portal.

Some Devices that are connecting to the network can support Native Supplicant Provisioning whereas some of the devices do not support Native Supplicant Provisioning. The Devices, which doesn't support Native supplicant provisioning, cannot be registered with Bring your Own Device Portal. An Alternate for those devices which does not support Native Supplicant or Do not have Web Browser, these devices can be registered using My Devices Portal.

When a Client is adding the device to access the network, Client must have to add the MAC address of the device. When Employee managing new device submit the MAC address the device using My Devices Portal and device is not statically added to any Endpoint identity group, ISE adds the device into the database of Endpoint as Registered Endpoint devices identity group.

If a user enters Multiple MAC addresses on My Device Portal for registering devices, using Username, Cisco ISE will consider these MAC address Associated with same User and merged them together as a single entry. If the User Registered Laptop with Wired Address and Wireless Address using same username, both addresses are

considered as single entry. Any Operation from Cisco ISE will act on both Addresses, For Example Removing the device will remove both addresses.

When a registered device is removed or deleted from database, Device Registration status is changed to Not Registered and BYOD registration status attributes is changed to "No". These attribute value are set for Employees device registration only. If a guest device is registered BYOD attributes remains unchanged.

Supplicant Provisioning:
Client Provisioning feature downloads the client provisioning resources and configure Agent profiles at User end. Agent profiles are for Windows Client, MAC OS clients as well as native supplicant profiles for devices. If Client provisioning option is disabled, user will show a warning message. Client provisioning enabled the network session when a client connects to the network. When Client attempts to connect the network, Client provisioning resources are downloaded to the client device.

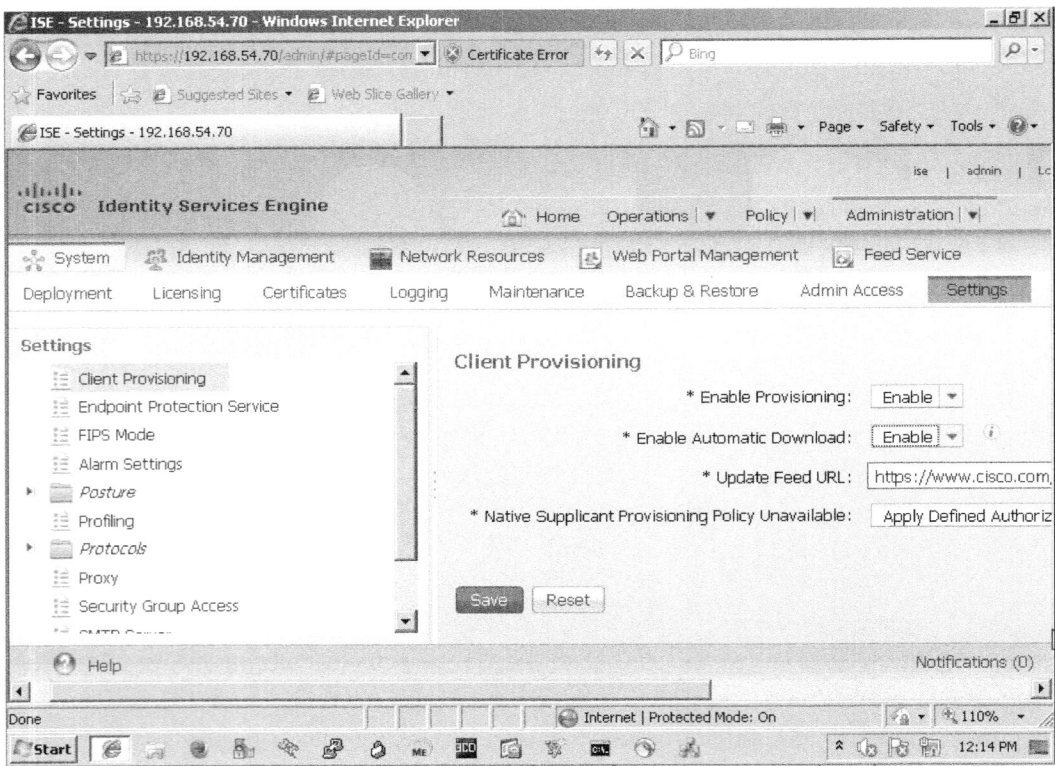

Figure 1-38. Client Provisioning

Configure Client Provisioning in Cisco ISE

1. Choose **Administration** > **System** > **Settings** > **Client Provisioning**.

2. From the Enable Provisioning drop-down list, choose **Enable** or **Disable**.
3. From the Enable Automatic Download drop-down list, choose **Enable.**
4. Update Feed URL—Specify the URL where Cisco ISE searches for system updates in the Update Feed URL text box. the default URL for downloading client-provisioning resources is https://www.cisco.com/web/secure/pmbu/provisioning-update.xml.
5. Click **Save**.

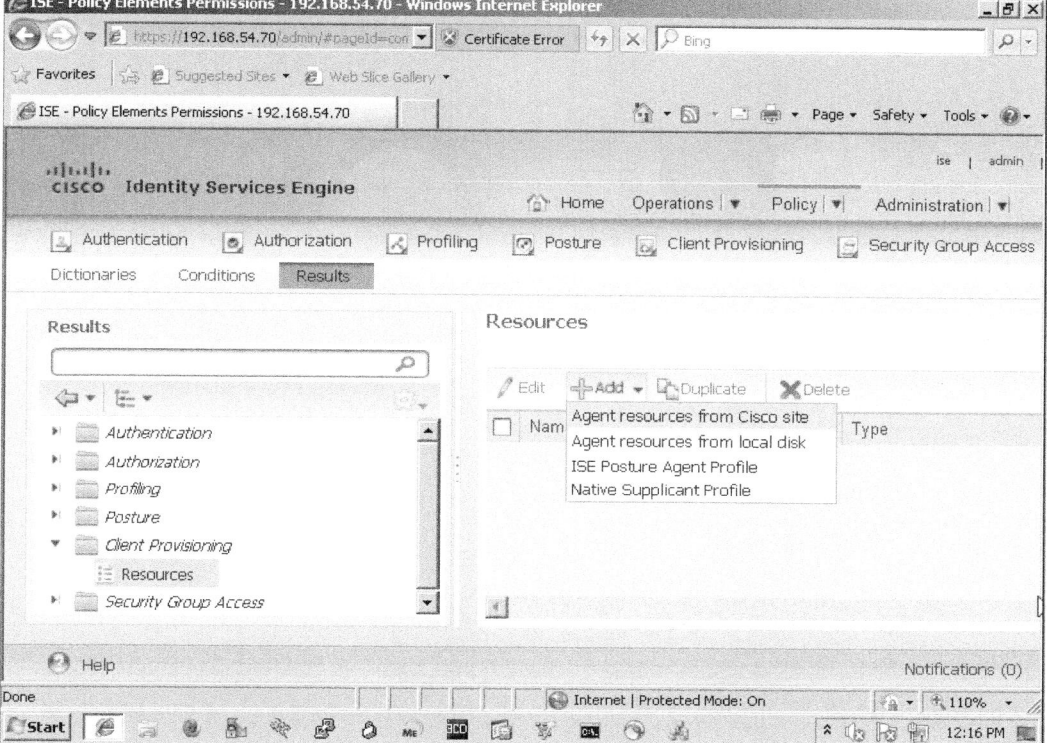

Figure 1-39. Client Provisioning Resources

Client provisioning resources are listed on **Policy Elements** > **Results** > **Client Provisioning** > **Resources**. The following resource types can be added to the list by clicking the **Add** button:

Options are

1. Agent resources from Cisco Site
2. Agent resources from local disk
3. ISE Posture Agent Profile
4. Native Supplicant Profile

Mind Map

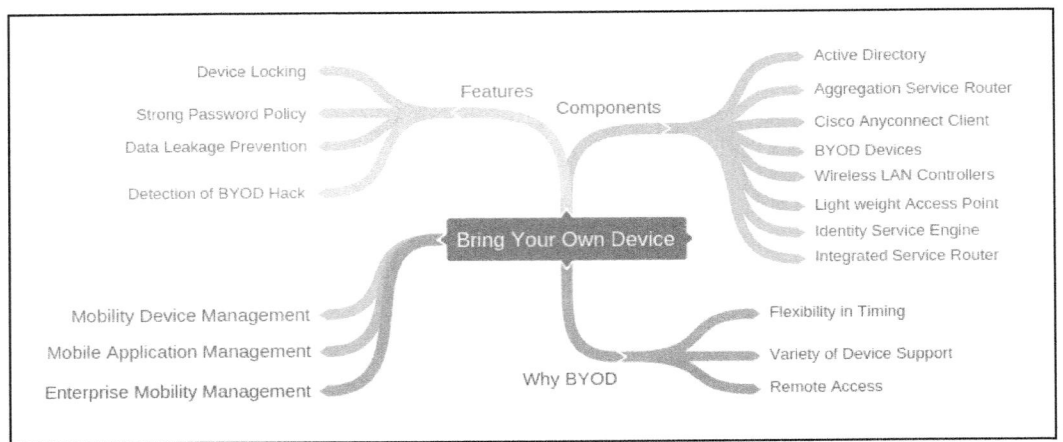

Chapter 2: Threat Defence

Technology Brief

TrustSec

Trust Security in short TrustSec is also known as Security Group Access (SGA). TrustSec or SGA offers Advance Access control mechanism, enforcement of Access control to secure the network. This Solution offers security solution to the rapidly growing network. TrustSec offers security by assigning a security tag known as Security Group Tag (SGT).

Security Group Tag (SGT) is a security tag, which is a 16-bit value that Identity Service Engine (ISE) assigns to the Endpoint device, or User upon login. When User, or Endpoint logs in from the initiation of session this security group tag is assigned and mapped over all traffic generating from that session.

By using the Cisco TrustSec technology, through Security Group Tags which requires hardware support to modify the Layer 2 Ethernet frame to add security group tag, access policies can be enforced associated with the security group tags (SGTs) as these tags are used by Switches, routers and firewalls as well for forwarding decision. Configuring Access Control list associated with the policy to isolate Security group to another security group can use Security Group tags.

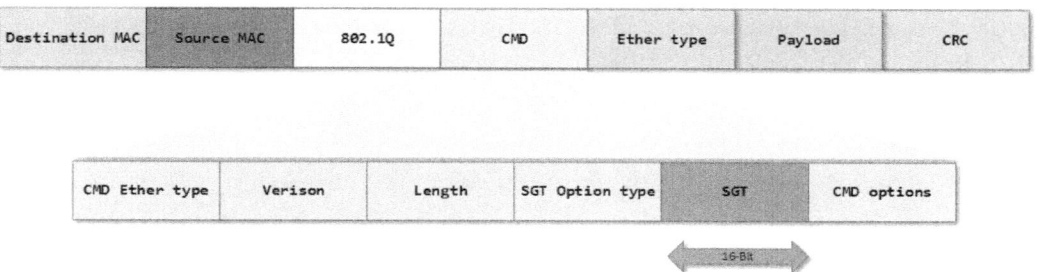

Figure 2-1. Ethernet Frame with TrustSec fields

Enforcement:

Cisco TrustSec Enforcement is offered by using tagging of Security Group tags on the ingress traffic to the Cisco TrustSec cloud. Ingress traffic in TrustSec Cloud is tagged with SGT and Security Group Number. At Egress point, Egress device uses Source Security Group tag and Security Group Number of destination for checking the condition against Access Control list entries. There are two types of Security Group Access Enforcement

1. Security Group Firewall (SG-FW)

2. Security Group Access Control List (SGACL)

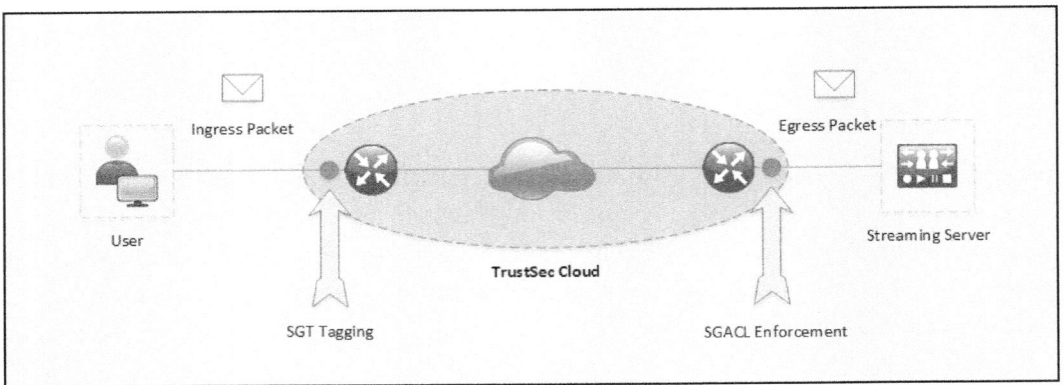

Figure 2-2. TrustSec Enforcement

Security Group Firewall (SG-FW)

Using Access Control List can do security enforcement but it can't not perform traffic filtering. Firewalls are the devices; whose purpose of deployment is to filter the traffic. Some Networks prefer Traffic enforcement by using Switching infrastructure. Firewall has the ability of traffic filtering, enforcing the traffic by Security group firewall (SG-FW).

This Firewall can be implement by using Cisco Adaptive Security Appliance (ASA) that is called as ASA Based SG-FW, another technique of implementation is by using Router-based SG-FW. By using Router Zone-based Policy Firewall implementation can also provide strong security feature to Security Groups. Integrated Service Router (ISR) and Aggregation Service Router (ASR) are also used for this purpose.

Security Group Access Control List (SGACL)

Security Group Access Control List, in short (SGACL) is control list which are associated with the Security Group access policy. These Access Control lists permits and restrict as ordinary Access Control List do, but SGACL permissions are associated with SGA Policy evaluation.

These Security Group ACLs performs permission and restriction over the user according to the role and responsibilities of that user instead of Logical Address (IP address and Subnet mask). These Security Group ACLs can be configured from Cisco Identity Service Engine (ISE) administrative user interface.

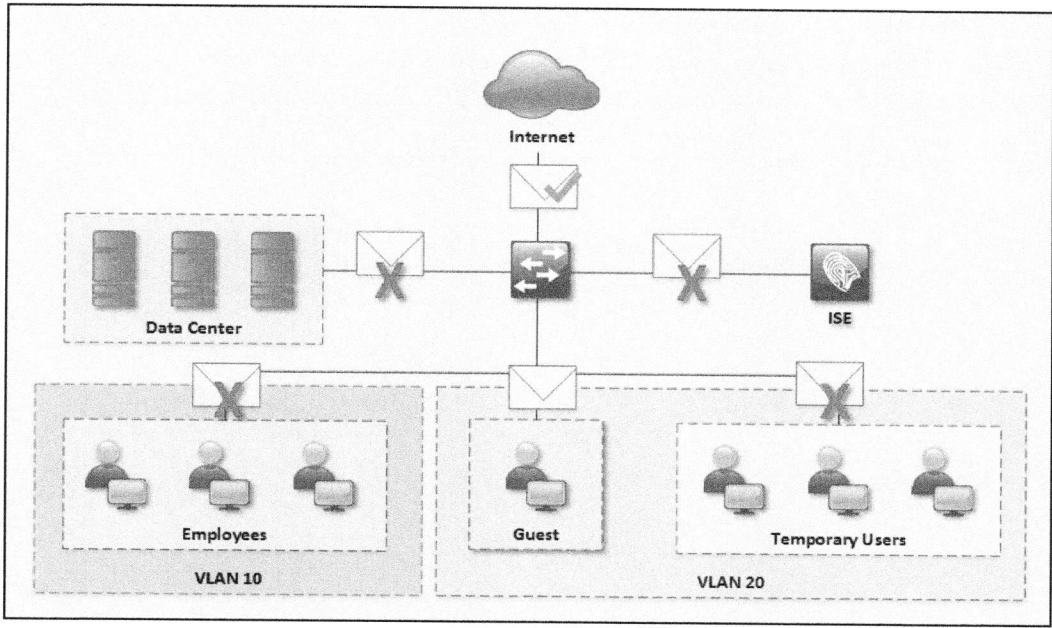

Figure 2-3. SGA ACLs

Consider a scenario of an organization that deployed Security Group Access Control List to secure its network and network resources. By Using SGACLs Guest user is restricted. The limitation of guest user is it can access the Internet service only. Guest user cannot communicate the Temporary Users which lies in the same VLAN as in Guest user is in. Guest is denied to communicate Employees of the organizations as well as they can't access Data Centre services.

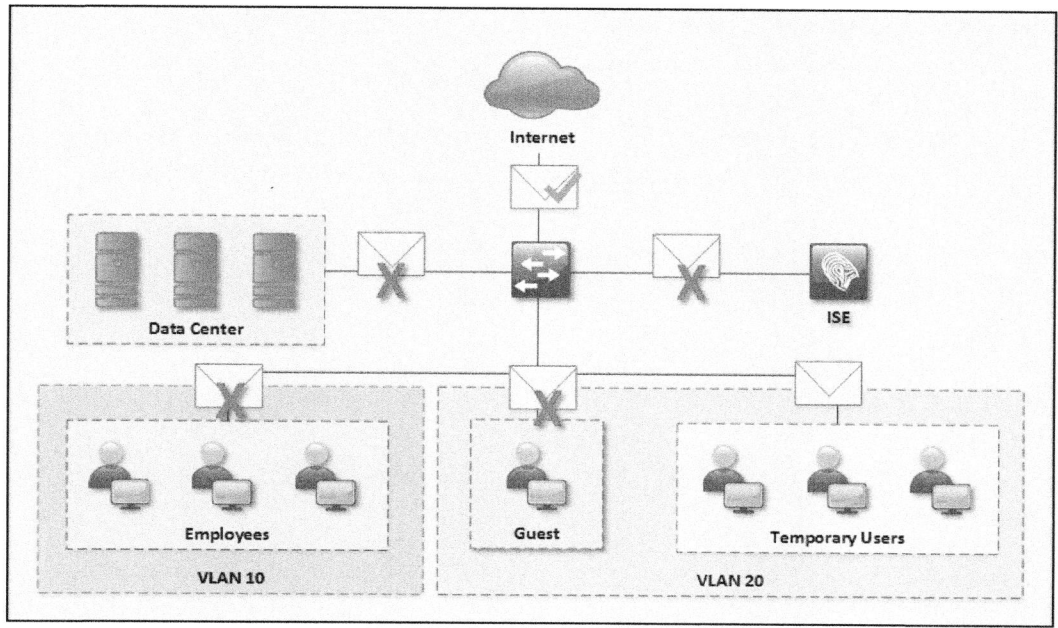

Figure 2-4. SGA ACLs

Similarly, Temporary users are restricted. Temporary User has validity of their Accounts little more than Guest user. They can use Internet services only as Guest User can. But they can't communicate with Guests or Employees as well as Data Centre.

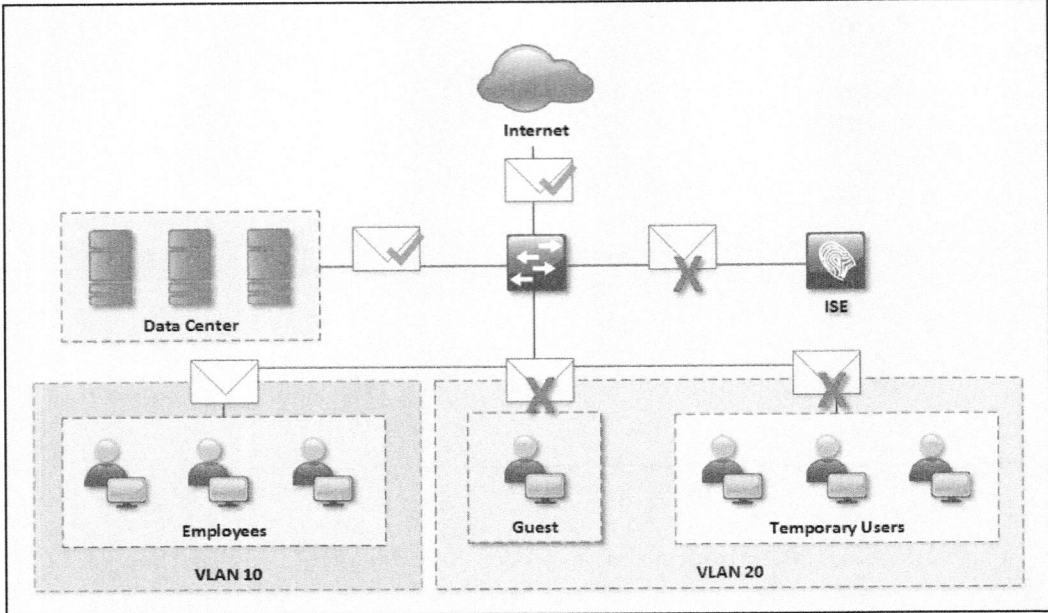

Figure 2-5. SGA ACLs

Employees of the Organization are authorized to access the Datacentres of the company. They can access the Internet as well.

Configuring Security Group Access Control Lists
1. Go to **Policy / Policy Elements / Results.**

2. In Results Navigation pane on left side, select > button next to **Security Group Access** and Select **Security Group ACLs**. SGAACL page will show with following options
   1- Name
   2- Description
   3- IP Version
   4- IPv4
   5- IPv6
   6- Agnostic

3. Click **Add** Button

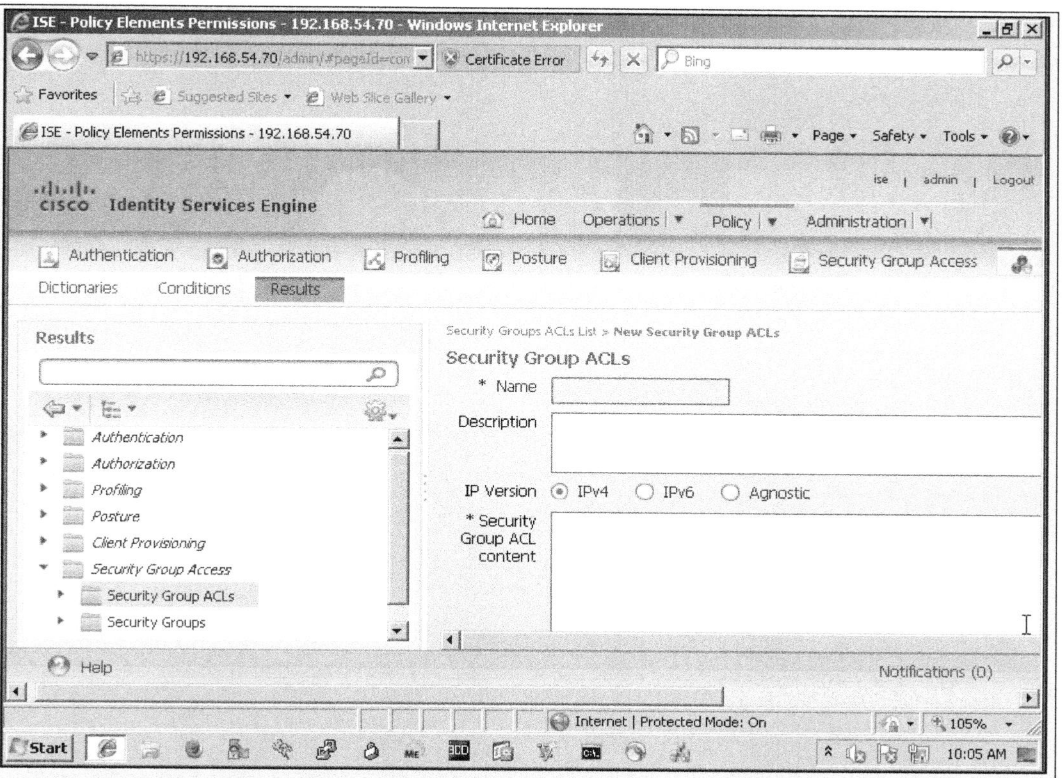

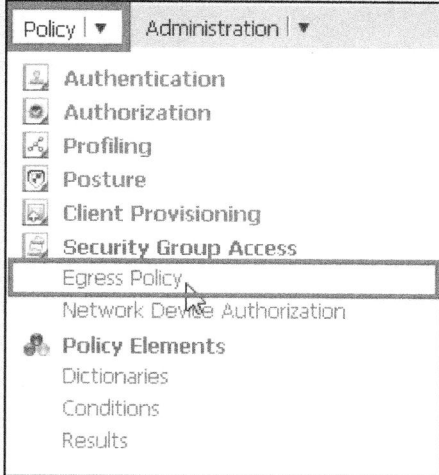

Figure 2-6. SGACL

Assigning SGACLs to Security Group Tags (SGTs)

1. Go to **Policy** > **Security Group Access** > **Egress Policy.**
2. Click **Add**

Figure 2-7. SGACL

Click on the **Policy** Tab on the Top of the Web page of ISE. Click **Egress Policy** in **Security Group Access** Section.

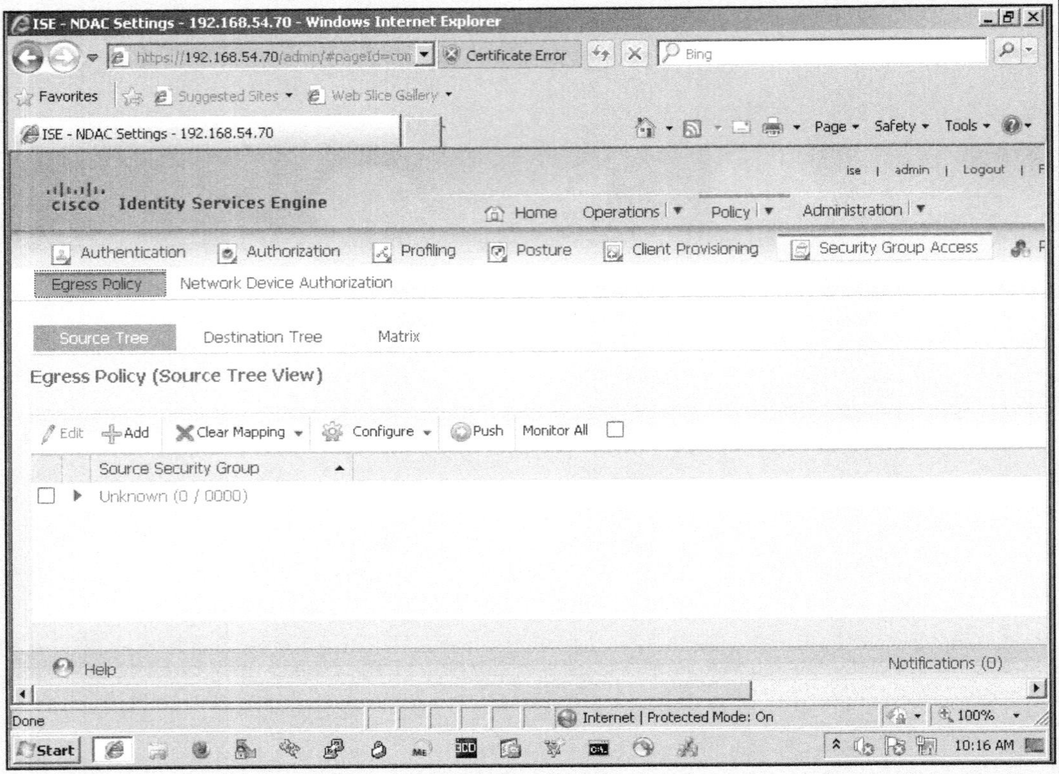

Figure 2-8. SGACL

Here Configured Egress Policies are listed (If Configured). You can add new Security Group Access Control List Mapping by click add button. For Modification of previously configured Security Group Access Control List Mapping, select desired Option and Click Edit option.

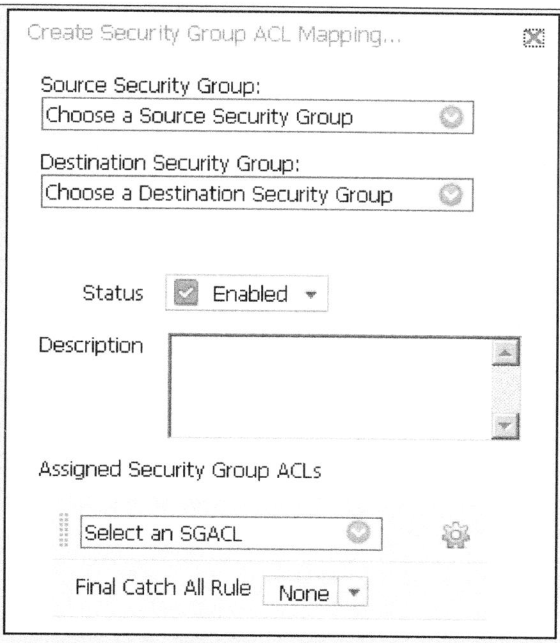

Create Security Group ACL Mapping...

Source Security Group:
Choose a Source Security Group

Destination Security Group:
Choose a Destination Security Group

Status ☑ Enabled ▾

Description

Assigned Security Group ACLs

Select an SGACL

Final Catch All Rule None ▾

Figure 2-9. SGACL

3. Select **Source and Destination Security Groups**
4. Enable the **Status**
5. Select **SGACL**
6. **Save** settings

Security Group Exchange Protocol
As we know that Security Group tagging requires Hardware support of the network device for tagging SGTs over Ethernet frame. Devices, which do not have hardware support for Cisco TrustSec, can also participate Cisco TrustSec by using Security Group Tag Exchange Protocol (SXP) which offers propagation of SGTs. IP Base or Service License is required for SGT Exchange Protocol deployment.

Cisco TrustSec or Security Group Access Cloud offers secure network by deploying a cloud of trusted device. Each device is the peer authenticates the trusted group. All communication between these secure devices of a trusted network group is secured and encrypted.

The Security Group Tag Exchange Protocol (SXP) uses TCP port 64999 as transport protocol to initiate connection. Message Digest 5 (MD5) algorithm is used by Security Group Tag Exchange Protocol to authentication and Integrity Check. Authentication process is started by "Speaker" which is the initiator of the authentication session which is replied by "Listener" which is waiting for Speaker to start session.

SXP protocol is also responsible for IP to Security Group tags binding across the TrustSec Cloud for the devices which are not capable of tag packets. These Tagged traffic is filtered at egress interface. Authentication process of an Endpoint to access the Cisco TrustSec is associated with Security Group tags, DHCP Snooping and IP device tracking. Cisco TrustSec Hardware capable devices maintain a table in which IP-SGT binding is record. At these Egress Device policies are enforced like SGACL.

Enable SXP and configure an SXP peer connection between Switch A, and Switch B. Switch A is Speaker and Switch B is listener

Configuring Switch A as Speaker

Switch(config)# cts sxp enable
Switch(config)# cts sxp default password Cisco123
Cisco123 is configured as password
Switch(config)# cts sxp default source-ip 192.168.1.1
Configure Source interface
Switch(config)# cts sxp connection peer 172.16.2.1 password default mode local speaker
Configure peer address, and mode

Configuring Switch B as Speaker

Switch# configure terminal
Switch(config)# cts sxp enable
Switch(config)# cts sxp default password Cisco123
Cisco123 is configured as password which must match on both devices
Switch(config)# cts sxp default source-ip 172.16.2.1
Configure Source interface
Switch(config)# cts sxp connection peer 192.168.1.1 password default mode local listener

Related Commands for Configuring SXP Protocol

Switch(config)# cts sxp connection peer peer-ipv4-addr [source src-ipv4-addr] password { default | none } mode { local | peer } { speaker | listener } [vrf vrf-name]

Switch(config)# cts sxp reconciliation period seconds
Changes the SXP reconciliation timer. The default value is 120 seconds (2 minutes). The range is from 0 to 64000.

Switch(config)# cts sxp retry period seconds

> Changes the SXP retry timer. The default value is 120 seconds (2 minutes). The range
> is from 0 to 64000.
>
> Switch(config)# cts sxp log binding-changes
> Enables logging for IP to SGT binding changes.

IEEE 802.1 AE (MACsec)

Securing Wired and Wireless Network is always remains on the top most priority. In a corporate Network, either Wired or Wireless, Security concerned are always requiring advanced and next level security solution to protect and secure the network infrastructure. Different techniques and security solutions are deployed to secure resources.

Authentication techniques and encryption algorithm are providing a certain level of security to the wired and wireless networks. As the Wired network are not transmitted on air, and due to advanced encryption and authentication techniques, they are assumed safe and secure as compared to Wireless network however various techniques and solution are also available for securing wireless networks like 802.1x authentication, Wi-Fi Protected Access (WPA/WPA 2) using Encryption algorithms like AES. As far as both of these wired and wireless networks are concerned, they have enough security solutions to secure transmission.

One of the Option for End to Endpoint security is by using End-to-End IPsec which is not a good solution in terms of QOS management, and filtering because everything will be encrypted between endpoints.

MACsec defined as IEEE 802.1 AE is a layer 2 encryption protocol which provide MAC layer Encryption for Wired Network. This Layer 2 Encryption uses Out-of-band management for Keying. In a LAN Network, hop by hop encryption is provided by IEEE 802.1 AE MACSec between Endpoints and Switches at layer 2. MACSec also support encryption between switches. MACSec process initiates after a successful authentication of 802.1x Extensible Authentication Protocol (EAP). Once device or devices are authenticated, these Endpoint devices are secured by using MACSec.

MACsec Key Agreement (MKA) protocol offers the management of Keys required in MACsec process. The keys required in 802.1 AE are
1. Session key
2. Encryption key

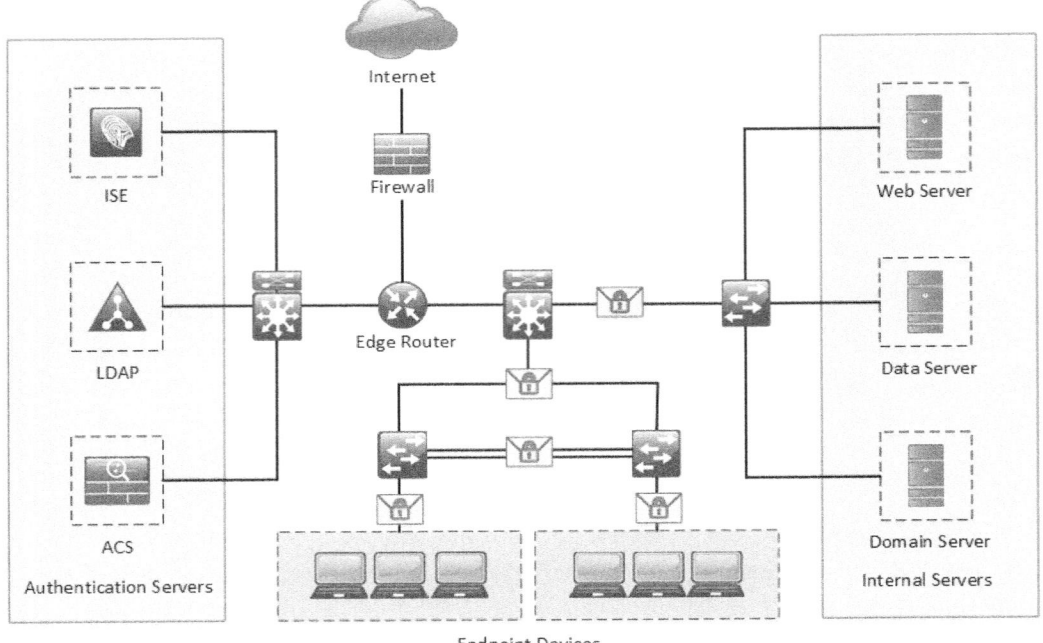

Figure 2-10. MACsec at Layer 2

Switch receives MACSec and Non-MACSec frame after authentication of endpoint devices, it can accept both depending over policies configured. MACSec frame are secured by encryption and Integrity Check value (ICV). Receiver switch will decrypt this MACSec packet and checks for Integrity Check Value for integrity of packet. This decryption process required decryption key (Session key) provided by MACSec key Agreement (MKA) Protocol. Frames that are not meeting the requirement for example if frame has difference in ICV will be dropped. These encrypted packets are transmitted out-of-band using Secured Port using session key.

In IEEE 802.1 AE MACSec protocol, the two main communication links are known as
1. Downlink MACSec
2. Uplink MACSec

Downlink MACSec
Downlink MACSec is IEEE 802.1 AE MACSec encrypted link that is established in between the Endpoint device authenticating to access the network resources and the Network Access Device that is Commonly a Switch. MACSec Key Agreement (MKA) Protocol is responsible for the encrypted communication between endpoint and switch through Downlink MACSec. For successful Downlink Communication, MACSec feature supported Network Access Device (such as Catalyst 3750-x) and MACSec Supplicant Endpoint is required. Endpoint device must be installed with Cisco AnyConnect Network Access Manager as MACSec Supplicant capability.

Force Encryption, Optional and Force Non-Encryption can be configured dynamically as well as per port basis. Integrated solution of MACsec with ISE offers Authorization profile and Encryption policy to control the Endpoint dynamically.

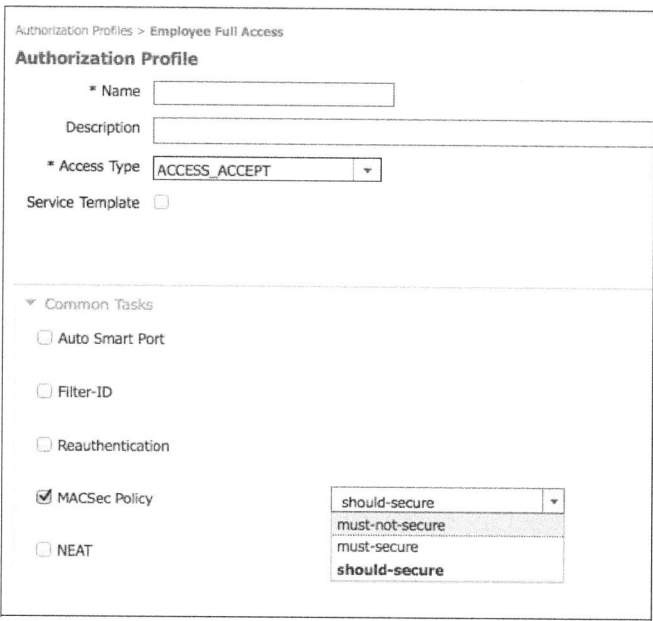

Figure 2-11. MACsec Policy Configuration

Go to **Policy > Policy Elements > Results.**

Select **Authorization Profiles.**

Edit an authorization profile to which you would like to add MACSec.

Under Common Tasks, scroll down to **MACSec Policy**.

Select **must-secure, should-secure, or must-not-secure** as required.

Click **Submit** or **Save** to save the change.

Interface Configuration for MACsec
Switch(config)# interface ethernet 0/0
Switch(config-if)# switchport access vlan 10
Switch(config-if)# switchport mode access
Switch(config-if)# switchport voice vlan 20
Switch(config-if)# ip access-group ACL-ALLOW in
Switch(config-if)# authentication event fail action next-method
Switch(config-if)# authentication event server alive action reinitialize
Switch(config-if)# authentication event linksec fail action next-method

```
Switch(config-if)# authentication host-mode multi-domain
Switch(config-if)# authentication open
Switch(config-if)# authentication order dot1x mab
Switch(config-if)# authentication priority dot1x mab
Switch(config-if)# authentication port-control auto
Switch(config-if)# authentication violation restrict
Switch(config-if)# macsec
Switch(config-if)# mka default-policy
Switch(config-if)# mab
Switch(config-if)# dot1x pae authenticator
Switch(config-if)# dot1x timeout tx-period 10
Switch(config-if)# spanning-tree portfast
Switch(config-if)# ex
```

Single Host Mode MACsec:

MACsec offers 802.1x Single-Host mode configuration, Multi-host Mode Configuration and Multi-Domain Authentication (MDA). MACsec does not support Multiple Authentication modes.

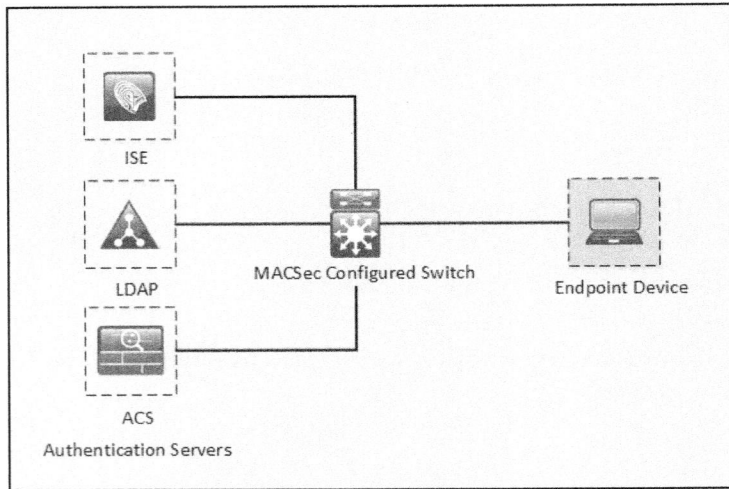

Figure 2-12. MACsec Single-Host Mode

Multi-Host Mode MACsec

802.1x Multiple Host based Authentication offers only two states of ports. Open and Closed with respect to single Authentication process. If Primary Host is authenticated, same network access is provided to the secondary host. If Secondary user is Supplicant, it will not be authenticated. This mode is not secure and hence not recommended to be use.

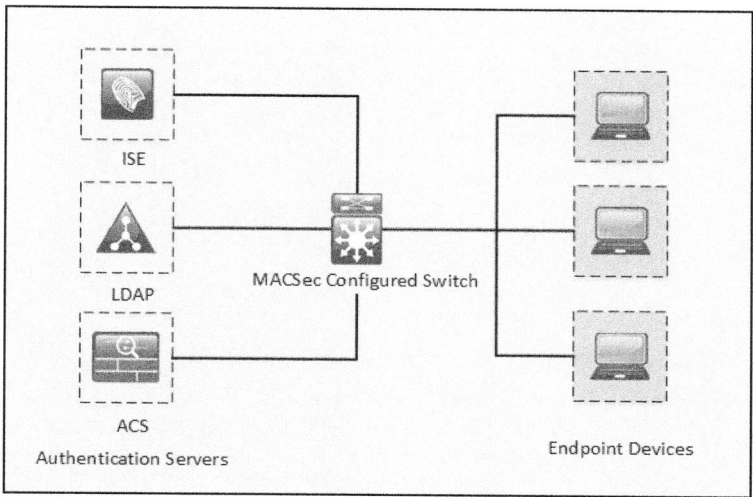

Figure 2-13. MACsec Multi-Host Mode

Uplink MACSec

Uplink MACSec are the encrypted links between Switches configured with IEEE 802.1 AE Protocol. The Encryption algorithm used for Uplink and Downlink MACSec is AES-GCM-128. Uplink MACsec can be configured manually or dynamically using IEEE 802.1x Port Based Authentication. Cisco Proprietary protocol SAP or MKA is used for keying mechanism. Cisco SAP is for Inter Switched links. SAP doesn't support Switch ports connected with Endpoint devices such as PC or laptops etc. MKA supports condition, Switch-to-Switch links as well as Switch connected with Endpoint Host. Downlink MACsec typically requires flexible authentication for supporting different heterogeneous devices. Cisco NDAC and SAP are for securing Uplinks with Network Edge Access Topology (NEAT)

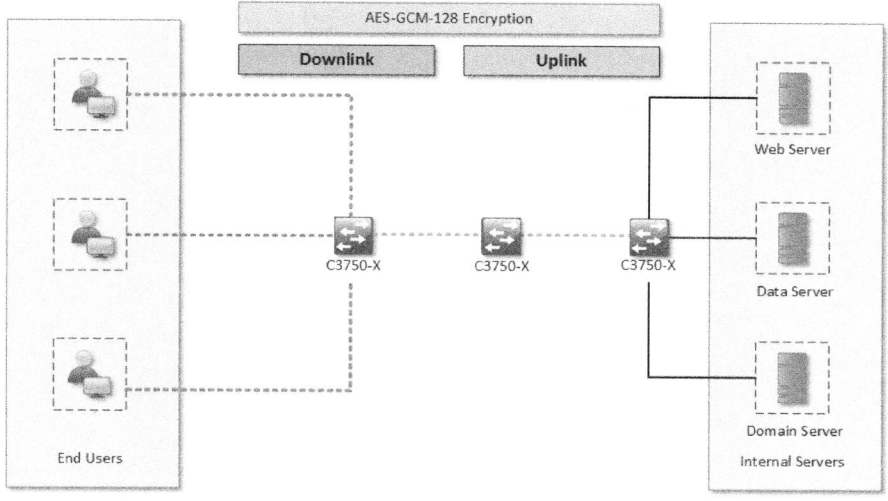

Figure 2-14. MACsec Links

Manual Configuration for MACSec Uplink Interface Configuration
Switch(config)# interface [Interface name]
Switch(config-if)# no switchport
Switch(config-if)# ip address [IP address] [Subnet Mask]
Switch(config-if)# cts manual
Enters Cisco TrustSec manual configuration mode.
Switch(config-if)#no macro auto processing
Disable macros feature
Switch(config-if)# policy static sgt [tag] trusted
Switch(config-if-cts-manual)# sap pmk [key] mode-list gcm-encrypt
(Optional) Configures the SAP pairwise master key (PMK) and operation mode. SAP is disabled by default in Cisco TrustSec manual mode.
Switch(config-if-cts-manual)#end

Chapter 3: Troubleshooting, Monitoring and Reporting Tools

Technology Brief

Introduction

Troubleshooting and Monitoring are very important in any of the Operation running on any device. For identity management Solution, Troubleshooting and Monitoring becomes much more important tool.

Using Cisco Identity Service Engine (ISE) these diagnostic and reporting tool become a comprehensive solution for ISE running service. The Process of Troubleshooting and Monitoring of services includes following key Operations

- Monitoring
- Troubleshooting
- Reporting

Monitoring

Monitoring Operation ensures the availability of all meaningful related data, real time presentation of this data in a readable format. Monitoring Operation presents the running operation logs in a way that administrator can easily interpret and control operations.

Troubleshooting

Troubleshooting may include certain event specific diagnostics or overall Operation processes troubleshooting. There are many troubleshooting tools are available for Endpoint devices, Troubleshooting commands for Network Access devices and Built-in troubleshooting services in Servers. Using these troubleshooting options actual fault can be determined causing failure or disturbance in the network.

Reporting

Reporting tools provides a report of the analysing logs of Network operations and processes. These reports are in standard form. These reports can be customized and stored for use.

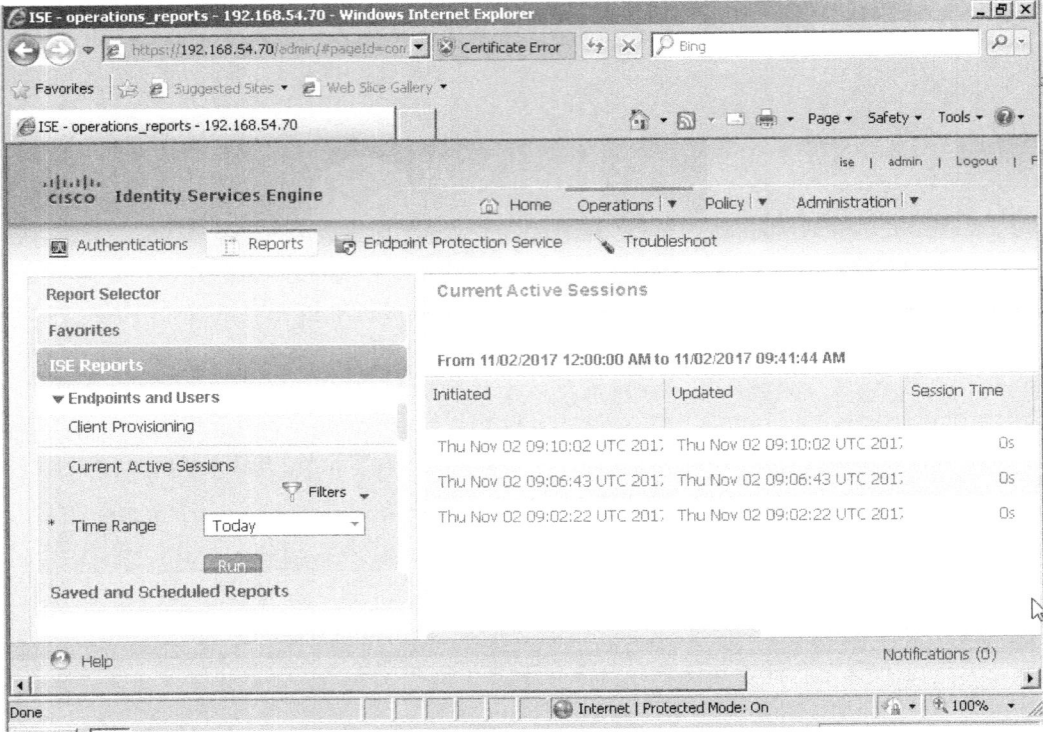

Figure 3-1. Cisco ISE reporting Services

Network Privilege Framework (NPF)

Dashboard of Cisco ISE has also a feature of Centralized Management recording and monitoring the Operations. This Centralized management offers real time monitoring data of running services within the network.

Dashboard uses Network Privilege Framework (NPF), which offers the detailed and comprehensive data and information for Monitoring Troubleshooting and Reporting. Network Privilege Framework (NPF) is depending upon the following conditions

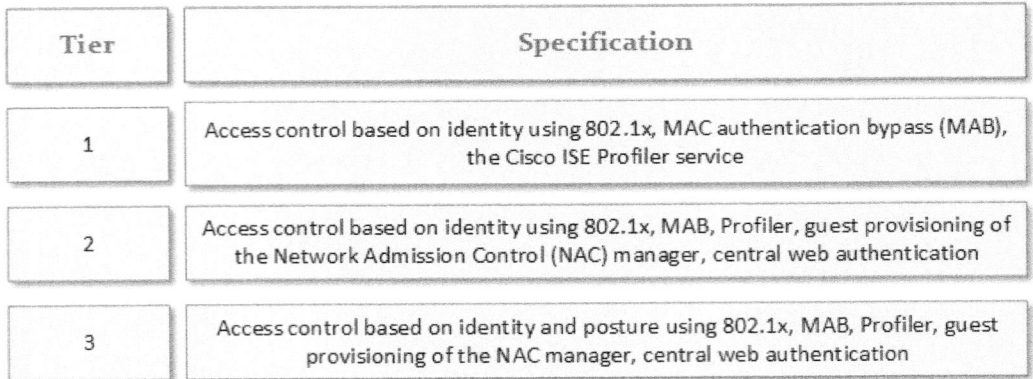

Tier	Specification
1	Access control based on identity using 802.1x, MAC authentication bypass (MAB), the Cisco ISE Profiler service
2	Access control based on identity using 802.1x, MAB, Profiler, guest provisioning of the Network Admission Control (NAC) manager, central web authentication
3	Access control based on identity and posture using 802.1x, MAB, Profiler, guest provisioning of the NAC manager, central web authentication

Figure 3-2. NPF Tiers

Monitoring:

Monitoring Endpoint from Server

Cisco Identity Service Engine (ISE) monitors the process and stores the information in its separate Monitoring database. For high monitoring traffic, and efficiency in Monitoring, Additional dedicated node may be required.

Monitoring Network Authentications

For Monitoring Authentication processes, including successful and failed Authentications, can be monitored form Authentication section. Real time authentication is reporting in Authentication dash let.

Monitoring Authentication in Cisco ISE

- Go to the Cisco ISE Dashboard.
- Expand the Authentications dash let. A detailed real-time report appears.
- Expand the data categories for more information.

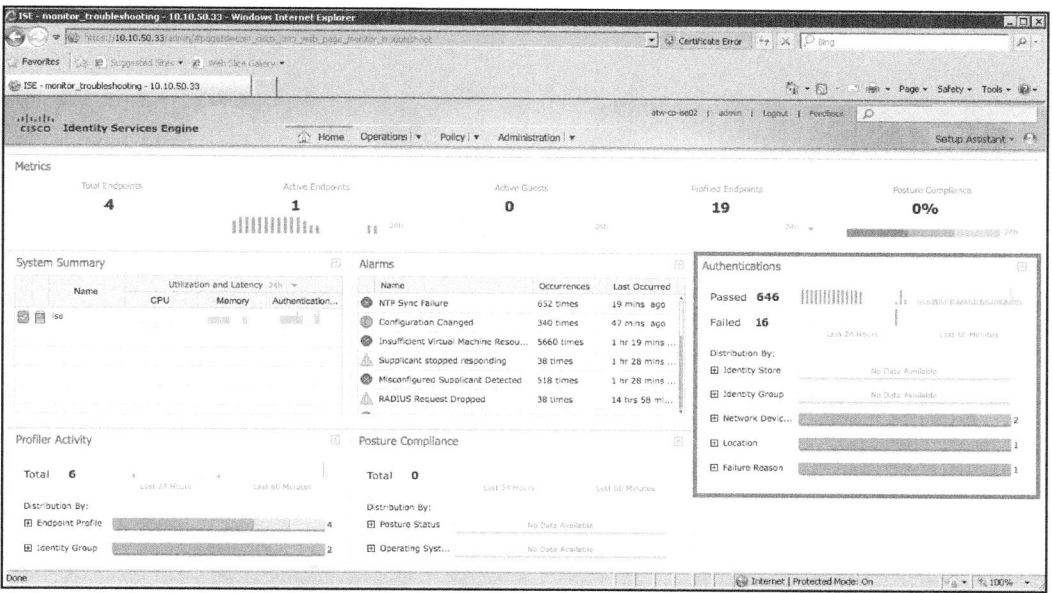

Figure 3-3. Monitoring Network Authentication

Profiler Activity

Profiled Endpoint section in the Cisco ISE dashboard monitors the Endpoint with in the network, which are authenticated, and Matched the Profile. This Profiler Activity Section provides Data each Endpoint Profile including Device type, Location and Address.

Monitoring Profiler Activity

- Go to Dashboard of Cisco ISE
- Check Profiler Activity Dash let
- Expand the Profiler Activity option for More information and real time data.

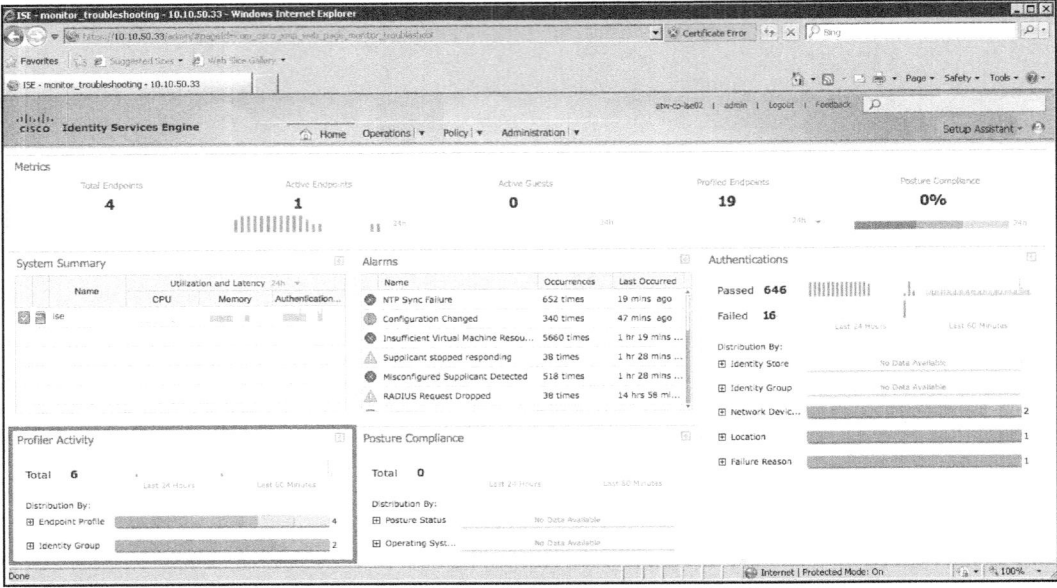

Figure 3-4. Cisco ISE profiler Activity

Posture Compliance:

Posture Compliance section in the Cisco ISE shows information and data of the Devices, which are accessing the network resources including the information of meeting, posture compliance or not.

Monitoring Posture Compliance

- Go to Dashboard of Cisco ISE.
- Check Posture Compliance Section.
- Expand the Option for Detailed information.

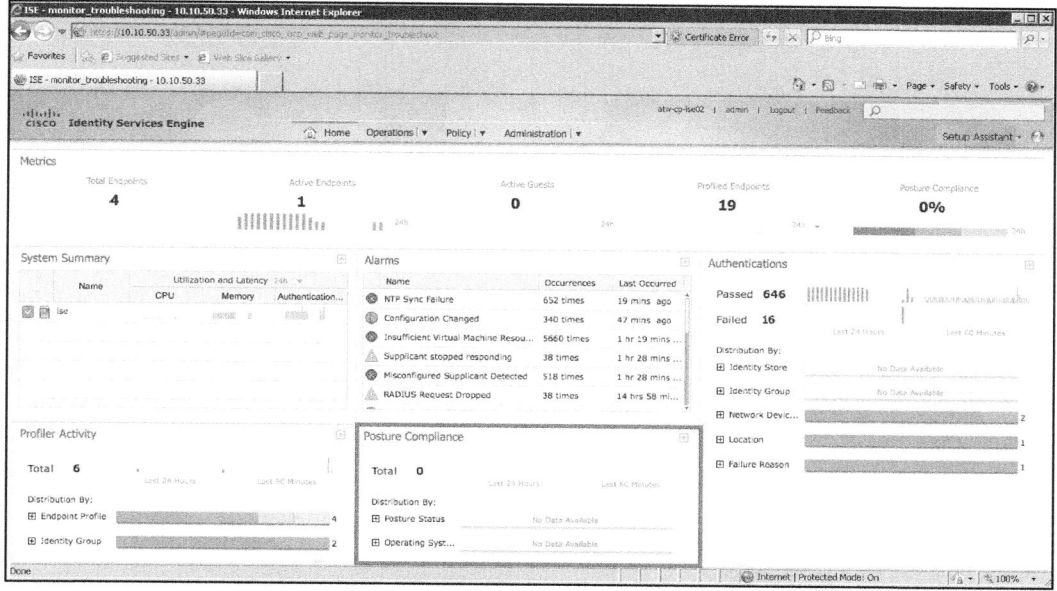

Figure 3-5. Cisco ISE Posture Compliance

Cisco ISE Alarm

Cisco ISE alarm option provide notification and update of certain critical conditions. Alarm option also provides presentation of information in Alarm Dash let. Information monitored by Alarm feature includes about System Processes, data purge event, CA server Up/Down, Identity Service unavailable, Misconfigured Supplicant Detection, RADIUS Request drop, SGAACL Drop, Supplicant Response stop, Unknown NAD, About System Health, Licensing, ISE Services as well as Administrative and Operational Management.

Configuring Alarm
  • Select **Administration** > **System** > **Settings** > **Alarm Settings**.   • Select an alarm from the list of default alarms and click **Edit**.   • Select **Enable** or **Disable**.   • Configure alarm threshold if applicable.   • Click **Submit**.

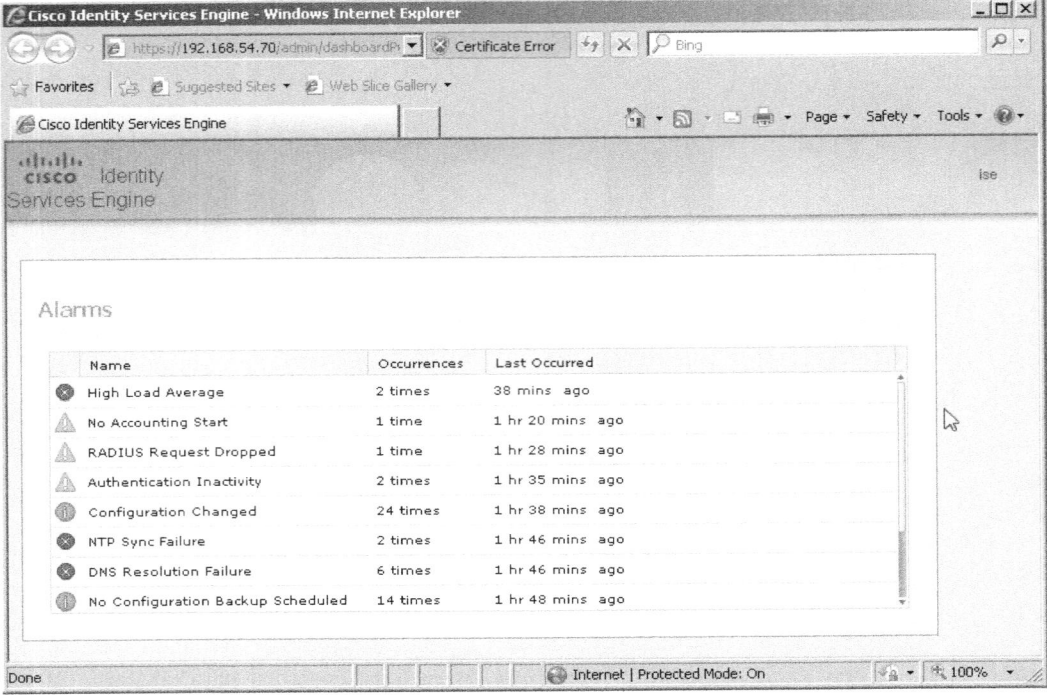

Figure 3-6. Cisco ISE Alarm Dash let

Logging

Cisco ISE also has Logging feature of its services and processes for Auditing, Monitoring, Troubleshooting, Reporting, and Management purposes. Logging is helpful for identification of errors, issues and faults in the network processes to be resolved. Virtual loopback address is configured for logging. Logging can externally collect using Syslog servers.

Configuring Logging

- Select **Administration** > **System** > **Logging** > **Local Log Settings**.
- Set logging period
- Click **Delete Logs Now** to delete the existing log files. Or log files will be deleted upon expiration of storage time for new storage
- Click **Save**.

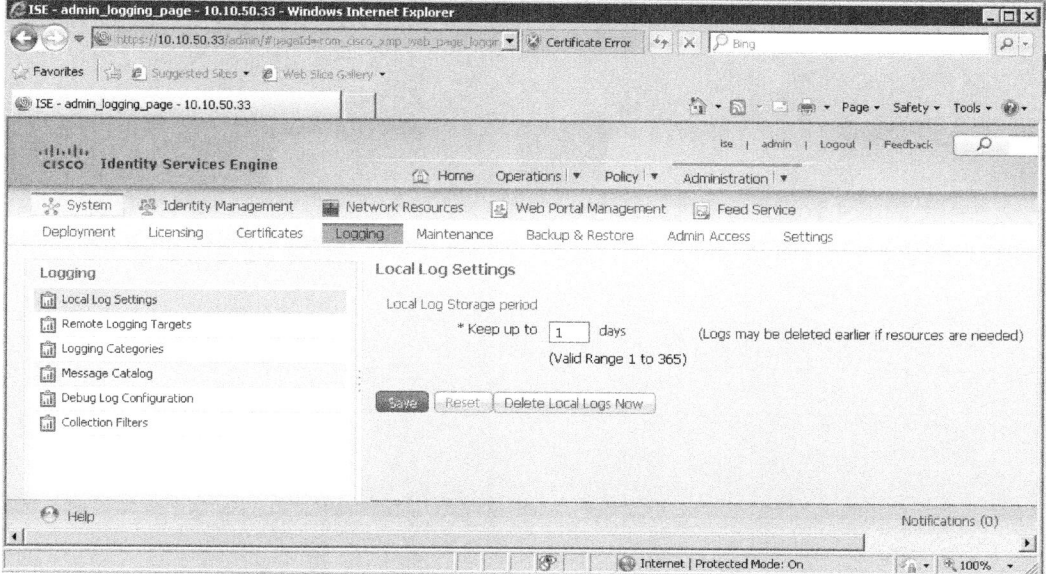

Figure 3-7. Cisco ISE logging

Session logging

Logging service of Cisco ISE also has Live session logging feature. Live logging only shown logs about the authentication process specially focusing over successful and failure of authentications. Live session logging shows information about sessions. Logging every state of a running session helps to troubleshoot in more focused way. Using session logging, step by step process from initiating of Authentication till starting of Accounting.

Remote Logging Targets

The ISE sends the logging information to the Monitoring and Troubleshooting Nodes. These nodes are introduced at **Administration > System > Logging > Remote Logging Targets.** The list of current logging targets can be observed as shown in the figure of the ISE showing its default configuration of Remote Logging targets.

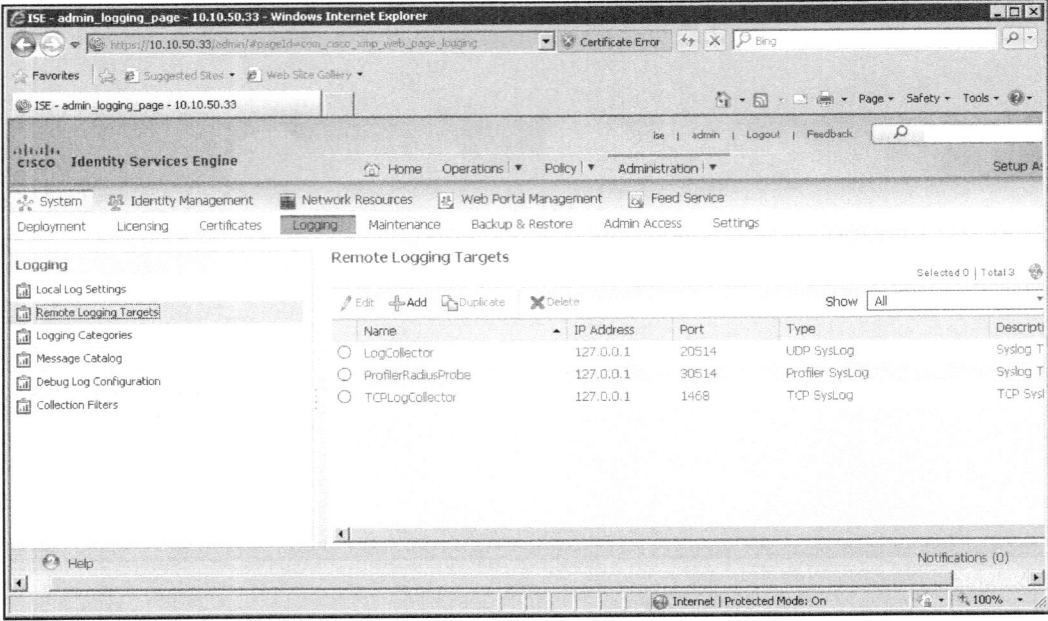

Figure 3-8. Cisco ISE Remote Logging Configuration

To add a logging device, click on the Add button and provide the attribute to configure remote logging. Security Information Event Management (SIEM) is one of the popular Syslog receivers. However, any other syslog receiver can also be used.

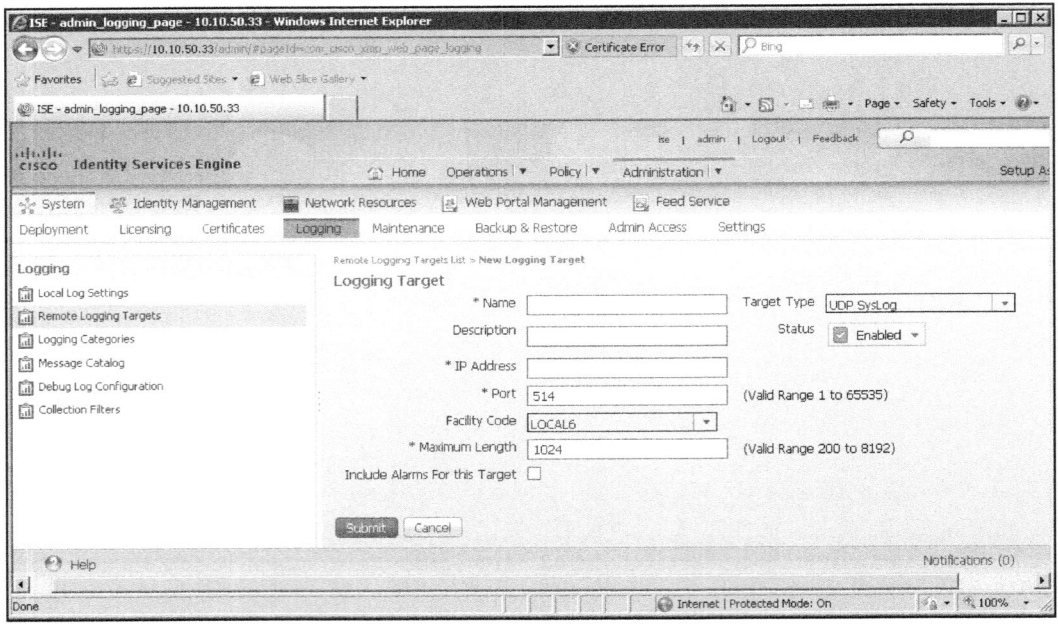

Figure 3-9. Cisco ISE Remote Logging Configuration

Configure Name, Description, IP address, Port and other attributes as required and save your configuration to add new target for logging.

Logging categories is another efficient and more focused option in logging environment. ISE offers categorized logging feature which allow the logging receivers to assigned particular category of logs. Administrator can configure multiple logging receivers for different categories of logs. Categories of logging classified by Cisco ISE can be observed from **Administration > System > Logging > Logging Categories**

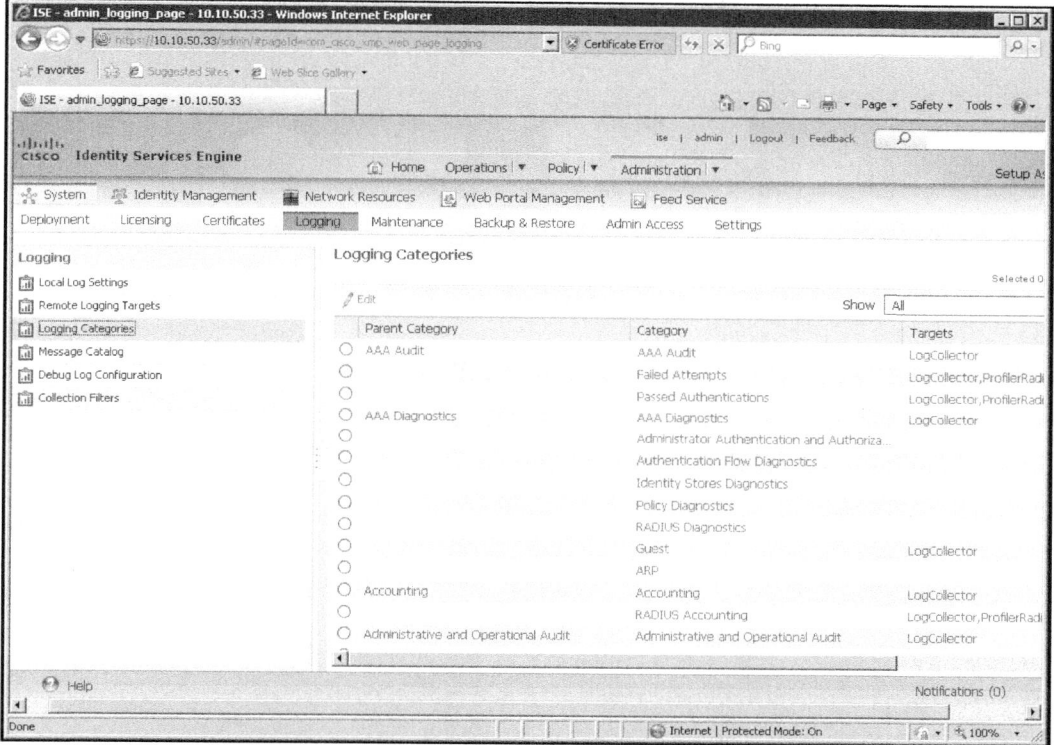

Figure 3-10. Cisco ISE Logging Categories

Monitoring Live Authentication Session

Cisco ISE provide feature of Monitoring of RADIUS authentication sessions on run time. Cisco ISE Live authentication features shows last 10 authentications within 24 hours. Two Entries are added upon single authentication of an Endpoint. One Entry for Authentication record and another one for Session records.

Monitoring Live Authentication
• Select **Operations** > **Authentications**. • Select a time interval from the drop-down list to change the data refresh rate. • Click the **Refresh** icon on the Live Authentications menu bar to manually update the data.

- Choose an option from the Show drop-down list to change the number of records that appear.
- Choose an option from the within drop-down list to specify a time interval,
- Click **Add** or **Remove** Columns and choose the options from the drop-down list to change the columns that are shown.
- Click **Show Live Sessions** to view live RADIUS sessions.
- Click **Save** at the bottom of the drop-down list to save your modifications.

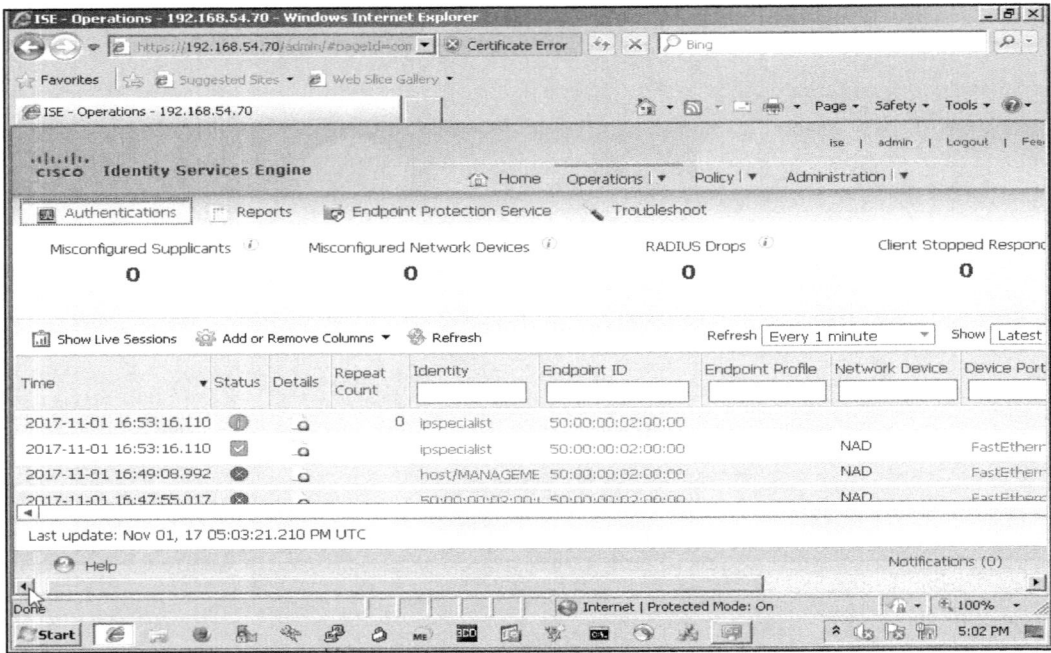

Figure 3-11. Authentication Sessions

Status

Status Section in live Monitoring shows Informational Event logs, Successful Authentication and Authentication Failure Logs.

- **Informational logs**

Logs with Blue icon in the Status column as shown in the diagram contains suppressed record including pass and fail. This suppression is enabled by default

- **Pass**

Successful Authentication Log entries are shown in green colour icon in status column.

- **Failure**

Failure logs are shown in red icon indicating logs associated with the authentication session lead to failure.

Repeat Count

Repeat count column with a value indicate the number of repeat count that is associated with a client-suppressed information. Whenever information is updated, such as when an Endpoint or User is re-authenticated, its repeat count value will rise.

Monitoring Network Access Device from Server

Network Access Device is also configured for Monitoring from Cisco ISE Server. For troubleshooting and diagnostics of Authentication and Authorization process of Endpoints, logs of Network Access device play important role. It also helps in diagnostic of problem, error and issues in Server to Network Access Device processes.

Configuring NAD for ISE Monitoring
Switch(config)# **epm logging** Switch(config)# **logging monitor informational** Switch(config)# **logging origin-id ip** Switch(config)# **logging source-interface** *[interface_id]* Switch(config)# **logging host** *[syslog_server_IP_address]* **transport udp port 20514**

Troubleshooting

Go to **Operations** > **Troubleshoot** > **Diagnostic Tools** >**General Tools**

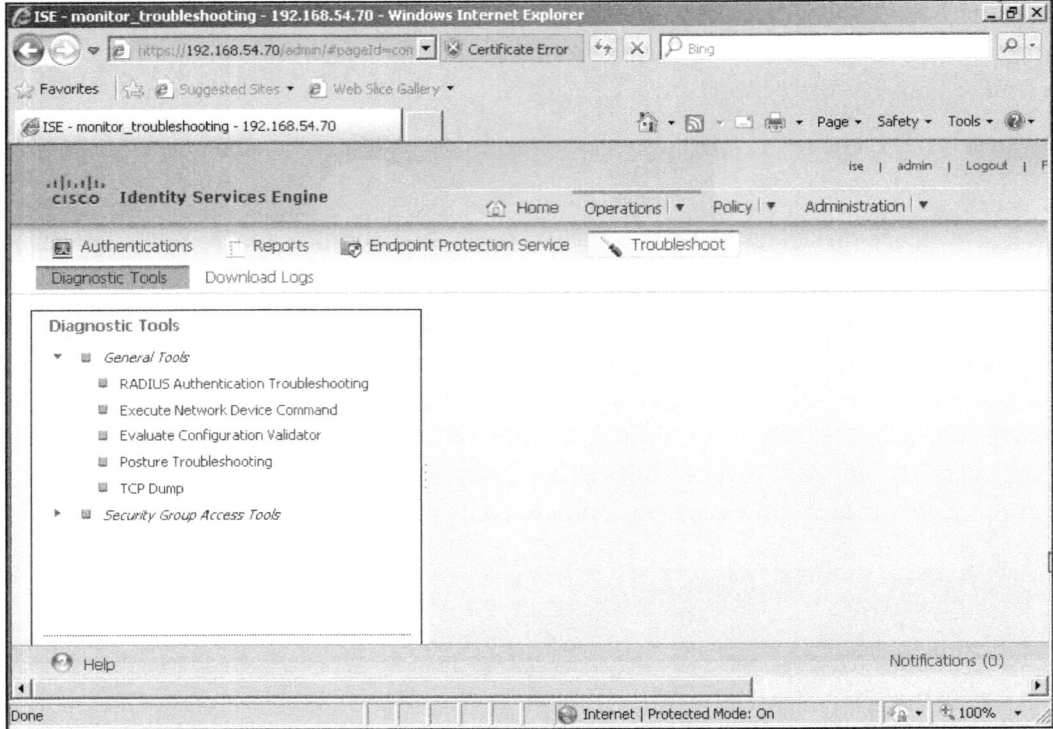

Figure 3-12. Troubleshooting Tools

Here you will find a lot of troubleshooting tools offered by Cisco ISE. List of troubleshooting tools offered by ISE are

1. RADIUS Authentication Troubleshooting
2. Execute Network Device Command
3. Evaluate Configuration Validator
4. Posture Troubleshooting
5. TCP Dumps

Troubleshooting RADIUS Authentication

RADIUS authentication tools allow you get results of unexpected authentications. Using RADIUS Authentication troubleshooting tool, Authentication result can be filtered with respect to Username, ID, Network Access Service IP address as well as reason of Authentication failure.

Troubleshooting Authentication options

- Choose **Operations** > **Troubleshoot** > **Diagnostic Tools** > **General Tools** > **RADIUS Authentication Troubleshooting.**
- Specify the search criteria in the fields as needed.
- Click **Search** to display the RADIUS authentications that match your search criteria.
- Select a RADIUS authentication record from the table, and click **Troubleshoot.**

- Click User Input Required, modify the fields as needed, and then click **Submit**.
- Click **Done.**
- Click **Show Results Summary** after the troubleshooting is complete.
- To view a diagnosis, the steps to resolve the problem, and a troubleshooting summary, click **Done**.

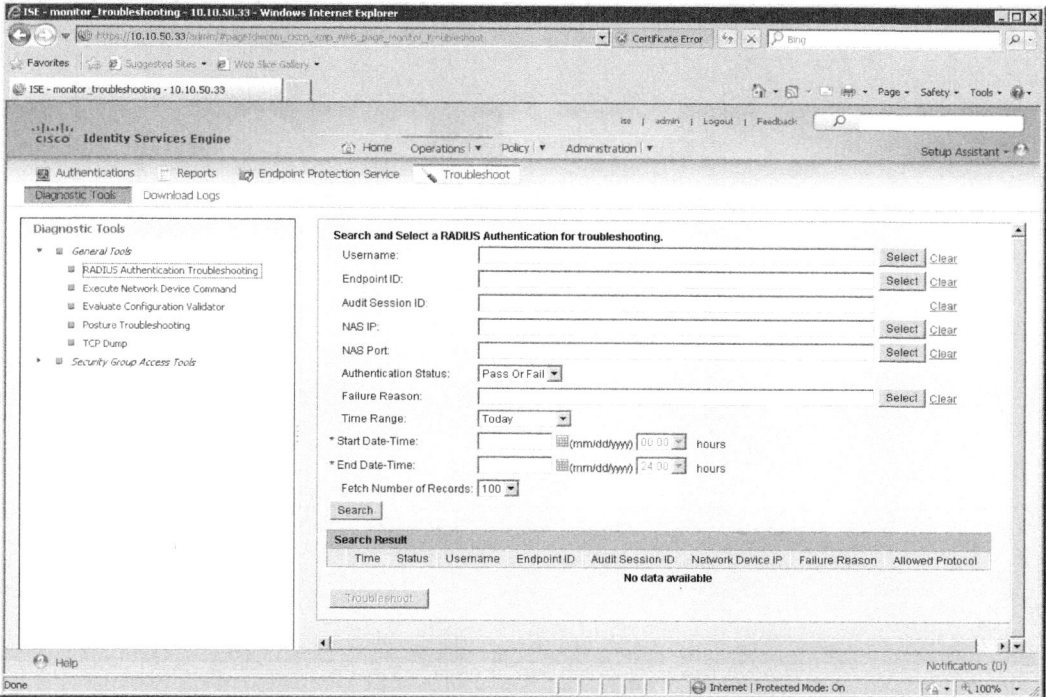

Figure 3-13. Cisco ISE RADIUS authentication troubleshooting panel

Network Device Configuration Validator Tool

A configuration validator tool in Cisco ISE is for Network Device configuration issues troubleshooting and diagnostics. This tools helps in diagnostics and evaluation of configuration of network access device and identification of the problem.

Step of Troubleshooting using Validator Tools

- Select **Operations > Troubleshoot > Diagnostic Tools > General Tools > Evaluate Configuration Validator**.
- Enter the Network Device IP address, and specify other fields.
- Select the configuration options to compare against the recommended template.
- Click **Run**.
- Click User Input Required, and modify fields.
- Check the check boxes you want to analyse, and click **Submit**.

- Click **Show Results Summary**.

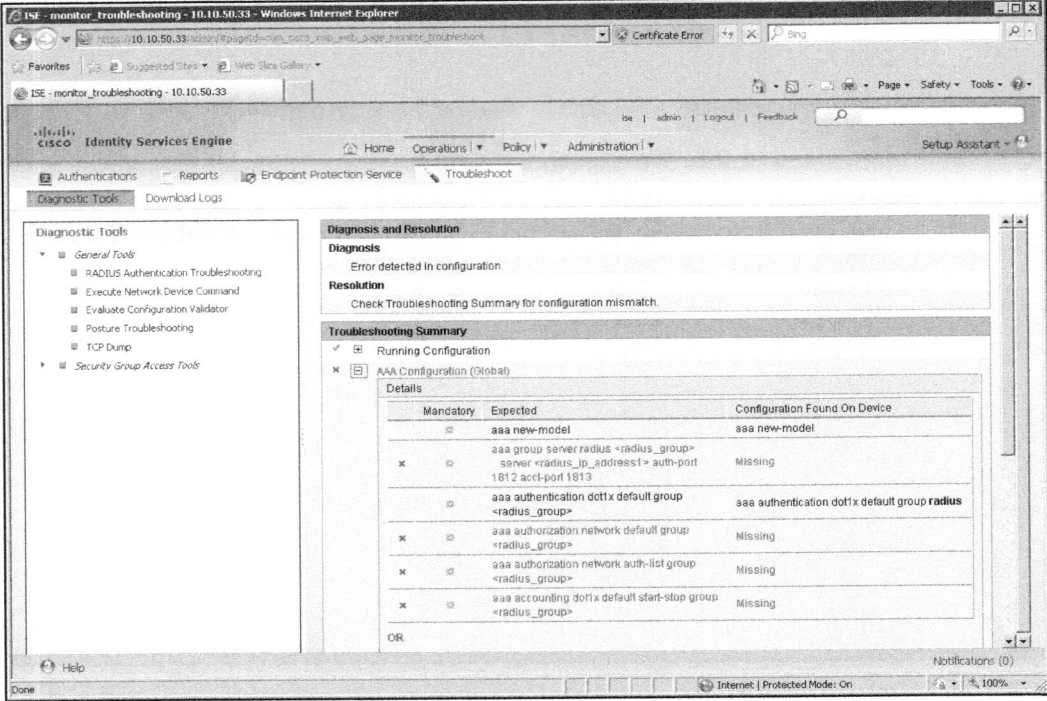

Figure 3-14. Cisco ISE Configuration Validator

Troubleshooting Posture

Endpoint Posture troubleshooting can be done by using Cisco ISE Posture Troubleshooting tool. Posture troubleshooting tools provides diagnostics of Posture failure. Endpoint with successful Posturing, and unsuccessful in posturing can be diagnosed. Failed Endpoint can be examined, as at which step of Posturing they are failed.

Steps of Troubleshooting Posturing

- Select **Operations** > **Troubleshoot** > **Diagnostic Tools** > **General Tools** > **Posture Troubleshooting**.
- Enter information in the appropriate fields.
- Click **Search**.
- Select the event in the list and click **Troubleshoot**.

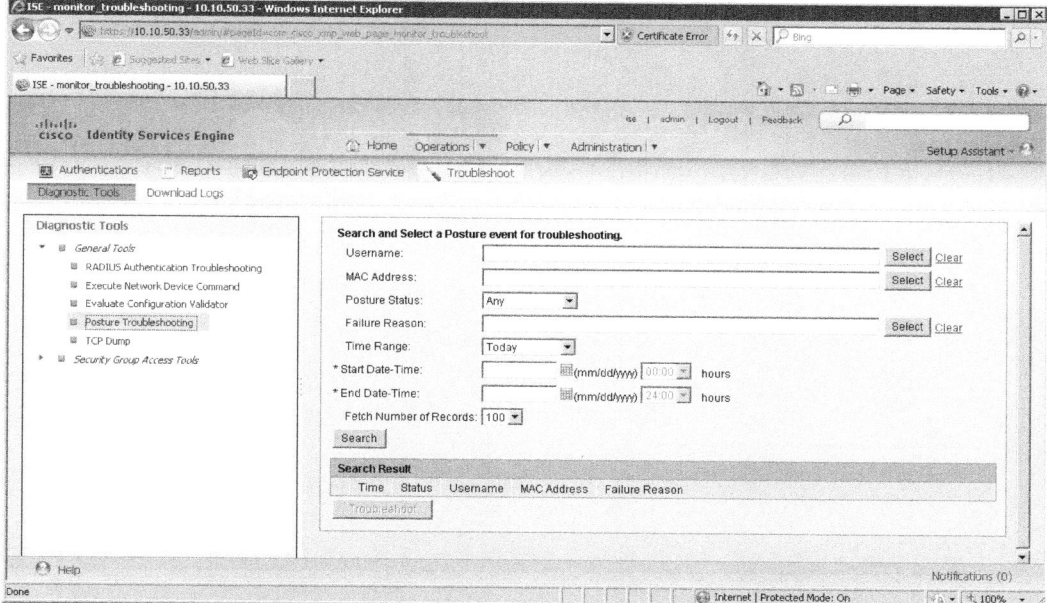

Figure 3-15. Cisco ISE posture Troubleshooting Panel

TCP Dump

TCP Dump diagnostics tool ensure that the traffic is reaching the Cisco ISE server. TCP Dump is Packet Sniffing tool. To ensure that any expected packet is reaching that node or not, TCP Dump can be use.

Step of Troubleshooting Using TCP Dump

- Select **Operations** > **Troubleshoot** > **Diagnostic Tools** > **General Tools** > **TCP Dump**.
- Select Host Name as the source. Inline Posture nodes are not supported.
- Select Network Interface to monitor.
- Set Promiscuous Mode by clicking the radio button to On or Off. The default is On (Recommended)
- In the Filter text box, enter a Boolean expression on which to filter.
- Click **Start** to begin monitoring the network.
- Click **Stop** when you have collected a sufficient amount of data, or wait for the process to conclude automatically after 500,000 packets.

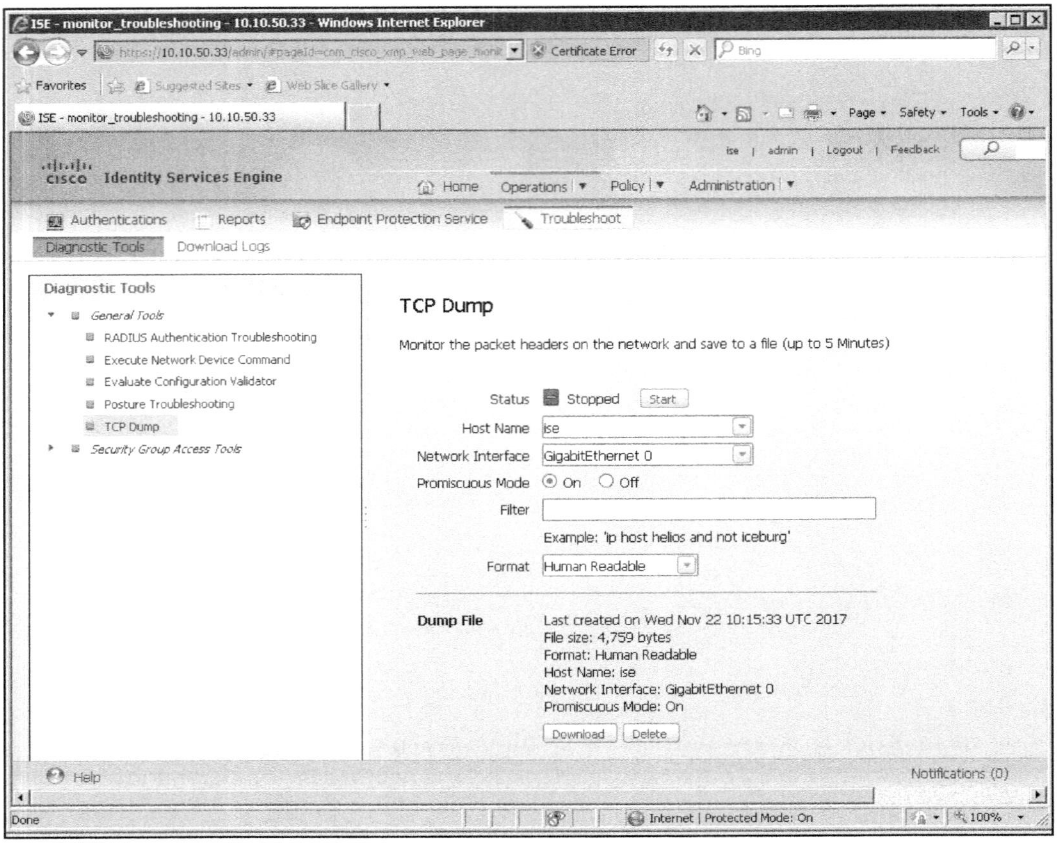

Figure 3-16. Cisco ISE TCP Dump panel

Network Device Troubleshooting

Network Device troubleshooting includes troubleshooting commands which helps in troubleshooting the authentication and authorization processes running when an Endpoint connects the network till authorized for using network resources. These commands include server Show commands issued on command line of Network access device.

Troubleshooting Commands

Switch# **show authentication sessions**

Switch# **show authentication sessions interface** *[interface]*

Switch# **debug client** *[MAC Address]*

Switch# **debug interface** *[interface]*

Switch# **debug authentication** *[all | errors | events | feature | sync]*

Switch# **debug epm** *[all | api | error | events | redirect]*

Switch# **debug dot1x** *[all | errors | events | packets | redundancy | registry | state-machine]*

```
Switch                                                        —    □    ×

Switch#show authentication sessions

Interface  MAC Address    Method   Domain    Status       Session ID
Et0/1      (unknown)      mab      UNKNOWN   Running      01010101000000000000002A4

Switch#show authentication sessions ses
Switch#show authentication sessions session-id 01010101000000000000002A4
            Interface:   Ethernet0/1
           MAC Address:  Unknown
            IP Address:  Unknown
                Status:  Running
                Domain:  UNKNOWN
       Security Policy:  Should Secure
       Security Status:  Unsecure
        Oper host mode:  multi-auth
      Oper control dir:  both
       Session timeout:  N/A
          Idle timeout:  N/A
     Common Session ID:  01010101000000000000002A4
       Acct Session ID:  0x00000001
                Handle:  0xE5000001

Runnable methods list:
      Method     State
      mab        Running

Switch#
```

Figure 3-17. NAD troubleshooting

This output shown in the figure shows the running process of authentication session in which Authentication session status is mentioned as running. Method is MAB authentication, along with session ID. When this Authentication process is complete, Status Option will change to Authorization successful or failure. Domain will be defined as Data or Voice.

Mind Map

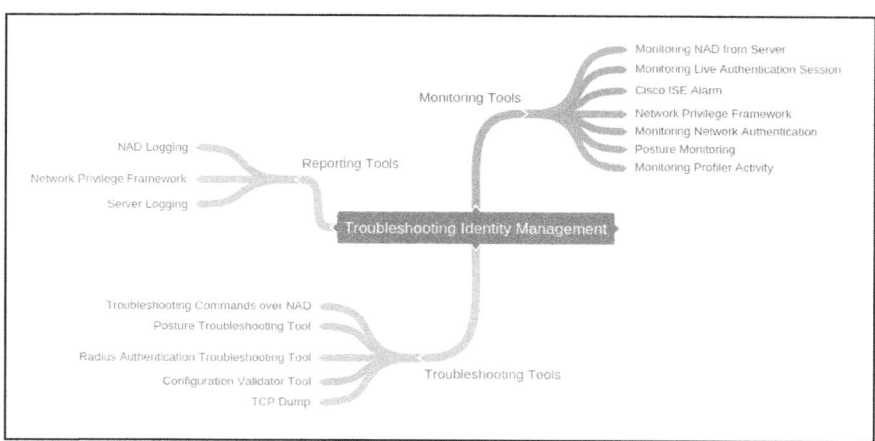

Chapter 4: Threat Defence Architectures

Technology Brief

Highly Secure Wireless Solution

The Design of Secure Wireless Solution Architecture means a Secure Wireless Network design from Security Threats Providing security across the network for all Network Devices and Endpoints. This Wireless Network Security offers core Components, which are as follows

- Cisco Unified Wireless Network Architecture
- Cisco Campus Architecture
- Cisco Branch Architecture

Cisco Wireless Network Solution Architecture offers security to the core mobility platform of Wireless Network. High Security and High Availability of network resources for Wireless Endpoints is main goal of this Solution. Cisco offers many integrated solutions, Network Devices, which dedicated for Wireless Network Security.

A Combined platform of Wired and Wireless Network with best Security elements offers Flexible, Scalable, Secure Wireless Network. This Secure Network Architecture for Wireless Network is dependent on Wireless Endpoint Devices, Access points, Wireless Controllers, Network Management Device, Mobility Services and Security Devices.

Wireless Network requires some unique and different security parameters to secure on air transmission.

- Monitoring of Endpoints, Managing and Controlling Wireless Users.
- Preventing Rogue Clients or Endpoint Users to access the network.
- Authentication of Network Access Device which are Wireless Access point to prevent rogue Access Points from accessing network resources.
- Denial of Service (Dos) attack prevention. DoS attack can stop Wireless Network Services.
- Securing from Reconnaissance, Eavesdropping, Traffic Monitoring, Packet Capturing and Other Wireless Attacks.

Secure Wireless Solution

In Secure Wireless Architecture, Wireless Local Area Network (WLAN) Security and Network Security Devices are used to provide security. In this Secure Wireless Architecture, Traffic from Lightweight Access Points, Lightweight Outdoor Mesh

Access Points and other access points are directed to the Cisco Wireless LAN Controller (WLC). This traffic from Access Point to Wireless LAN Controller is tunnelled. Wireless LAN Controller offers a Central Management and Controller over Wireless Network by using Security Services such as Network Access Control (NAC), Intrusion Prevention System (IPS) or firewall. Cisco also offers several other Wireless Network Security Devices that can be used depending upon the scalability, Flexibility, requirement and Cost effectiveness with respect to the network deployment.

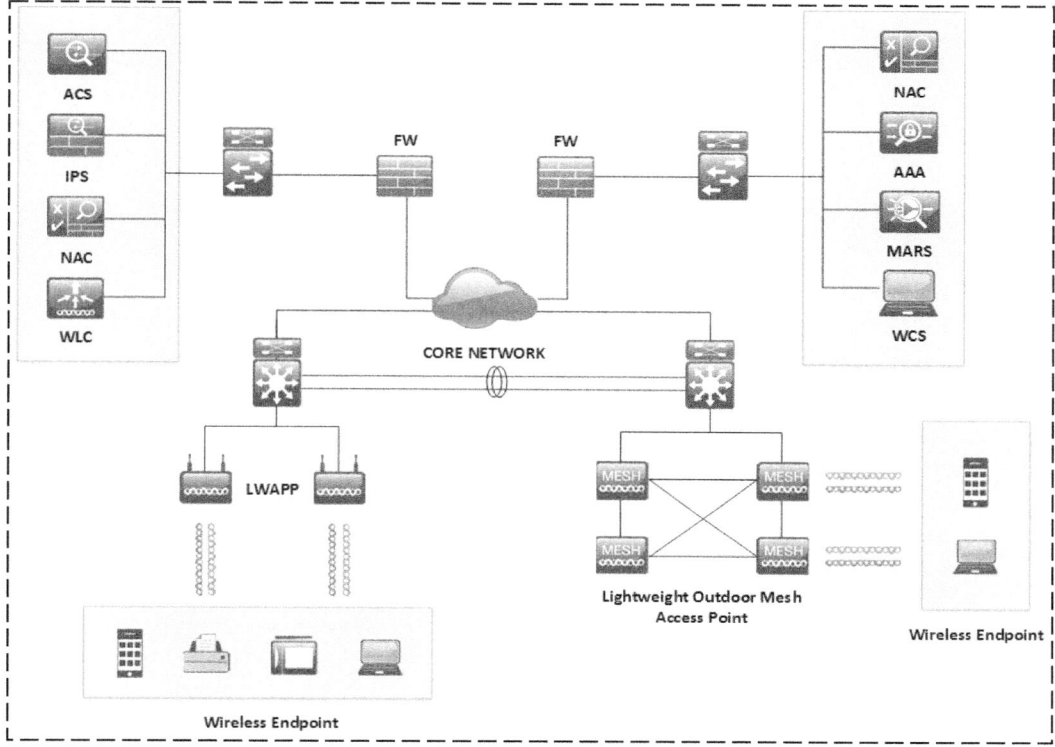

Figure 4-1. Highly Secure Wireless Network Architecture

Wireless Access Points (AP): Cisco wireless access points (APs) provide wireless connectivity to the corporate network for above defined BYOD devices. Access points are installed physically at campus, branch office, or even at home office to facilitate the employees.

1. **Light Weight Access Point Protocol (LWAPP)**

   Lightweight Access Point Protocol (LWAPP) is a Protocol use for secure communication between Wireless edge devices such as Access point (AP) and Wireless LAN Controller (WLC). LWAPP can use Layer 2 or Layer 3 transport mode. Layer 2 messages are encapsulated in Ethernet Frames while Layer 3 utilized Layer 3 IP Network and messages are encapsulated in UDP packets. There are two Channels used by LWAPP. LWAPP Control Channel is used

when an Access point communicates with Controller. Another Channel is LWAPP Data Channel containing Data.

2. **Light Weight Outdoor Mesh Access Point**

   Light Weight Outdoor Mesh Access Points are more flexible, scalable, secure devices that are most appropriate for Metropolitan Area Network (MAN). These Outdoor Mesh Access Point are designed for Large Scale Deployment. This Wireless Mesh Access Point ensures accessibility over wide range. Places where Wired Networking is difficult or costly, this Wireless Network can be deployed. Cisco Mesh Network for Outdoor Access Point offers robust Network, great capacity, up time, Security, Mobility and reliability.

Wireless LAN Controllers: Wireless LAN Controller is the important device in Wireless Secure Network Architecture. These Wireless LAN Controllers are deployed with Light Weight Access Points. These Access points offer endpoint connectivity. On the other end these access points are connected directly (next hop) or indirectly (through the network) to the Wireless LAN Controller. Wireless LAN Controllers offers HTTP or HTTPS Web User interface for configuring and monitoring WLC. Command Line Interface is also available with Wireless LAN Controllers. Main Function of Wireless LAN Controllers is Monitoring and Controlling of Endpoint Clients. Monitoring of Access point if any rogue access point is connected.

A WLAN controller provides centralized management and monitoring of Cisco WLAN solution. WLAN are integrated with Cisco Identity Service Engine to enforce the authorization and authentication on end-point devices.

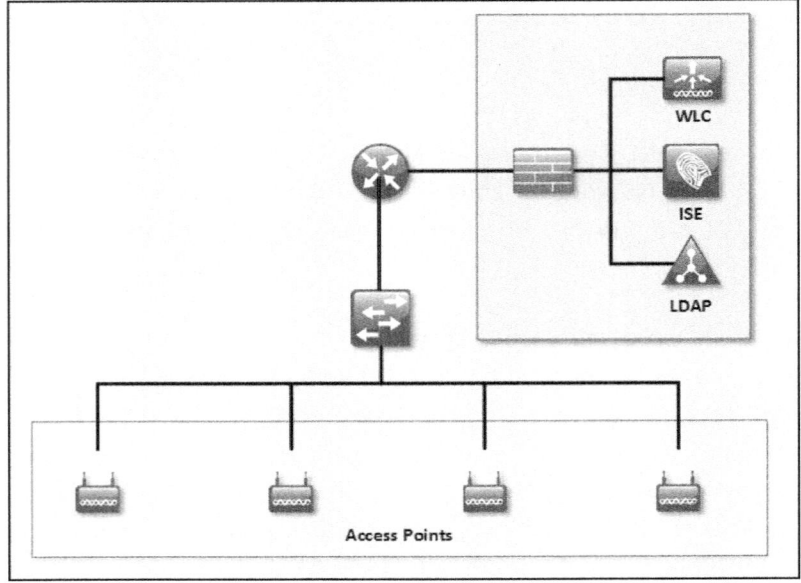

Figure 4-2. Wireless LAN Controller

Cisco Wireless Control System

Cisco Wireless Control System (WCS) is very efficient and comprehensive tools in today's world. Wireless Control System is very efficient Monitoring, diagnostic and troubleshooting, Reporting tools with Robust management. It is very easy tools of administrator to deploy wireless network in indoor or outdoor environment. Wireless Control System can scale Small, Medium, Large Wireless Network. Cisco Wireless Control System can manage Hundreds of Cisco Wireless LAN Controllers along with thousands of Light Weight Access points connected with these Wireless LAN Controllers. Cisco Wireless Control System Navigator offers the following key features:

- Network monitoring
- Aggregated alarm notifications
- Automated browser redirect
- Simplified setup and configuration
- Quick and advanced searches
- Location tracking of client, Wi-Fi, and rogue devices
- Inventory reports
- Secure administrative access

Network Admission Control (NAC)

Cisco NAC stands for Network Admission Control (NAC), also called, Cisco Clean Access (CCA) formerly is an appliance deployed in a network infrastructure to apply security policies over the devices connecting or attempting to gain access. Cisco Network Admission control can be deployed for authentication of users, Authorization, identification of wire or wireless, Local and remote user before getting access to the network resources. User can be identified along with their devices and roles. Security policies can be enforced on the user connecting to the network.

Cisco Adaptive Wireless Intrusion Prevention System (IPS)

Cisco Wireless IPS or Cisco Adaptive Wireless Intrusion Prevention System leads to advance security of the Wireless Network including Dedicatedly monitoring and detection of Wireless Network threats. It also controls Access to the network, and attacks. Cisco Adaptive Wireless Intrusion Prevention System (IPS) offers visibility and control over the wireless network. Wireless IPS can trace locate and capture RF events. These forensic events are available for Analysis and reporting. Alarm configuration, threat detection and reporting are also offered by Wireless IPS as its key features.

Cisco Security Monitoring, Analysis and Reporting System (MARS)

As logging and debugging of Network processes generates Hugh amount of data, which is difficult to handle and filter to find appropriate results. In between these logs

filtering the data of an attack is difficult enough. Cisco Security Monitoring, Analysis and Response System known as Cisco (MARS) offers identification of security threats within the network by monitoring topology and behaviour of the network. It also recommends for mitigation of these attacks according to the ability of visualizing attack path and source.

Other Network Security Devices for Wireless Architecture

Cisco Mobility Services Engine (MSE)

The Cisco Mobility Services Engine (MSE) platform gives you a centralized way to deliver and monitor the services like Base Location services to capture and aggregate key information such as location of a device, Information of RF spectrum, and interference sources. Cisco MSE also offers real-time location services (RTLS). Cisco Connected Mobile Experiences (CMX) delivers customized location-based mobile services. Cisco MSE secure wireless users and your network. Cisco MSE Adaptive Wireless Intrusion Prevention System helps protect the network from rogue wireless devices, denial-of-service (DoS) attacks, and other wireless threats.

Adaptive Security Appliance (ASA): Cisco ASA provides the standard security solutions at the Internet edge of campus, branch and home office networks within BYOD architecture. Apart from integrating IPS/IDS module within itself, ASA also act as termination point of VPN connections made by *Cisco AnyConnect Client* software over the public Internet to facilitate the BYOD devices.

ASA features and services: Although ASA as a product provides many security features. It may be very difficult to highlight every single feature in this workbook. Following are the most prominent features of ASA firewalls:

- **Packet filtering:** Simple packet filtering techniques like Access-Lists (ACL) can be used to perform traffic control by using layer 3 and layer 4 information. The main difference between ACL on a routers/switches and on ASA is the firewall uses subnet mask instead of wild card mask as in routers and switches.
- **Stateful filtering:** By default, Stateful packet filtering is enabled on ASA, which mean that firewall will keep track of every session initiated from trusted network to untrusted network. For example, a connection is made from client, say 10.0.0.2:800 to destination address, say 12.12.12.1:9090. Let's assume TCP socket connection is established. When the first packet from source hits the trusted interface of ASA, its entry will be made in Stateful database. The reply traffic of connection will only be allowed when source address and port number matches the saved state in the stateful table.
- **Inspection at application level:** In some cases, multiple ports pairs are used for over communication. For example, a client from inside zone trying to use FTP service. Now FTP uses port 21 for initial connection but uses port 20 for data

transfer. If stateful inspection is working then the return traffic from data port which is 20 will be dropped in return. BY application inspection, ASA firewall learns dynamically about these ports and allow traffic from extra ports as well.

- **NAT, DHCP and IP Routing:** Cisco ASA firewalls also support multiple features of Layer 3 routing devices like NAT, DHCP and routing protocols like RIP, EIGRP and OSPF.

- **Layer 3 and Layer 2 Operational mode:** One way of ASA deployment is to assign IP address to different interfaces and it will appear an extra hop in end-to-end traffic path. This mode is known as traditional mode. Another case would be to deploy the firewall in transparent mode, in which no IP address is assigned to the interfaces of ASA and it will act as multiport bridge with an ability to inspect the overall traffic just like traditional mode. The advantages of using the transparent mode is that end-users will be unaware of new addition in the network topology.

- **VPN Support:** ASA can also be used to implement the Site-to-Site or SSL VPNs. The number of VPN connections ASA can made may depend on the purchased license

- **Mitigation against BOTNET:** A BOTNET is a group of infected computers, who can perform under a centralized command from an attacker. Most of the DDoS attacks are generated by BOTNETs. Cisco ASA can be configured to get regular updates related to BOTNET Traffic Filter Database from Cisco Systems Inc in order to mitigate latest attacks.

- **Advanced Malware Protection (AMP):** Cisco Next Generation Firewalls(NGFW) provides the traditional firewalls feature along with some advanced malware protection features in a single device.

- **AAA Support:** Just like routers and switches, authorization, authentication and accounting features can also be implemented either locally or in integration with some specialized hardware like Access Control Server (ACS).

Cisco Wireless Bridging

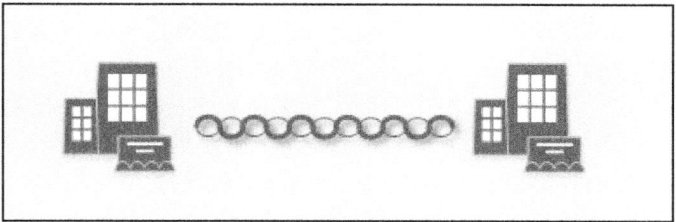

Figure 4-3. Wireless Bridging Point to Point

Cisco Offers Wireless Bridging Device, which offers High speed, efficient performance device which can connect several LAN in Metropolitan area. Using Cisco Aironet Series Wireless Bridging Device is very easy, flexible and meet security requirement within Wide Area. Wireless Bridging offers Point to Point and Point to multipoint connections. High Speed Data Transfer up to 54 Mbps. Security standard supported by

wireless bridging is 802.11 and 802.11i. This Options can be used as backup link, Redundant path as well as Primary or sole connection.

Figure 4-4. Wireless Bridging Point to Multi-Point

Identity Management

As we know, Security of a network is very important to secure not only the secret information but also your network devices and the control over it. In Security, the main component over which the entire security concept is dependant is Identity. Identity of Users, Endpoints Device and Network Devices are very important. Any misconfiguration is identification of User or Endpoint devices will lead to permit any unknown, rouge access to the resources as well as any legitimate user can also be denied to access the corporate network.

Internal & External Identity Stores

Cisco Identity Service Engine (ISE) focused over Identity management to provide secure access to the wired and Wireless network. Cisco ISE flexible, scalable and enhanced feature provide strong protection against rough access of User, Endpoints and network devices as well. Cisco ISE is scalable in terms of Integration with External Identity Store like Active Directories (AD) and Lightweight Directory Access Protocols (LDAP) including its internal Identity stores offering local users and Endpoints database.

Not Only the Cisco Identity Service Engine (ISE) offers identity management but also Cisco Secure Access Control (ACS) offers Internal identity store for authentication of Endpoints and User and it can also integrate with External Identity store such as Active Directories and others, also provide One-time Password (OTP) Smart Card, Certificate and other method for Secure Access controlling.

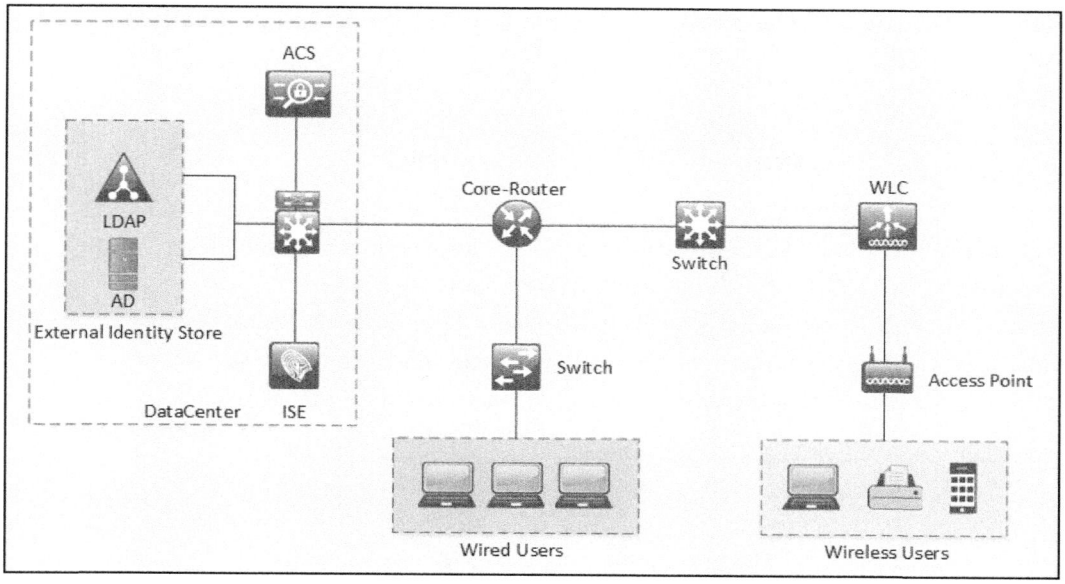

Figure 4-5. Wireless Network with External Identity Store

Authentication and Authorization

AAA Authentication is another important component that is associated with the Identity management. AAA offers the Authentication, Authorization and Accounting process for identity management. To identify the Endpoint device or User, AAA using RADIUS protocol, which is flexible as it is used for Network Access offering combined Authentication and Authorization process. As RADIUS packets has only encrypted payload, it is used as transport protocol for EAP and other authentication protocol.

IEEE 802.1x Port-Based Authentication

Now a day, Basic technology of WLAN which is commonly and widely deployed and still being in used all over the world is IEEE 802.11. The Authentication Option for IEEE 802.11 network is Shared-Key-Authentication mechanism or WEP (Wired Equivalency Privacy). Another option is to Open Authentication. These Options are not capable to secure the network hence the IEEE 802.11 is remaining unsecure.

These two authentication mechanism Open and Shared Authentication cannot efficiently secure the network because WEP key is required, and in Shared-Key Authentication, Challenge is forwarded to the client which can be detected by hacked which can detect clear text challenge packet and Encrypted packets.

IEEE 802.1x comes with an alternative Wireless LAN Security feature that offers more enhanced user authentication option with Dynamic key distribution. IEEE 802.1x is focused solution for WLAN framework offering Central Authentication. IEEE 802.1x is deployed with Extensile Authentication Protocol (EAP) as WLAN Security Solution.

The major components on which this enhanced WLAN Security solution IEEE 802.1x with EAP depends are

1. Authentication
2. Encryption
3. Central Policy

Authentication: Mutual Authentication process between Endpoint User and Authentication Server RADIUS i.e. commonly ISE or ACS.

Encryption: Encryption keys are dynamically allocated after authentication process

Central Policy: Central policy offers management and Controlling over re-authentication, session timeout, regeneration and encryption keys etc.

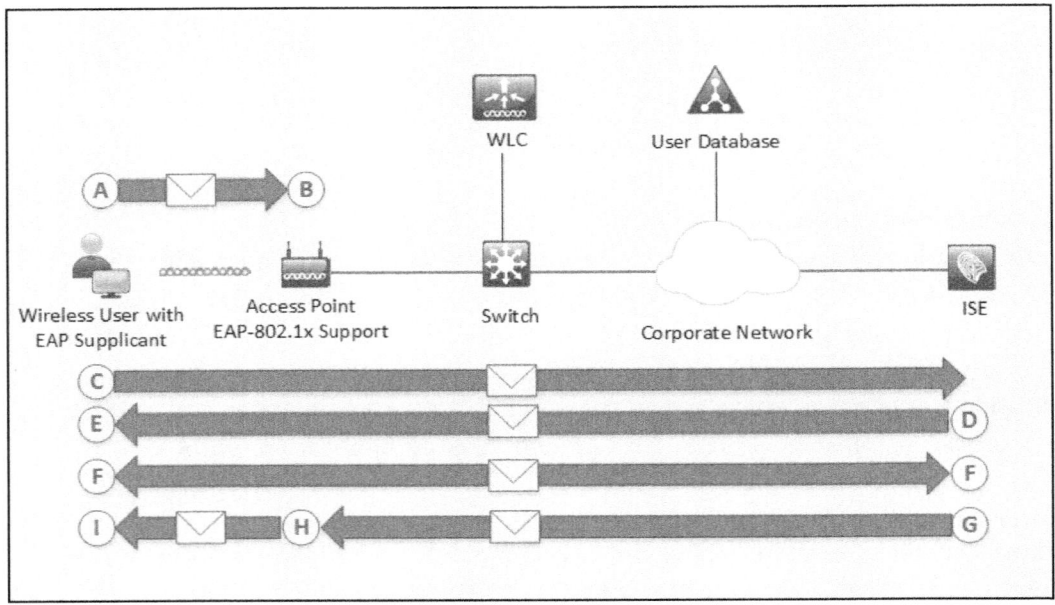

Figure 4-6. IEEE 802.1x-EAP Authentication Flow

Wireless 802.1x –EAP Authentication Flow

A. In the above figure, Wireless User with EAP Supplicant connects the network to access the resources through an Access Point.

B. As it connects, and link turns up, Access point will block all traffic from recently connected device until this user logs in to the network.

C. User with EAP Supplicant provide login Credentials that commonly are Username and Password but it can be User ID and One-Time password or combination of User ID and Certificate. When User provides login credentials, these credentials are authenticated by the Authentication server that is RADIUS server.

D. Mutual Authentication is performing at point D and E between authentication server and Client. This is a two-phase authentication process. At first phase, server authenticates User.

E. At the second phase User authenticates Server or vice versa.

F. After the mutual authentication process, mutual determination of WEP key between server and client is performed. Client will save this session key.

G. RADIUS authentication server sends this session key to the Access point.

H. At the end, Access point now encrypt the Broadcast key with the session key and send the encrypted key to the client.

I. Client already has Session key, which will use for decryption of encrypted broadcast key packet. Now Client can communicate with the Access point using session and broadcast keys.

EAP Authentication Protocol

EAP protocol offers some other Authentication method as well for user authentication over LAN and WLAN. Authentication options offered by EAP are

- EAP-Cisco Wireless (LEAP)
- EAP-Transport Layer Security (EAP-TLS)
- Protected EAP (PEAP)
- EAP-Tunnelled TLS (EAP-TTLS)
- EAP-Subscriber Identity Module (EAP-SIM)

Cisco Lightweight Extensible Authentication Protocol (LEAP)

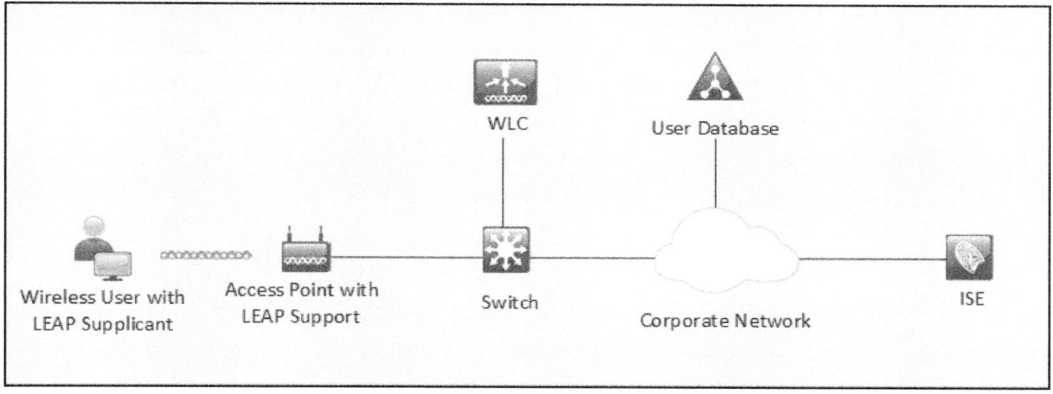

Figure 4-7. IEEE 802.1x LEAP Authentication

The Authentication procedure using Cisco Lightweight Extensible Authentication Protocol (LEAP) is the same as implementation of Cisco EAP but the basic difference is this authentication is used in Cisco Aironet WLANs. It encrypts data transmissions using dynamically generated WEP keys, and supports mutual authentication. Heretofore proprietary, Cisco has licensed LEAP to a variety of other manufacturers through their Cisco Compatible Extensions program. LEAP Mutual Authentication process depends upon Shared Secret. RADIUS server sends challenge to the client to

authenticate it. Client performs one-way hash and send the response to the server. Server gets the information about the client from its database (Internal or External data stores) and creates a response and compares them to authenticate the client. Upon Successful comparison, EAP-Success message is send to client and Client and server mutually derive the WEP key.

Cisco Extensible Authentication Protocol Transport Layer Security (EAP-TLS)

Figure 4-8. IEEE 802.1x EAP-TLS Authentication

EAP-TLS is an Internet Engineering Task Force (IETF) standard (RFC 2716). EAP-TLS uses Digital Certificates for the Mutual Authentication process between Client and RADIUS Authentication Server. RADIUS Authentication server sends its digital Certificate towards the Client known as Server Side TLS. Client when receive the Digital Certificate, it validates the certificate. After validation Client sends its certificate to the server known as Client Side TLS. Both of these TLS Certificates are validates by verification of issuer (Certificate Authority) and Validation of components of Certificate. Upon successful authentication, Dynamic WEP key is generated by Mutual agreement.

Cisco Protected Extensible Authentication Protocol (PEAP)

Cisco Protected Extensible Authentication Protocol (PEAP) is a combined Security Solution from IETF, RFC, Cisco, Microsoft and RSA. Authentication process of PEAP uses Digital Certificate from RADIUS Authentication server. PEAP Authentication supports multiple EAP Encapsulation methods. In Phase 1 of Authentication process, Server-Side TLS is send to client. When Client Authenticate the Server using Server-Side TLS, an encrypted TLS Tunnel is creating for phase 2. In Phase 2, the server uses another EAP encapsulation method for authentication of Client. The server authenticates using a method like One-Time password through EAP-GTC client. Upon successful authentication process, Dynamic WEP key is determined.

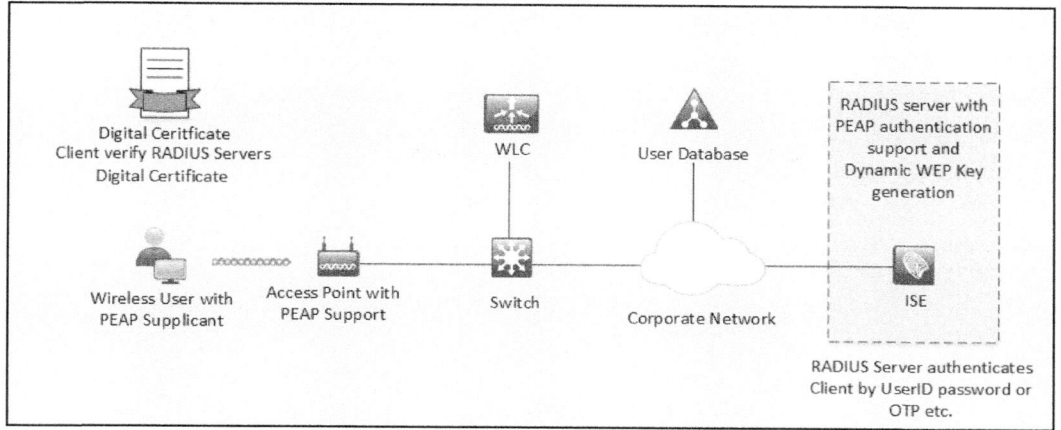

Figure 4-9. IEEE 802.1x PEAP Authentication

MAC Authentication Bypass (MAB)

MAC Authentication Bypass (MAB) is an Authentication bypass operation in which authentication process is bypass to the Authentication server instead of local Authentication by Network Access device. Another Methods similar to MAB Authentication are Port Security, Cisco VLAN Management Policy Server (VMPS) and User-Registration tools (URT). MAB Authentication process supports both Wired and Wireless Network deployment. Basic Operation of MAC Authentication Bypass depends upon PAP Authentication process between Client and Authentication Server i.e. RADIUS Server. Deployment in Wired Scenario bypass the Network Access Device i.e. Switch that support MAB features. In Wireless network, Endpoint device is connected through an Access point associated with Wireless LAN Controller. When Wireless Access point detects the Endpoint Device connecting the network, PAP Authentication initiates which put MAC address as in Username and Password fields. RADIUS Server extracts these attributes and authentication is processed by identifying the Endpoint in database. Depending only upon MAC Authentication is not a good approach because it is potentially a security risk for the corporate network, more in wireless scenario. MAC address Spoofing is not a big deal to break this security. MAC authentication can be configured as alternative, or backup authentication option in the Network.

As we know in Wired Network scenario, 802.1x Authentication is the first method applied on the Client connecting the network. Upon timeout of 802.1x Authentication, Next authentication method is MAB for which Switch listen for. In Wireless Deployment, MAC check can be configured before 802.1x authentication. Following are some reason ensuring the need of MAC Authentication Bypass (MAB).

- Additional Authentication process using Extensible Authentication Protocol (EAP).

- Additional Authentication process to behind IEEE 802.1x Port-Based Authentication.
- Provide Authentication for the device, which do not support 802.1x Authentication.
- Migration form Port Security, VMPS and URT.

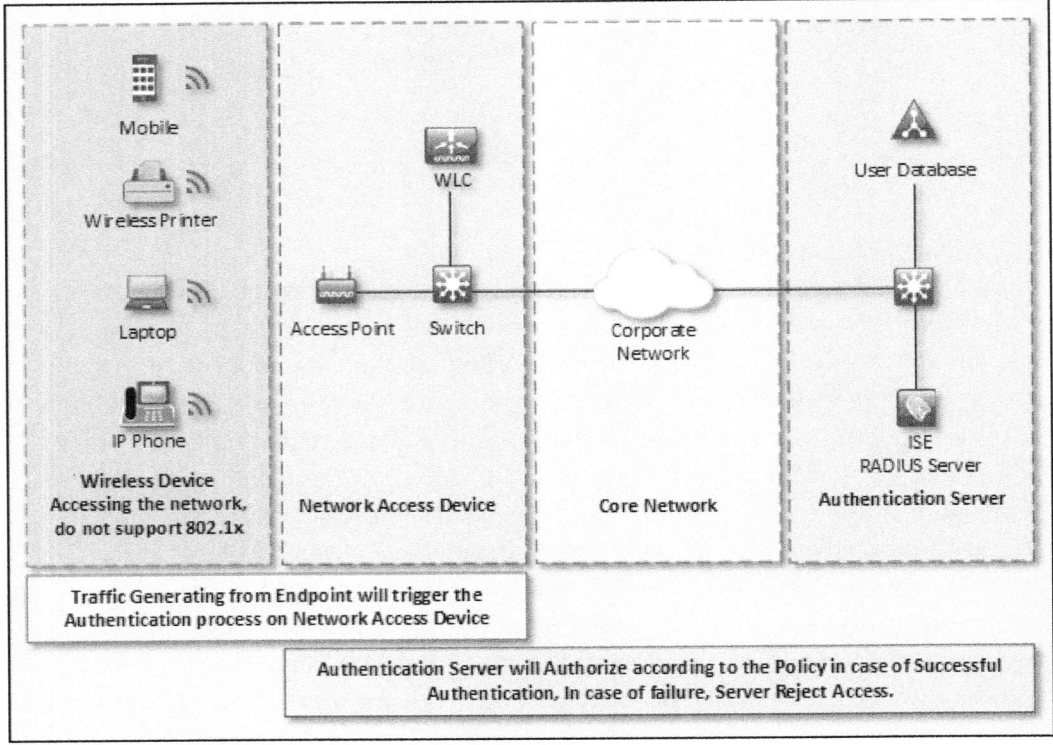

Figure 4-10. MAC Authentication Bypass

MAB Capable Recommended Device
- Catalyst 6500—CatOS 8.5(1)
- Cisco Catalyst 4500/4948—12.2(31)SG
- Cisco Catalyst 3750-2960—12.2(25)SEE
- Cisco Catalyst 2940—12.1(22)EA9

MAB with Guest VLAN
Guest VLAN is normally configured as Backup in case of MAC Authentication failure. When an Endpoint is failed to be authenticated using 802.1x and MAB respectively, Guest VLAN configuration enable the Unknown Wireless or Wire Endpoint device to get limited access. When Network Access device detect the link turns up, it triggers 802.1x authentication. In case of timeout, MAB Authentication is initiated. If MAB is also timeout Port goes into HELD state. When HELP state is completed, the re-authentication starts and 802.1x authentication is attempted again. Here Guest VLAN offers the condition for new Endpoints whose identities are not authenticated by

Identity store. Port can be dynamically assigned to a VLAN referred as Guest VLAN, which may have limited access over the corporate network.

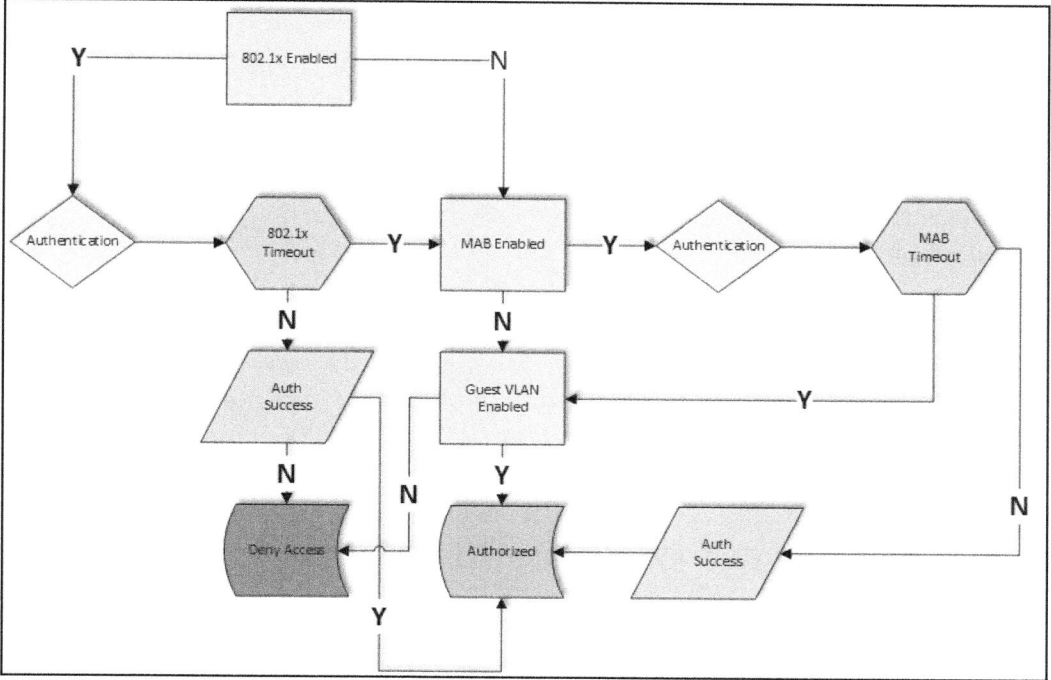

Figure 4-11. Guest VLAN with MAB Process flow

Network Authorization Enforcement

Authorization stands for Allowing, permitting or granting someone for something. If Network Authorization Enforcement, Authorization means permitting or granting the Endpoint device or Endpoint user which can connected through wired or wireless access towards the network resources. Granularity of the Authorization is associated to the Policies and enforcements. Using Authentication, Authorization feature of AAA Authentication server, Authorization enforcement can be done including layer 2 segmentation using enforcement of Dynamic VLANs, Filtering at layer 3 using Downloadable Access Control Lists (dACLs) and layer 7 entitlements.

Authentication only / Null Authorization:

Basic Authorization configuration in AAA is Null Authorization. When 802.1x or MAB authentication is deployed, default configuration upon successful authentication leads to full network access. When a AAA Authentication server performs Authentication of a client or an Endpoint device, and it found it trusted upon successful authentication, it permits the client as connected to the Trusted Home network where no layer 2 segmentation or layer 3 filtering is required as default configuration. This default configuration must be modified and a strong authorization policy must be configured to secure the network from any security threat.

Dynamic VLAN Enforcement

In Network Authorization Enforcement, Segmentation of Layer 2 enhanced the security and protection by securing the device at layer 2. Dynamically allocation of VLAN associated with the Authorization profile enforces upon successful authentication of Wired or Wireless Users or Endpoint devices is an efficient way to not only manage the network access and allocation of VLAN but also secure the network from Unknown access. Authentication Server can dynamically allocate employees, Temporary Users, and Guest User to their respective VLANs automatically after Authentication process.

Downloadable Access Control Lists

Downloadable ACL are the key Component Securing the Network Access using AAA. Downloadable ACL offers layer 3 filtering, which controls the authorization and restrict the User by downloading on Network Access Device such as Routers, Switches and Security Gateways etc. These downloadable ACLs are configured over AAA RADIUS server with an authorization profile associated with the Endpoints, User, or group of User or Endpoints. Authorization profile configured with Downloadable ACL and Dynamic VLAN enforce aggregate authorization to host or range of host granting access of service or list of service towards specified destination for entire VLAN.

Central Web Authentication

Central Web Authentication offers Central Authentication of Users over Web. Centralized Authentication ensures accounting and Authorization enforcement through an Authentication Server i.e. RADIUS Server. Security Solution recommends Web Authentication in case of failure MAB. IEEE 802.1x Authentication is recommended as Primary Authentication protocol for Users. Database holding attributes of trusted users like Username, Passwords and other optional and mandatory attribute is required for 802.1x Authentication. MAC Authentication Bypass should be used as backup or alternate for the device, which does not support IEEE 802.1x Authentication. Trusted MAC database is required for MAB Authentication. Web Authentication is the third option, which is generally setup for unknown or guest users.

Deployment Scenario for Web Authentication

Temporary User Authentication:

Organization demanding mobility and security also requires Temporary User in their corporate network. These temporary users are Guests, Contractors or other user, which need to access the network. As these are temporary Users, they may have 802.1x capable device or may not which leads to Central Web Authentication, which is an easy method for these user to authenticate themselves.

Fall Back Authentication

Central Web Authentication can also be used for Normal User like employees of an organization, which may use Central Web Authentication in case of failure of other Authentication mechanism like 802.1x. This could be due Misconfiguration of supplicant, Password Expiry, Certificate Expiry or any other reason. This fall back method will resolve these issues, which can be handled by the Administrator later.

Device Registration.

Another deployment scenario is Bring Your Own Device where users are allowed to register their Mobile phone, tablets, laptop and other Wireless devices. Demand of Mobility and BYOD can be fulfilled by Central Web Authentication which not only Register and Authenticate the Devices also manage the Control and Logging of these devices.

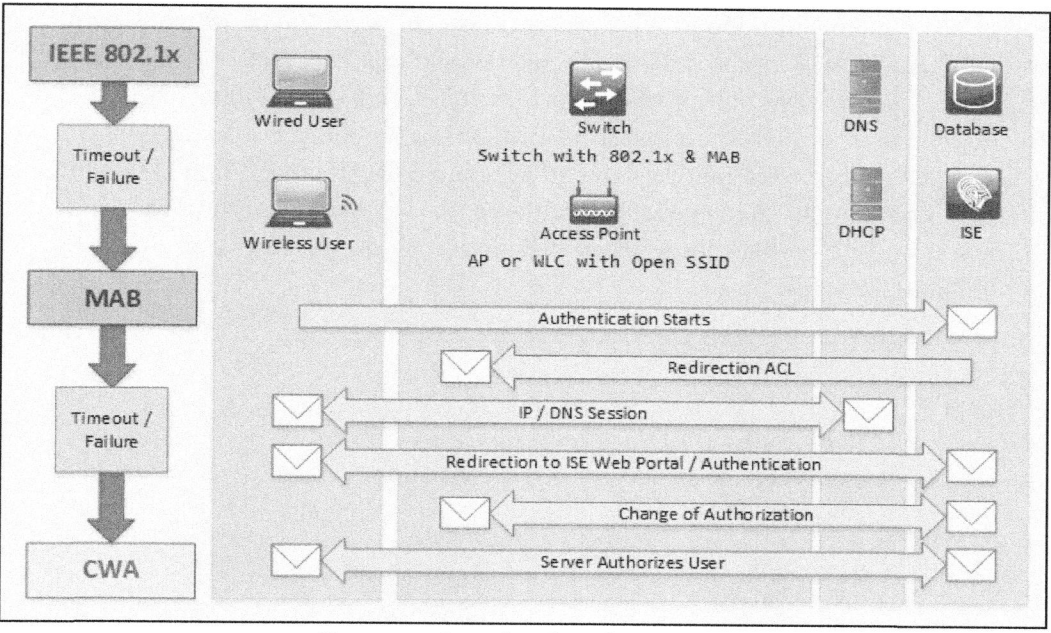

Figure 4-12. Central Web Authentication

Web Authentication Flow

Central Web Authentication is conducted by Central Authentication Server i.e. RADIUS server like Cisco ISE. When a wire or Wireless user is connected, it triggers authentication. Upon failure of 802.1x, MAB leads to Central Web Authentication, which redirect the User to a Web Page. This Redirected Web page allows the User register itself. Central Web Authentication Support Network Authorization enforcement such as Downloadable ACLs, Dynamic VLAN Assignment, Change of Authorization, Posturing and Guest Services. For the Wireless User Central Web Authentication is associated with Open SSID, which is specially configured for CWA.

Profiling
Profiling Solution Overview:
Profiling ensures the dynamic detection and identification of the Endpoint devices or Users connected to the Network. Using MAC address can uniquely identify endpoint and their Login Credentials can identify User. Classification and identification of Endpoints requires collection of various attributes associated with predefined or user defined policies such as a wide variety of devices including mobile of different Operating Systems, Desktop Operating System, Printer and other devices. Once the User or Endpoint is authenticated and identified using Probes, it can be authorized according to the profile matches the condition.

Profiling Policy Architecture and Components
As we know Profiling depend upon Probes, which collect the attribute information of Endpoints. Different Probes are responsible for collection of different type of Endpoint attributes. Cisco ISE probes collects information, After Collection of Information, Attribute are compared against the configured rule. Each matching condition has a certainty factor (CF), which differentiates the appropriate matching condition for the classification of Endpoint to the associated profile because matching conditions can match in more than one profile. Association of Endpoint to the respective profile is the result of highest CF value.

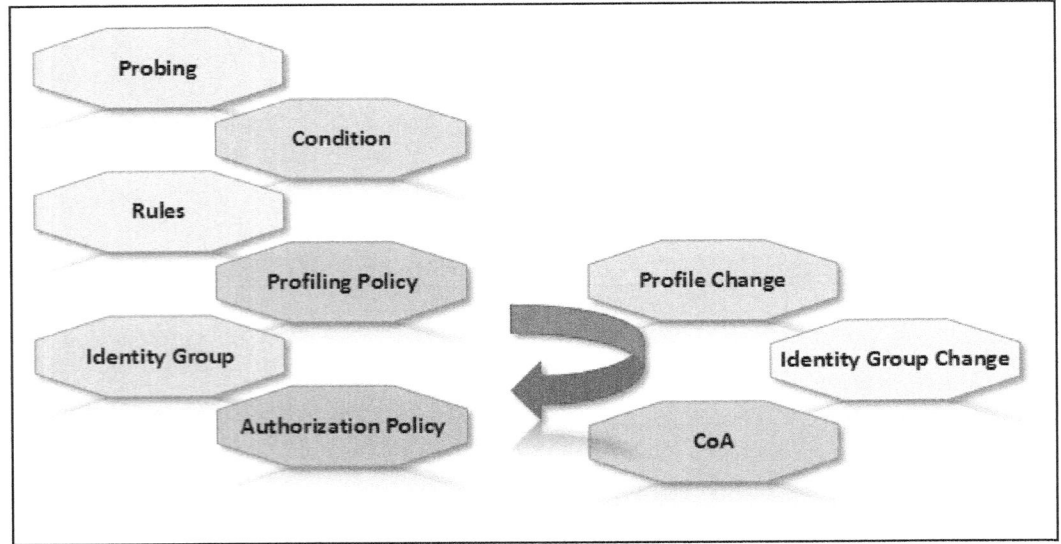

Figure 4-13. Profiling Policy Architecture and Components

Profiling Using RADIUS Probe
RADIUS probe in Profiling is use to Collect attributes from the RADIUS Attributes coming from Endpoints through Wired or Wireless Network Access devices such as Switches or Wireless LAN Controllers towards the RADIUS authentication server. ISE standard RADIUS ports include UDP port 1645 or 1812 used for Authentication and

Authorization whereas UDP port 1646 and 1813 are used for accounting by RADIUS. RADIUS probe collecting information from RADIUS packets does not mean that RADIUS probe can directly capture information from RADIUS packets. It extracts the information from the packet send to syslog on UDP Port 20514. This RADIUS Probe also collects other information from accounting packet of RADIUS like CDP, LLDP and DHCP attributes.

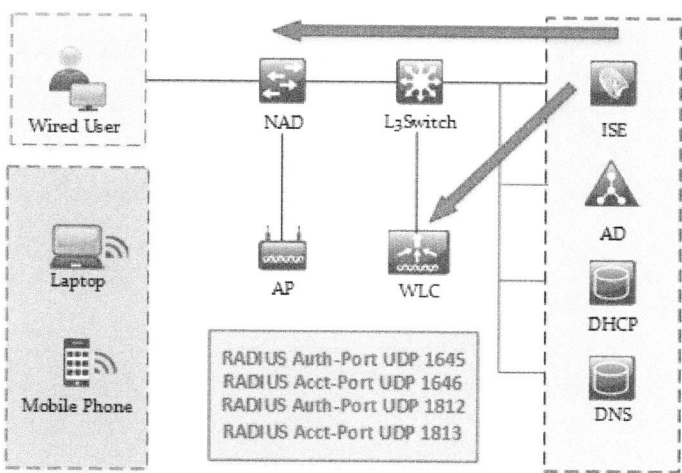

Figure 4-14. RADIUS Probe

Profiling Using SNMP Query Probe

SNMP Query Probe send query packets known as SNMP GET Requests, to the access devices such as Switches, Access point etc. Other Network devices can also be configured to collect relevant information. SNMP query is further classified into two types

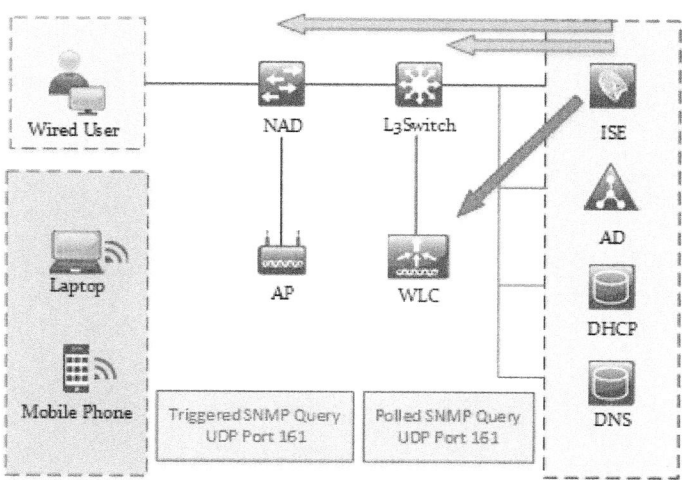

Figure 4-15. SNMP Query Probe

1. System Query

System Queries are periodic depending upon Polling interval. The key attributes collected by System Query are
• Bridge, IP (ARP)
• CDP Cache Entry (Wired only)
• LLDP Local System Data (Wired only)
• LLDP Remote Systems Data (Wired only)
• cldc Client Entry (WLC only)

2. Interface Query

Interface Queries are generated either when RADIUS Accounting Starts or when SNMP detect linkup. Recommended is to reduce then traffic overhead and use SNMP Query based on RADIUS accounting Start message. Attributes collected by Interface Query are
Interface data (ifIndex, ifDesc, etc)
• Port and VLAN data
• Session Data (if interface type is Ethernet)
• CDP data (Cisco devices)
• LLDP data

Profiling Using DHCP Probe

Configuring DHCP Packets forwarding directly to the ISE or RADIUS Server uses DHCP probe. Relay Function obtains this within the network. An additional helper address is configured over layer 3 interface for forwarding the requests to ISE. The actual DHCP server will respond the DHCP requests where is due to additional Helper address packets are forwarded to ISE which does not reply these packets but collect attribute from them.

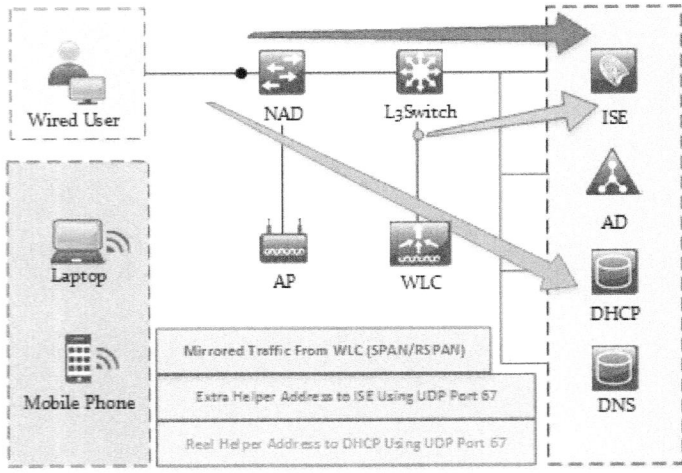

Figure 4-16. DHCP Probe

DHCP SPAN Probe is the also the option for the devices where DHCP Relay is not possible or required. Using Switch Port Analyser (SPAN) and Remote Switch Port Analyser (RSPAN), probing can be done for Wireless Device connected through the

WLC where DHCP Relay is not configured, or cannot be configured due to any limitation. Recommended best practice is use any of the one Option for Probing either DHCP Helper Probing or DHCP SPAN probing. If DHCP Helper option is available, it is more preferred option than SPAN because it has less traffic overhead on ISE.

Guest Services

Cisco ISE offers the feature of Guest Service, which ensures the secure and visible access of Guest users and temporary client of an organization within the corporate network. Traffic generating from these guest users are segregated from internal networks, regular employees and secure internal Servers. Using Cisco ISE Guest Services, a Centralized management for these Guests is offered which can be deployed over wired and Wireless network requirement. It can also integrate with Customized or Third party access portals. HTTPS port 8443 is used for redirection to Guest and Sponsor Portal by default.

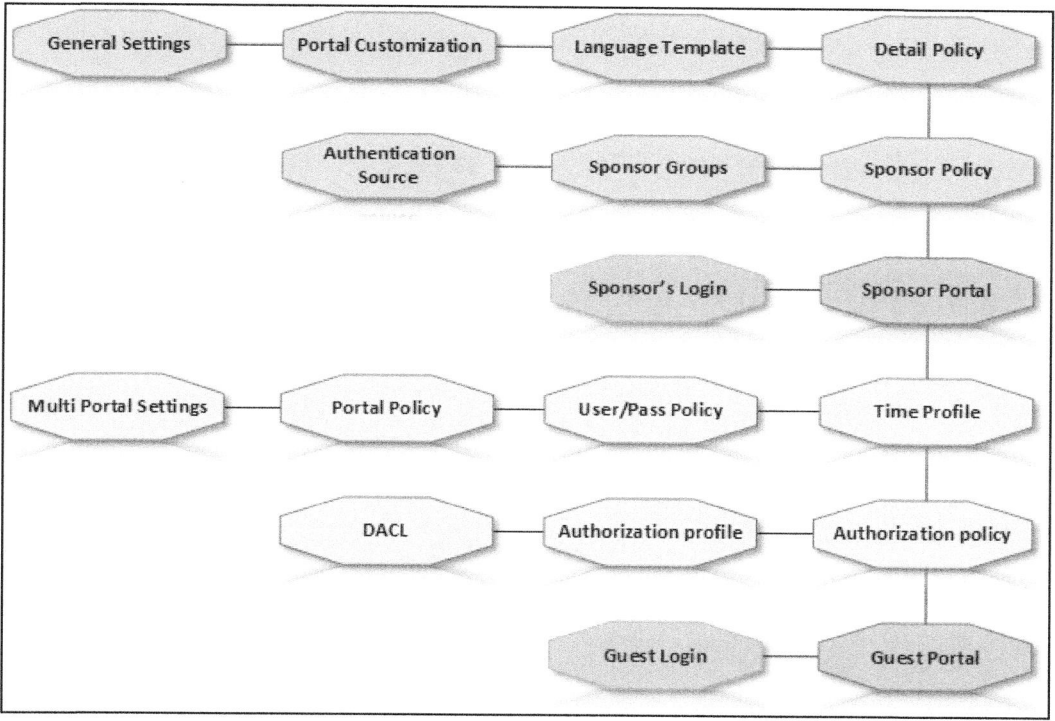

Figure 4-17. Guest Service Operation Flow

Cisco ISE brings the Guest user, visitors and temporary clients to the Web portal, which is known as Guest User portal to login for accessing the network. Using dynamic VLANs, Downloadable ACLs configuration Network Access Device restricts the access of guest users.

Sponsors Portal

Sponsor Portal offered by Cisco ISE provide the option for Sponsoring the guest User account on the behalf of the sponsor which has privileges. Sponsors using Sponsor portal login to the network and create guest user account and provide the credentials to the guest by Email, messaging to any other out of band way.

Guest Self Service

Cisco ISE also offer Self Service for Guest to register themselves. Redirection page having a link to create an account will bring them to the web page where they will provide attribute and upon successful submission of required field an automatic Username and Password will be generated for them. Guest user will have to note these credentials because they will be redirected to Guest Portal again to login with these credentials.

Wireless Guest Service Overview

- Dedicated Guest WLAN SSID is configured within the organization for guest access.
- Guest traffic is segregated using Layer 2 and Layer 3 techniques
- Downloadable Access Control List is configured for controlling access functionality.
- Guest User Authentication using AAA or other Management System.

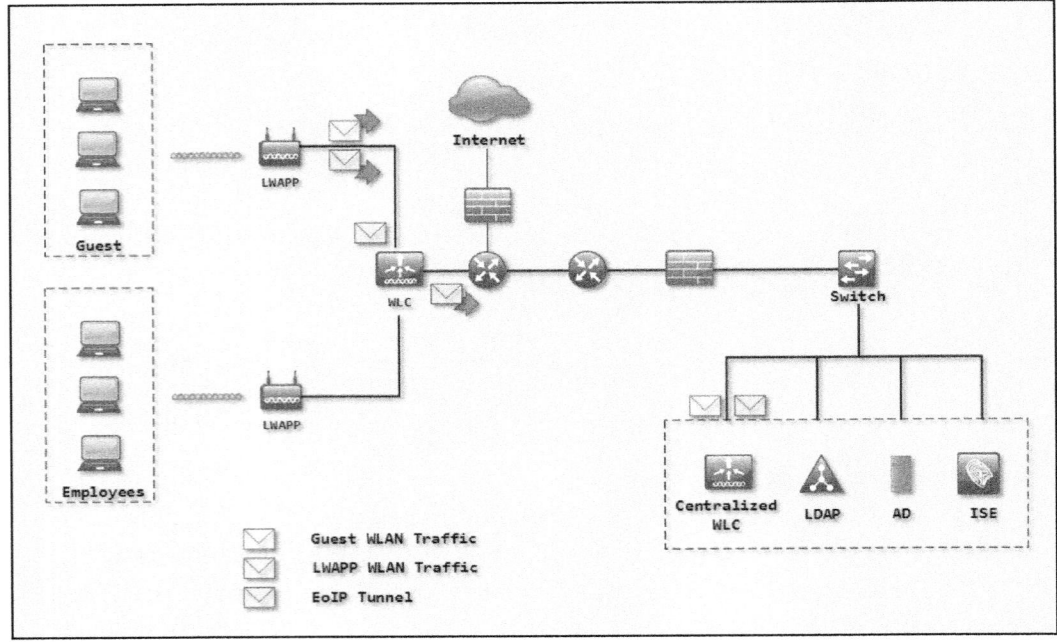

Figure 4-18 Centralized WLC Communication

Centralized Wireless LAN Controller

Using a Centralized Wireless LAN Controller in Wireless Guest Service Architecture offer flexibility in deployment. Ethernet in IP (RFC3378) tunnels communication between Wireless LAN Controllers in Layer 3 Network.

Wireless Controller Guest Access feature of Cisco offers the independent solution for Guest services. Cisco Wireless Controller Guest Access has eliminated the need of external ACL, Web Authentication Portal, AAA servers. All these functions are implemented in a Single Wireless LAN Controller. Tunnelling, Web Authentication, ACL are supported by

- CISCO 4440 Series
- Cisco 6500 Series (WiSM)
- Cisco 3750 with Integrated WLC

Posturing

Posture is a Cisco ISE service that allows the administrator to configure the policies that automatically checks for compliance by the Endpoints connecting the network with Security policies. Posture Assessment checks the Endpoint device through an Endpoint agent for the requirements configured at Authentication Server i.e. Cisco ISE.

Components of Posture Service

Posture Administration Services

Posture Administration Services requires advanced license installed in Cisco ISE. Posture Administration Services ensures back end support for Posture Conditions, remediation action associated with Posture services.

Posture Run Time Service

Posture Run Time Service ensure secure communication between NAC agent and Cisco ISE by encapsulating SWISS protocol and other communication for Posturing.

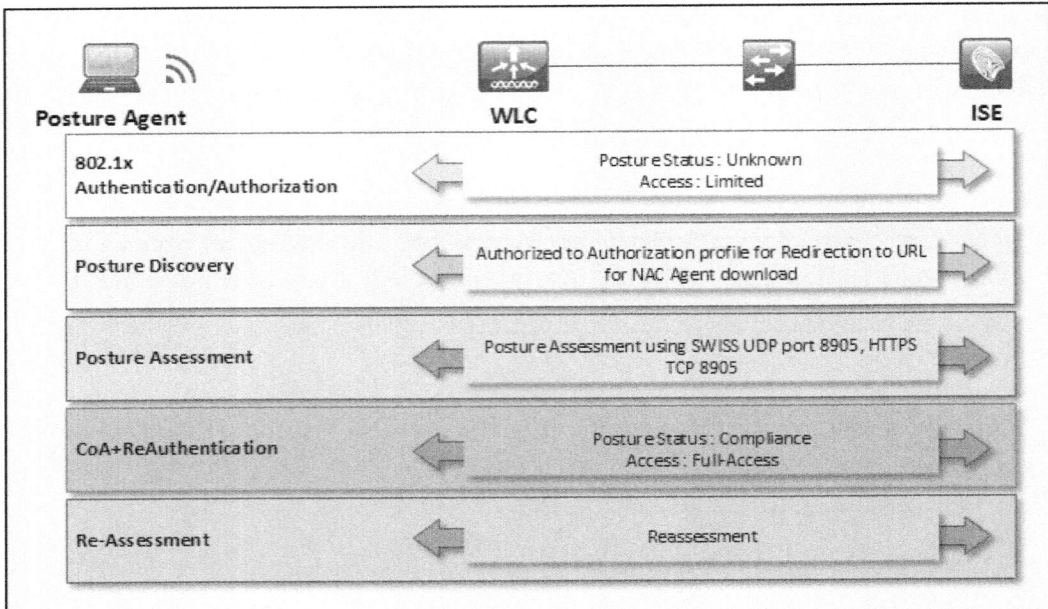

Figure 4-19. Posturing Work flow

Posture assessment service operation depends upon three major configuration steps

1. Client Provisioning
2. Posture Policy
3. Authorization Policy

Client Provisioning

To deploy the posture assessment in a network for the determination of the Endpoint regarding their compliance state according the policy of the corporate network, an agent is required at Endpoint, which inspect the Endpoint device for Posture assessment on the behalf of Authentication server. Network Admission Control (NAC) agent is responsible for the checking the Endpoint for the compliance. This NAC agent is automatically downloaded when user logs in through portal.

Posture Policy

Posture Policy is the combination the requirements configured for the Endpoint at Authentication server as a condition of compliance. Posture Policy conditions may include presence of a file, availability of an Application, Operating System requirement, Antivirus or Firewall and others rules. This Posture policy is enforced on the Endpoint to check compliance status. There are three types of Compliance status.

1. **Unknown**

   Posture Assessment was not done successfully or failed to collect data for assessment.

2. **Non-Compliance**

When Endpoint device is failed to meet all requirements of Posture Policy

3. **Compliance**

When Endpoint device meet all requirements of Posture Policy

Authorization Policy

Authorization policy enforces the granularity of the Network access that is to be enforced to the Endpoint based on the Status of Posture assessment. Normally in case of Non-Compliance network access is limited or denied. If remediation by ensuring the requirement by the agent is successful, network access is granted.

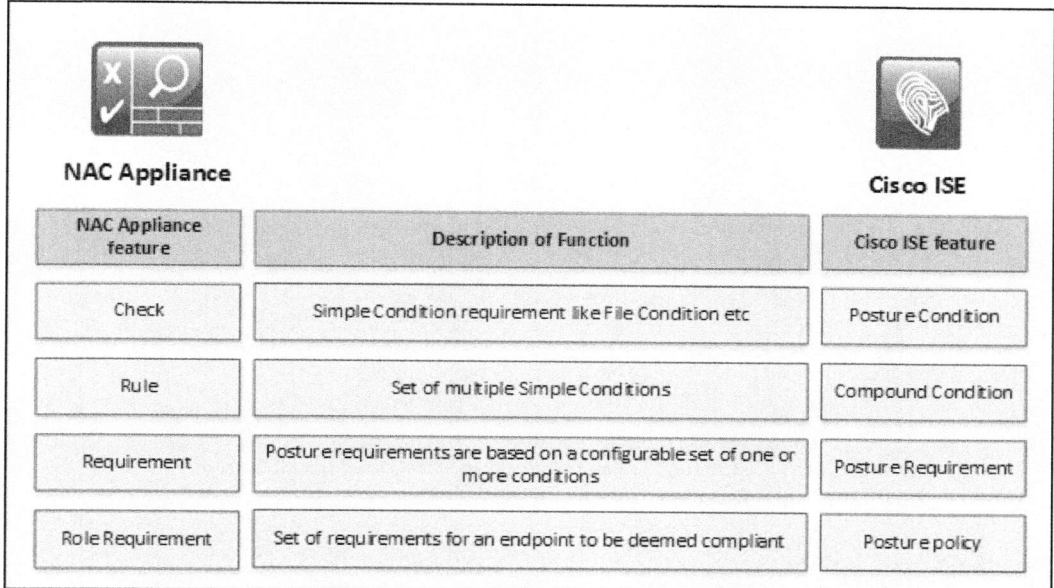

NAC Appliance feature	Description of Function	Cisco ISE feature
Check	Simple Condition requirement like File Condition etc	Posture Condition
Rule	Set of multiple Simple Conditions	Compound Condition
Requirement	Posture requirements are based on a configurable set of one or more conditions	Posture Requirement
Role Requirement	Set of requirements for an endpoint to be deemed compliant	Posture policy

Figure 4-20. NAC Appliance vs Cisco ISE

Chapter 5: Identity Management Architectures

Technology Brief

Cisco ISE Nodes

Cisco ISE can be deployed in different Nodes. Nodes offered by Cisco ISE are
1. Policy Service Node (PSN)
2. Policy Administration Node (PAN)
3. Monitoring & Troubleshooting Node (MnT)
4. pxGrid Controller

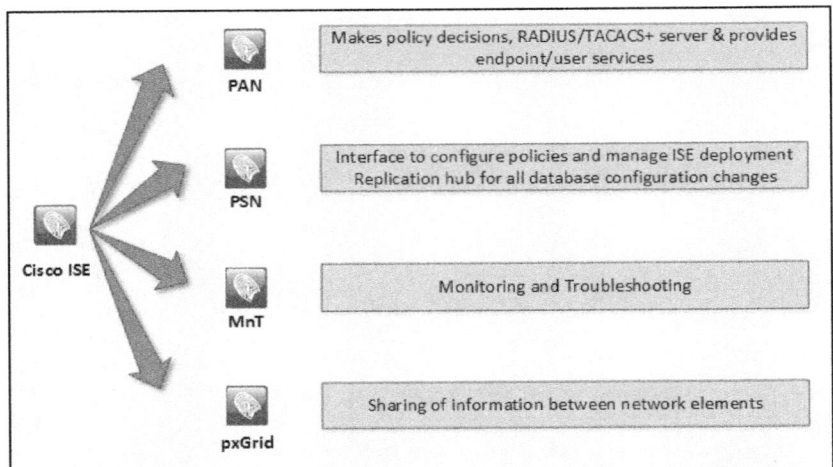

Figure 5-1. Cisco ISE Nodes

Policy Service Node (PSN)
Policy Service Node (PSN) of Cisco ISE offers the service offered by Cisco ISE like Network Access, Guest Access, Client Provisioning, Posture, Profiling and Policy services. Policy Service Node (PSN) ensure the evaluation of Policies and taking action based of configured profile. In a distributed deployment, Multiple Policy Service Node (PSN) can be configured using Load balancer. Failure of any node in this environment will be backed up by another node and take handover of the session.

Policy Administration Node (PAN)
Cisco Identity Service Engine with Administrative Node offers all administrative controlling and Operation over Cisco ISE. It is responsible for system configuration associated with functions of ISE services such as AAA. The Administration node can be configuring as standalone, primary, or secondary role. Distributed deployment offers maximum of two ISE administration nodes.

Monitoring and Troubleshooting Node (MnT)

Cisco ISE with Monitoring and Troubleshooting Node offers the features of Monitoring, Controlling, Troubleshooting and Visibility over corporate network. Various features offer by Cisco ISE for Monitoring and troubleshooting like Log collector, logging, troubleshooting tools offers advanced and enhanced control over the network. These effective tools also offer proper reporting for records as well as for other legal actions. Cisco ISE configuration with Monitoring and Troubleshooting node offer maximum of two nodes deployment as Primary and secondary nodes for high availability.

Cisco recommended deployment scenario is dedicated deployment of Cisco ISE Monitoring Node for maximum performance instead of deploying Monitoring and Troubleshooting Node with Policy Service Node.

pxGrid Controller

pxGrid node configuration over Cisco ISE offers sharing of sensitive information from Cisco ISE to the other Cisco platforms. This information may be context sensitive extracted form Session directories. pxGrid is also offers sharing of other information like sharing of configured policies, other configuration data between Cisco ISE nodes or associated third party platforms. Cisco pxGrid functionality depends upon Policy Administration Node because replication of information is through PAN. If PAN goes down, pxGrid also stops its functions. Manual promotion of PAN brings pxGrid server active.

Cisco ISE deployment Modes

There are two types of deployment modes of Cisco ISE
 1. Standalone Deployment
 2. Basic 2-Node Deployment
 3. Distributed Deployment

Standalone Deployment

Cisco Identity Service Engine ISE Standalone deployment has only one Cisco ISE node that performs all function of Administration, Policy Service, pxGrid and Monitoring Node. Standalone deployment can support up to 2000 Endpoints.

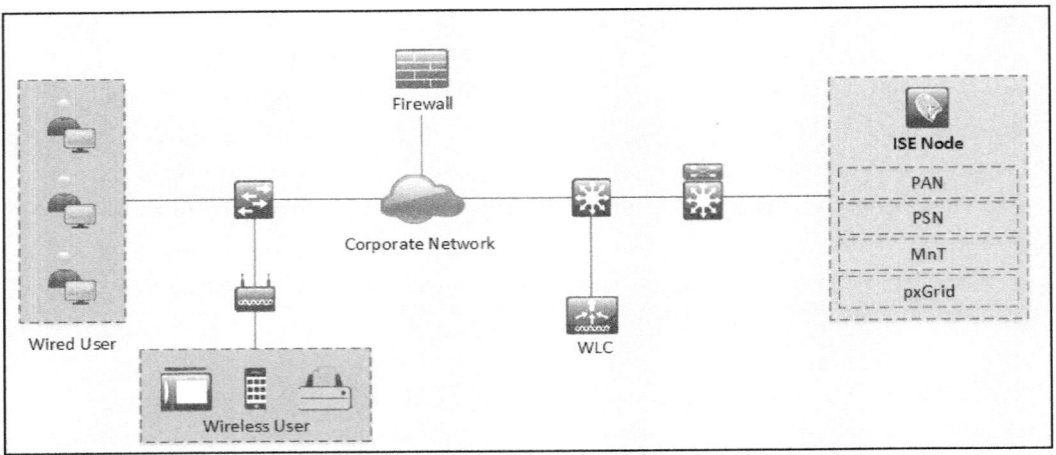

Figure 5-2. Standalone Deployment

Basic 2-Node Deployment

Basic 2-Node Deployment run all service as standalone but in redundancy. It can also support up to 2000 Endpoints.

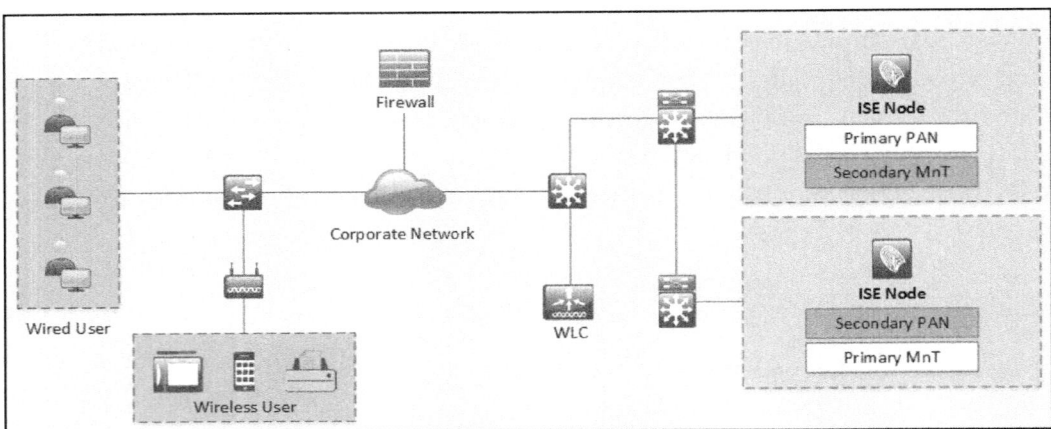

Figure 5-3. Basic 2-Node Deployment

Distributed Deployment

Cisco Identity Service Engine ISE Distributed deployment has more than one Cisco ISE node, which ensure failover support for high availability and performance. ISE node can be assumed with any persona like PAN, PSN or monitoring. Distributed Deployment support two Admin nodes, Two Monitoring node configured as Primary and Secondary Nodes along with up to 40 Policy Service Nodes facilitating up to 100,000 Endpoints.

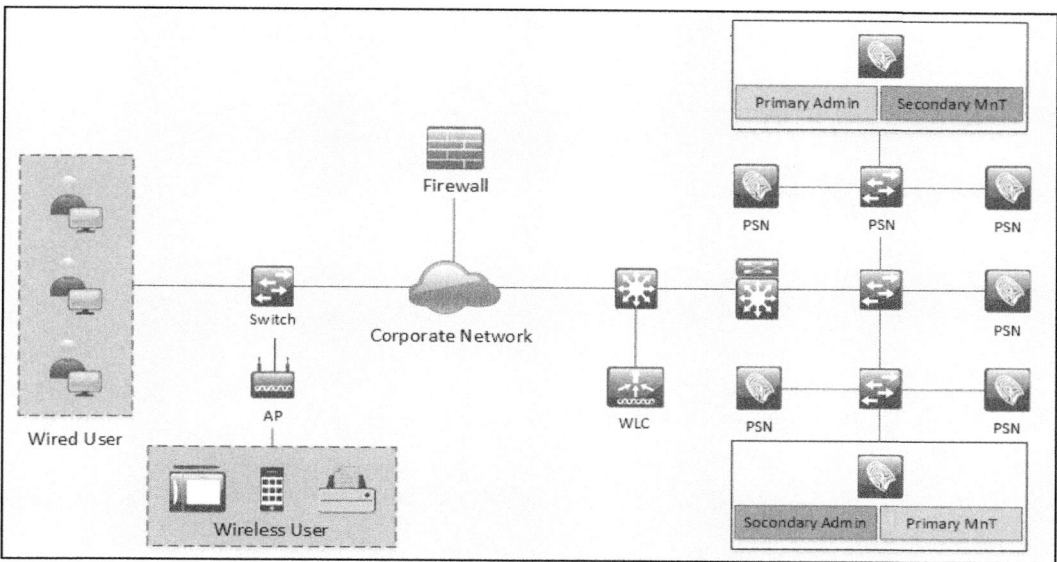

Figure 5-4. Distributed Deployment

Designing Security Solutions

AAA Security Solution

AAA is all about implementing the goals, which are Authentication, Authorization, and Accounting within a network with centralization command and control. Let say an organization has several devices located at different locations geographically, one method is to access these devices one by one and add a local database containing usernames and passwords of all authorized persons. The second solution is to have a centralized server containing the database with each device pointing to server for taking decision.

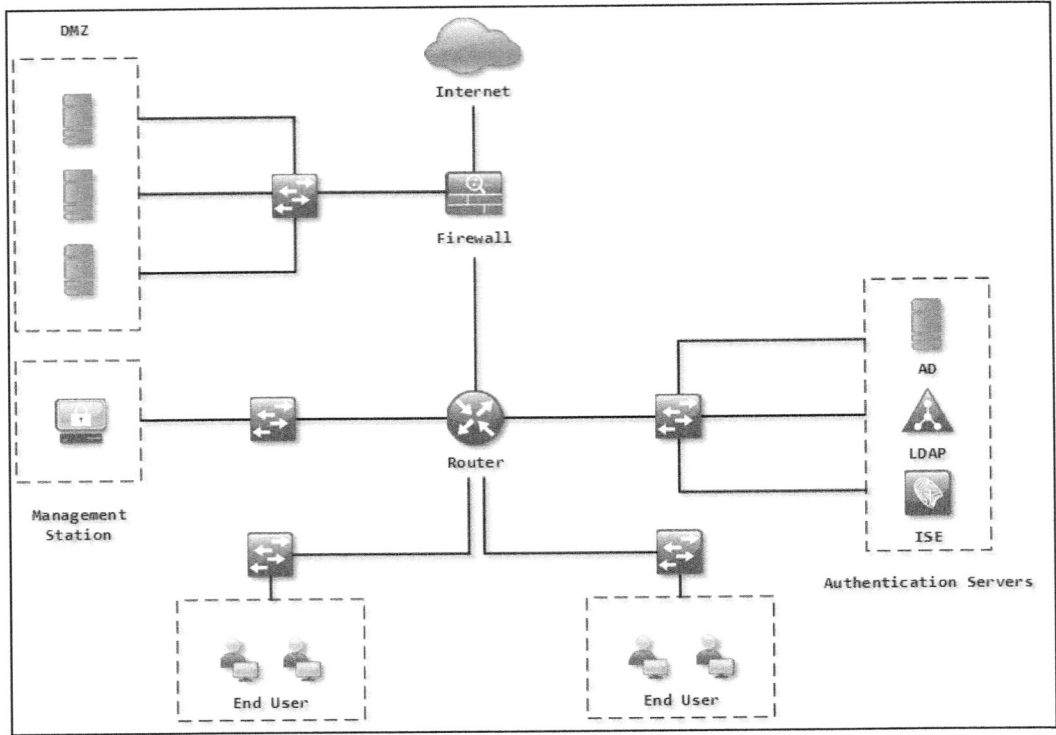

Figure 38. AAA Security Solution

Identity Service Unit (ISE)

ISE is used for secure access management like ACS. It is a single policy control point for entire enterprise including wired and wireless technologies. Before giving access to endpoints or even networking devices itself, ISE checks their identity, location, time, type of device and even health of endpoints to make sure that they comply with company's policy like antivirus, latest service pack and OS updates etc. Most of the time people prefer ACS over ISE, although ISE can implement AAA but it is not a complete replacement of ACS.

TACACS+ vs RADIUS

Two protocols used in ACS as a language of communication between a networking device and ACS server are RADIUS and TACACS+. TACACS+ stands for *Terminal Access Control Access Control Server* and it is Cisco proprietary. Anytime TACACS+ is used for communication between device and server, it will encrypt the full payload of packet before sending it over the network.

Another possible protocol to be used is RADIUS, which is an acronym for *Remote Authentication Dial-in User Service*. RADIUS is an open standard meaning that all vendors can use it in their AAA implementation. One main difference between RADIUS and TACACS+ is that RADIUS only encrypts password and sends other RADIUS packets as clear text over the network.

Active Directory

Active Directory provides centralized command and control of domain users, computers, and network printers. It restricts the access to network resources only to the defined users and computers

Profiling Security Solution
Overview

Cisco Identity Services Engine (ISE) offers wide and robust services for authentication and authorization of Endpoint devices accessing the network. Cisco ISE is very Popular and being used in network security for securing devices accessing the network resources.

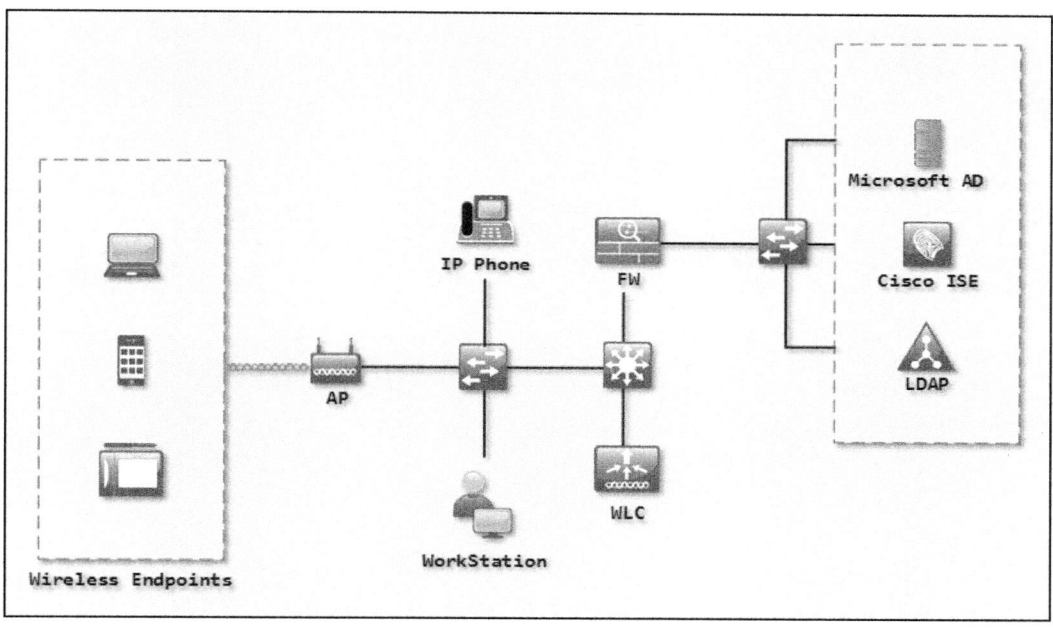

Figure 39. Cisco ISE Profiling Topology

It dynamically detects the connecting devices to access the network and classify these Endpoints. MAC address plays an important role in this classification to uniquely identify these Endpoint devices. Cisco ISE does not only depend on the MAC addresses of the Endpoint devices, it also investigates for certain set of attributes and compare against the entry in database. This collection of attribute can be stored in Internal Datastore as well as External Datastore. Cisco ISE checks and verify the attributes of the Endpoint devices against these pre-configured attributes, conditions and policies. These set of attributes are correlated to the Profile configured in ISE. These profiles can be configured to operate along 802.1x Port-based Authentication, MAC Authentication Bypass (MAB) as well as Network Admission Control (NAC). Profile contain information of Endpoint devices like type of devices connecting the network such as Mobile Phones including Android MAC, and Blackberry etc., Android Tablets, iPads, MAC OS and other along with their Operating System information.

Designing of Profiling Security solution must include a key step prior to the configuration and deployment of the Security solution is to get information and understanding about the number of devices and device type Endpoint using to access the network. This information of Endpoint devices will help in planning to deploy the network as well as in profiling configuration on Cisco ISE. Administrator can make a list which device can support 802.1x Port-based Authentication, Web Authentication and which device may need to be authenticated using MAC authentication Bypass MAB.

Profiler Policy List > **New Profiler Policy**

Profiler Policy

* Name	Android Phone	Description	New Android Device Configuration
Policy Enabled	☑		
* Minimum Certainty Factor	10	(Valid Range 1 to 65535)	
* Exception Action	NONE ▼		
* Network Scan (NMAP) Action	NONE ▼		
Create an Identity Group for the policy	○ Yes, create matching Identity Group		
	◉ No, use existing Identity Group hierarchy		
* Parent Policy	Android ▼		
* Associated CoA Type	Global Settings ▼		
System Type			

Rules

If Condition AndroidRule1Check1 ⊕ Then Certainty Factor Increases ▼ 10

⚙ ▼

Submit Cancel

Figure 40. Example of Profiling Android Device

When devices are known which are connecting to the network, information of devices is required to profile the Endpoints. If all required attribute about certain Endpoint is updated in database, when device try to authenticate itself, it will be identified and profiling probe will profile the Endpoint device. List of Endpoint devices, which are unknown, can also profiled. This Endpoint unknown devices may include Printers, Phones, Fax devices or advanced IP enabled devices. Using Monitor Mode, attributes of these unknown devices can be learned and can be denied using enforcement mode. Cisco Wireless LAN Controller offers Wireless Profiling using 802.1x Port-Based Authentication and MAC address Filtering. Cisco ISE can also learned about the Wired devices in Discovery mode before authenticating and authorizing these devices.

Probe	Profiling Attributes
RADIUS	MAC Address (OUI), IP address, CDP LLDP

	DHCP
SNMP	MAC Address, OUI, CDP, LLDP, ARP tables
DHCP	DHCP
NMAP	Operating System, Common ports, Endpoint SNMP data
DNS	FQDN
Netflow	Protocol, Source/Destination IP, Source/Destination /Ports
HTTP	User-Agent

Table 7 Profiling Probe and related Attribute

Cisco ISE Licenses for Profiling

Profiling Service in Cisco ISE requires license, which must be installed in Policy Administration Node PAN. License that support ISE profiling feature are

- Advanced Endpoint license (for wired or wireless deployments)
- Wireless Only license (for wireless only deployments)

Posturing Security Solution

Overview

Posturing feature ensure the states of endpoints connecting to the network according the security policies configured. Using Posturing services, Administrator can control the access of clients to sensitive, restricted and protected areas in a network.

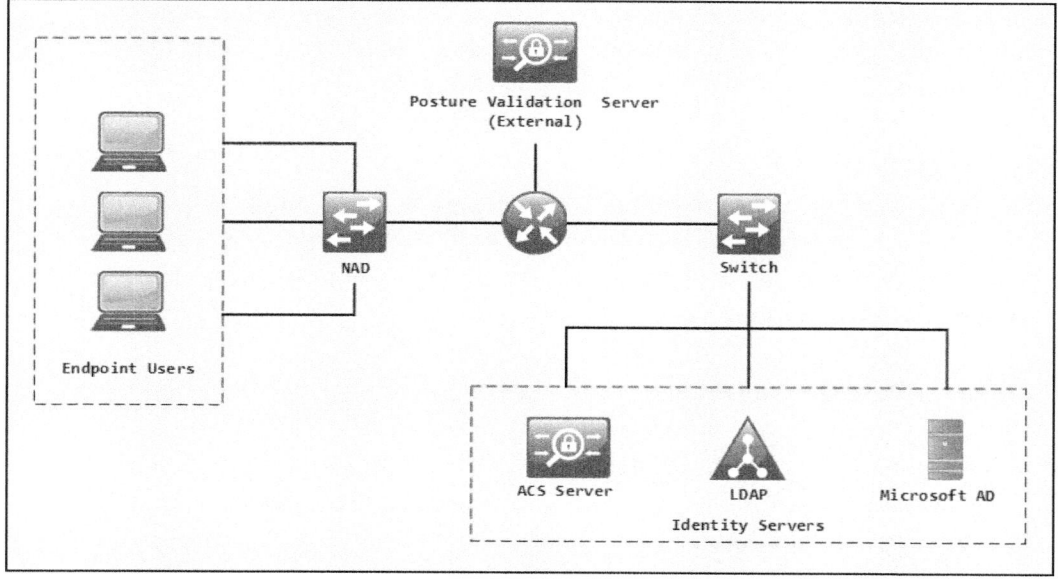

Figure 41 Posturing Solution Design

Network Access Control (NAC)

Network Access Control (NAC) or Network Admission Control is a Security Solution by Cisco for the Endpoint devices connecting to the network infrastructure for

accessing the network resources to apply Security policies on these Endpoints. Network Infrastructure with NAC deployment offers Network access to trusted and secures Endpoint Devices as well as restricts Non-Secure Endpoints. This will limit emerging security threats. Network Admission control can be deployed for authentication of users, Authorization, identification of wire or wireless, Local and remote user before getting access to the network resources.

Key features of Network Access Control
- It Ensures and Improve Network Security by Confirming Security Applications, Antivirus Software at the Endpoint devices.
- It Ensures and Improve Network Security by applying Security Policies to the Endpoint devices.
- It can Protect the Network infrastructure from worms, spywares, viruses and other malicious programs.
- It is scalable and applicable for LAN, WAN, Wireless and Remote Network Infrastructure.

Components of Network Access Control

1. **Endpoint Device**

   An Endpoint device normally knows as Client, Host or a User accessing the Network Locally, Remotely, through LAN or WAN, using Wire or Wireless Connection from any device like Mobile Phones, Tablets, PCs, Laptop. For NAC deployment, These Endpoint Users must have Cisco Trust Agent (CTA) application software.

2. **Cisco Trust Agent (CTA)**

   Cisco Trust Agent (CTA) is an application software of the Endpoint devices which collects the required attributes, Posture data from these Endpoint Devices. It can also fetch posture data from NAC Compliance application running of these Endpoint devices.

3. **Network Access Device (NAD)**

   A Network Access Device is required for the Deployment of Network Access Control (NAC). This Network Access Device (NAD) is basically a device through which Endpoint is connected, and accessing the network resources. This Network Access device is AAA Client device. Network Access Device can be the device such as Switch, Router that can support NAC Enforcement policies.

4. *Cisco Secure Access Control System (ACS)*

Cisco ACS is the device, which validates these Endpoint devices. Policies are configured in Cisco ACS known as Internal Policies, as well as an External Policy can also be used.

5. *Remediation Servers*

Remediation servers are those servers, which repair and upgrade the Endpoint which are not complying Network Admission policy.

BYOD Security Solution

BYOD Devices: These endpoint devices are required to access the corporate network for daily business need. BYOD devices may include both corporate and personally owned devices, regardless of their physical location. At day, they may be at corporate office and at night, they may be some café or food restraint. Common BYOD devices include smartphones, laptops etc.

Wireless Access Points (AP): Cisco wireless access points (APs) provide wireless connectivity to the corporate network for above defined BYOD devices. Access points are installed physically at campus, branch office, or even at home office to facilitate the employees.

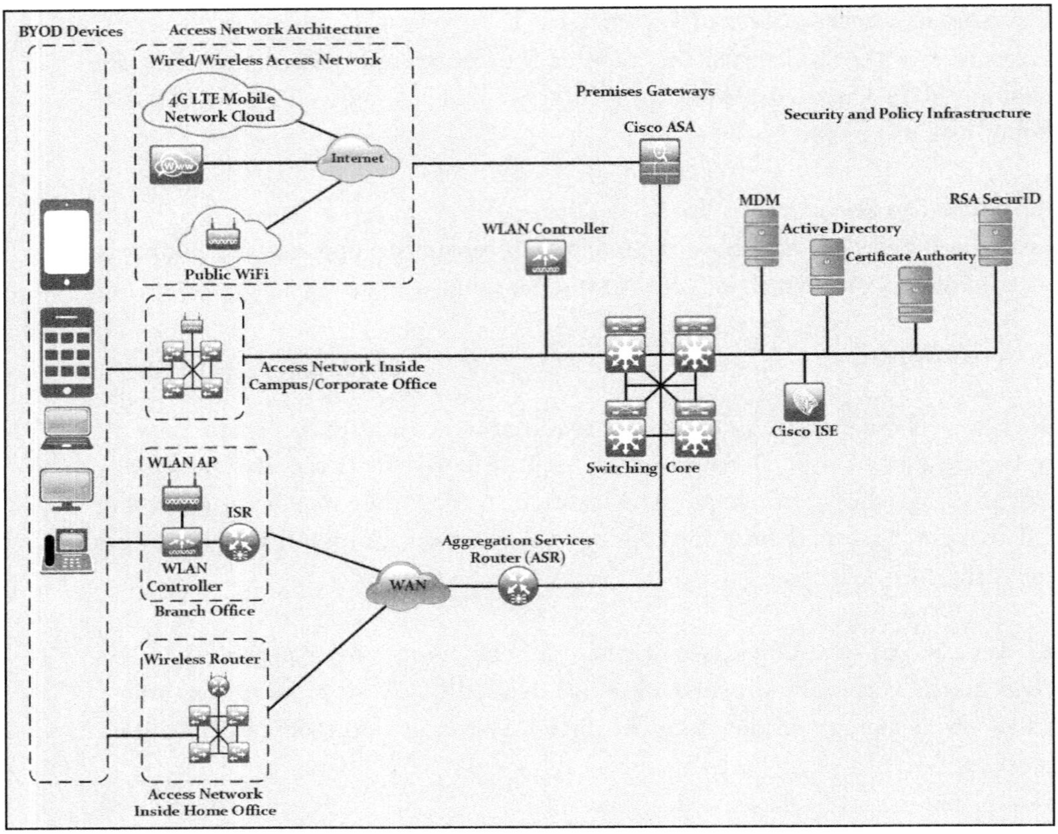

Figure 42 BYOD Solution Design

Wireless LAN Controllers: WLAN controllers provide centralized management and monitoring of Cisco WLAN solution. WLAN are integrated with *Cisco Identity Service Engine* to enforce the authorization and authentication on BYOD end-point devices.

Identity Service Engine (ISE): ISE is one of the most critical elements in Cisco BYOD architecture as it implements Authentication, Authorization, and Accounting on BYOD end-point devices.

Cisco AnyConnect Secure Mobility Client: Cisco AnyConnect Client software provides connectivity to corporate network for end users. Its uses 802.1x features to provide access with in campus, office or home office network. When end users need to connect over public Internet, AnyConnect uses VPN connection to make sure the confidentiality of corporate data.

Integrated Services Router (ISR): Cisco ISR routers are preferred in BYOD architecture for proving WAN and Internet access for branch and home office networks. They are also used to provide VPN connectivity for mobile BYOD devices within organization.

Aggregation Services Router (ASR): Cisco ASR routers provide WAN and internet access for corporate and campus networks. They also act as aggregation points for connections coming from branch and home office to the corporate networks of Cisco BYOD solution.

Cloud Web Security (CWS): Cisco Cloud Web Security provides enhanced security for all BYOD devices which access Internet using public hotspots and 3G/4G networks.

Adaptive Security Appliance (ASA): Cisco ASA provides the standard security solutions at the Internet edge of campus, branch and home office networks within BYOD architecture. Apart from integrating IPS/IDS module within itself, ASA also act as termination point of VPN connections made by *Cisco AnyConnect Client* software over the public Internet to facilitate the BYOD devices.

RSA securID: RSA securID generates one-time password (OTP) for BYOD devices that need to access the network applications that require OTP.

Active Directory: Active Directory provides centralized command and control of domain users, computers, and network printers. It restricts the access to network resources only to the defined users and computers.

Certificate Authority: Certificate authority can be used to allow access of corporate network to only those BYOD devices, which have valid corporate certificate, installed on them. All those devices without certificate may be given no access of corporate network but limited Internet connectivity as per defined in corporate policy.

Mobile Device Management

The basic purpose of implementing mobile device management (MDM) is deployment, maintenance, and monitoring of mobile devices that make up BYOD solution. Devices may include the laptops, smartphones, tablets, notebooks or any other electronic device that can be moved outside the corporate office to home or some public place and then gets connected to corporate office by some means.

The following are some of the functions provided by MDM:
- Enforcing a device to be locked after certain login failure attempts.
- Enforcement of strong password polices for all BYOD devices.
- MDM can detect any attempt of hacking BYOD devices and then limiting the network access of these affected devices.
- Enforcing confidentiality by using encryption as per organization's policy.
- Administration and implementation of *Data Loss Prevention (DLP)* for BYOD devices. It helps to prevent any kind of data loss due end user's carelessness.

Guest Services Security Solution

Overview

Guest Services offers New Endpoint Users Limited Network Resources. In this Guest Service, Endpoint guest users are authenticated and authorized depending upon the conditions configured for guest policy or network requirement. Using Guest services is risky, Administrator has to secure its internal data, Secure and secret information's, Core Network from access of these guests. Guest account is created for new users accessing through guest ports redirected to Web Portal to register them. After registering, according to conditions, Policies, Downloadable ACLs, Dynamic VLANs, these Guest Endpoint are restricted. For Wired Guest Users, Network Access Devices such as Router or Switch are used whereas for Wireless guest access, Wireless LAN Controller with LWAPP is used.

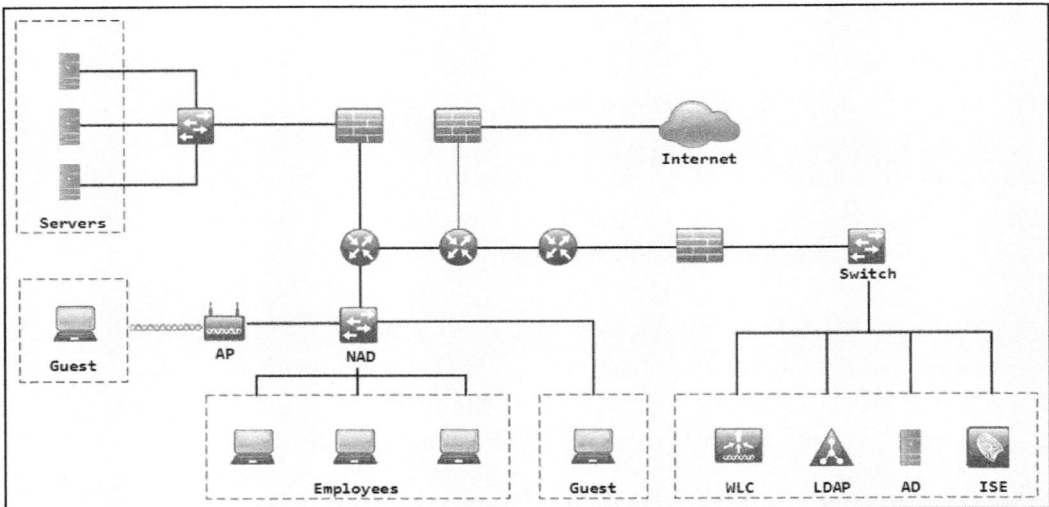

Figure 43 Guest Service Security Solution Design

Advantages of Guest Services

- Authentication of Wired and Wireless Guest Endpoints.
- Authorization of Wired and Wireless Guest Endpoints depending over various variables and policies.
- Accounting and Audit for Monitoring and Reporting Guest User using resources.
- Wireless Guest Feature eliminates the need of Designated Port, Designated Location for Guest User access.

Wired Guest Service Overview

- Dedicated Location for Guest user for Wired Access.

- Dedicated VLAN for Guest service is to be configured which is dynamically assigned to the guests.
- Downloadable ACL is to be configured to control functionality of guest users.
- Configuration of HTTP or HTTPS for Web Authentication redirection.

Mind Map

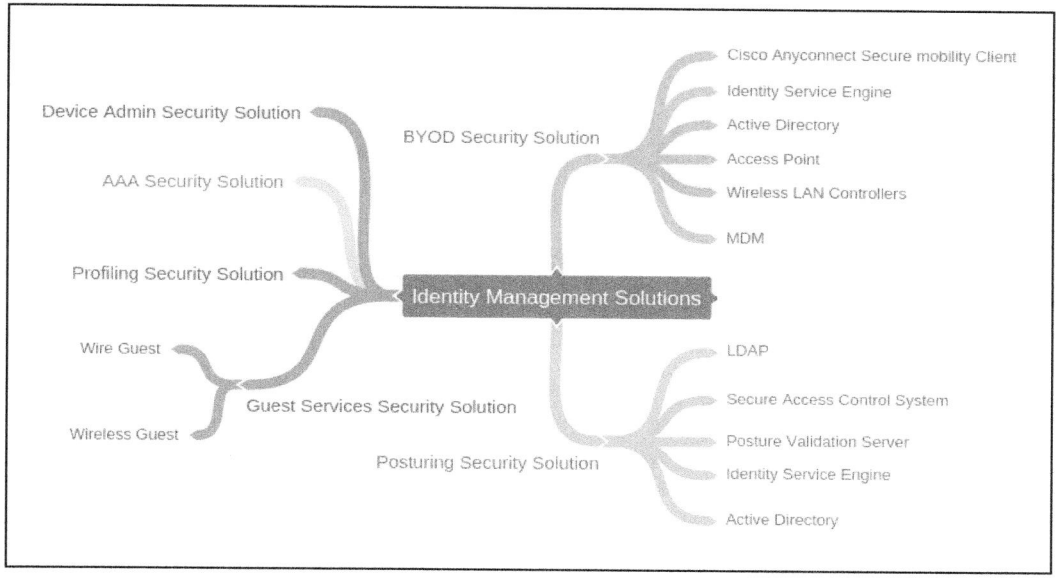

References

www.cisco.com

https://msdn.microsoft.com

www.intel.com

https://meraki.cisco.com

https://en.wikipedia.org/wiki/Computer_network

http://www.computerhistory.org/timeline/networking-the-web/

http://www.computerhistory.org/timeline/networking-the-web/

http://www.thetechnicalstuff.com/types-of-networks-osi-layersrefernce-table/

http://www.utilizewindows.com/data-encapsulation-in-the-osi-model/

http://www.cisco.com/c/en/us/td/docs/solutions/Enterprise/Campus/campover.html#wp737141

http://www.cisco.com/web/services/downloads/smart-solutions-maximize-federal-capabilities-for-mission-success.pdf

http://www.diffen.com/difference/TCP_vs_UDP

http://www.cisco.com/c/en/us/support/docs/availability/high-availability/15114-NMS-bestpractice.html

http://www.wi.fh-flensburg.de/fileadmin/dozenten/Riggert/IP-Design-Guide.pdf

https://www.google.com/url?sa=t&rct=j&q=&esrc=s&source=web&cd=1&cad=rja&uact=8&ved=0ahUKEwihpKO8lozQAhVDkRQKHeAzA_IQFggnMAA&url=https%3A%2F%2Fwww.cisco.com%2Fc%2Fdam%2Fen%2Fus%2Ftd%2Fdocs%2Fsolutions%2FCVD%2FOct2016%2FCVD-Campus-LAN-WLAN-Design-2016OCT.pdf&usg=AFQjCNHwUZXUr3QCKlzXFtBEfV-HJ7OiVw&sig2=lSO526GEgDoomeEfiSFolA&bvm=bv.137132246,d.d24

http://www.ciscopress.com/articles/article.asp?p=2180210&seqNum=5

http://www.routeralley.com/guides/static_dynamic_routing.pdf

http://www.comptechdoc.org/independent/networking/guide/netdynamicroute.html

http://www.pearsonitcertification.com/articles/article.aspx?p=2168927&seqNum=7

http://www.cisco.com/c/en/us/td/docs/wireless/prime_infrastructure/1-3/configuration/guide/pi_13_cg/ovr.pdf

http://www.cisco.com/c/en/us/products/security/security-manager/index.html

http://www.cisco.com/c/en/us/about/security-center/dnssec-best-practices.html

https://en.wikipedia.org/wiki/Malware

https://en.wikipedia.org/wiki/Security_information_and_event_management

https://en.wikipedia.org/wiki/Malware

https://ikrami.net/2014/05/19/siem-soc/

http://www.cisco.com/c/en/us/td/docs/ios-xml/ios/sec_usr_ssh/configuration/15-s/sec-usr-ssh-15-s-book/sec-secure-copy.html

https://en.wikipedia.org/wiki/IEEE_802.1X

http://www.ciscopress.com/articles/article.asp?p=25477&seqNum=3

https://www.paessler.com/info/snmp_mibs_and_oids_an_overview

http://www.firewall.cx/downloads.html

https://en.wikipedia.org/wiki/Threat_(computer)#Threat_classification

http://www.cisco.com/c/en/us/products/security/ids-4215-sensor/index.html

https://en.wikipedia.org/wiki/Brain_(computer_virus)

Note from the Author:

Reviews are gold to authors! If you have enjoyed this book and helped you along certification, would you consider rating it and reviewing it?

Link to Product Page: https://www.amazon.com/dp/B077ZKV394

About this Workbook

This workbook covers all the information you need to pass the Implementing Cisco Secure Access Solutions 300-208 Exam. Everything you need to prepare and quickly pass the tough certification exams the first time.

Printed in Great
Britain
by Amazon